The Second
Fly-Tyer's Almanac

Dave Whitlock

Also by the authors
The Fly-Tyer's Almanac

The Second Fly-Tyer's Almanac

Robert H. Boyle
and Dave Whitlock

J. B. LIPPINCOTT COMPANY · Philadelphia and New York

Copyright © 1978 by Robert H. Boyle and Dave Whitlock
All rights reserved
First edition
9 8 7 6 5 4 3 2 1
Printed in the United States of America

U.S. Library of Congress Cataloging in Publication Data

Main entry under title:

The Second fly-tyer's almanac.

Bibliography: p.
Includes index.
1. Fly tying. 2. Flies, Artificial. 3. Stone-flies.
I. Boyle, Robert H. II. Whitlock, Dave.
SH451.S42   688.7′9   78-24254
ISBN-0-397-01286-1

To JOAN WHITLOCK
and KATHRYN BELOUS-BOYLE

Contents

Introduction	9
I. Stoneflies	
1 The Super-Segmented Swannundaze Stonefly Nymph by Frank Johnson	13
2 Dave's Stoneflies by Dave Whitlock	17
II. Mayflies	
3 Tarcher Nymphs and Flies by Ken Iwamasa	25
4 Mini-Spinners by Del Bedinotti	28
5 The XT System Mayflies by R. K. (Ray) Dolling	34
6 Skip's Inverta Dun by Layton B. (Skip) James	39
7 The L&L Mayfly by Hank Leonhard and Bill Luzardo	43
III. Caddis	
8 The L&L Caddis by Hank Leonhard and Bill Luzardo	49
9 A Quartet of New Adult Caddis by Gary Borger, Jay Buchner, Mike Lawson and Bill Hunter	53
IV. Fly-Tyers East and West	
10 East: Ted Niemeyer by Robert H. Boyle	57
11 West: The Buchners by Dave Whitlock	65
V. Saltwater Flies	
12 Lew Jewett's Blue Crab by Lew Jewett	79
13 The Bally Hoo Tail Streamer by Mike Praznovsky, Jr.	82
14 The Mono-Body Knot by Captain Rick Ruoff	86

VI. Unique Flies
15 Latex Roly-polies by A. L. (Tony) Shuffrey — 91
16 The Omelet Series for Steelhead, Salmon and Trout, Part 1: Egg and Egg-Sperm Flies by Dave Whitlock — 96
17 The Omelet Series for Steelhead, Salmon and Trout, Part 2: Fry Flies by Don Hathaway — 101

VII. Streamers
18 The Rabbit Muddler by John Tibbs — 107
19 The Kat's Meow by Dmitri (Mitya) Kotyik — 112
20 The Whitlock Prismatic Marabou Shad by Dave Whitlock — 115

VIII. Materials of the Art
21 Genetic Hackle by Howard West — 119
22 New Materials and Tools by Dave Whitlock — 133

IX. A Special Section on Stoneflies
23 The Plecoptera, or Stoneflies by Stephen W. Hitchcock — 151
24 Glossary of Descriptive Terms — 169
25 Selected References — 175
26 Portraits of Members of the Nine Families of Plecoptera — 177

Appendixes
Dealers in Fly-Tying Materials, Tools, New Books and Accessories — 185
Dealers in Out-of-Print Books — 197
Periodicals of Interest to Fly-Tyers — 200
Notes on the Contributors — 202

Index
219

Introduction

The Second Fly-Tyer's Almanac is part of a continuing series of books appearing every two or three years to note new patterns, advances, materials, techniques, tools and other information of pertinence and value. It is a book for fly-tyers by fly-tyers, many of whom would never write books on their own but who have something to say that merits publication in permanent form. The contributors represent a diversity of occupations: a physicist, art professor, truck driver, harpsichord player, exterminator, etc.—and, of course, professional fly-tyers. They are you, the readers, and we hope you enjoy what they have written.

Ever since the publication of the first *Almanac* in 1975, both of us have been keeping an extra-sharp eye on developments and trends in fly-tying. Although hard figures are lacking, there is no doubt that interest in tying continues to boom. We can see this from public reaction and the sales of books and materials.

In large part, the booming interest in fly-tying is attributable to the ever-increasing popularity of fly-fishing. Not only is fly-fishing a sporting, compelling, graceful and even elegant way of angling, but the very physical act of casting a fly is, unlike spinning or bait casting, distinctly pleasurable in and of itself. Fly-fishing is fulfilling, somewhat akin to hitting a baseball or kicking a football, even when the fish fail to respond. Fly-tying is equally compelling.

- Fly-tying has gained such a large market that it can now support new materials and tools specifically created for that market. Instead of scrounging a lipstick case, we can now choose from a variety of hair stackers especially designed for tying, not for rugmaking. The same is true of other tools, and within the field of tying itself we can now pick and choose among new vises, such as those designed by Bill Hunter and Al Price. That also goes for materials, as witness the hackle herders described by Howard West in Chapter 21, who are raising super chickens with super feathers.
- Fly-tying is breaking loose from some of the tighter fetters of tradition. Tradition is a hallowed part of fly-tying, but tying would not grow in innovation or appeal if we adhered to the practices of ancient Macedonians or fifteenth-century English nuns or even to the dicta of the sainted Theodore Gordon. Gordon himself broke the rules by adapting the flies of British waters

to those of the Catskills. So be it; and in line with this, let us note that although natural materials will always have a revered place, tyers have been quick to embrace workable synthetics. We expect that this will be the case with Swannundaze, which we are pleased to introduce in Chapter 1.

• Fly-tying, for all the devotees of the impressionistic keep-it-simple school, is attracting more and more buffs of the exact (or almost exact) natural-imitation school, as exemplified by the fresh- and saltwater ties given in this second volume of the *Almanac*. We don't have a bias in favor of either school. What works, works. As the saying goes, you can't knock the trapper with the skins on the wall. Lew Jewett's Blue Crab, to cite only one tie, is an example of the naturalistic trend that is coming on strong in saltwater fishing, hitherto dominated by impressionistic flies.

• Fly-tying is becoming more international in scope. There is "feedback" (horrible word) between tyers in different countries. Tony Shuffrey in England got hipped on the latex caddis ties presented by Raleigh Boaze, Jr., in our first volume, and now he offers his Roly-poly ties. Similarly, John Tibbs has adapted a New Zealand pattern to serve up his Rabbit Muddler for your delectation. We have never seen a sexier streamer.

• Fly-tying offers a unique way of making a living. This applies not only to the Buchners, profiled in Chapter 11, but to other folks, particularly the housewife or teenager seeking to make an extra buck. Indeed, fly-tying (or making jigs or other lures) must have been the kind of thing the late E. L. Shumacher had in mind when he wrote *Small Is Beautiful*. Fly-tying and the packaging of materials and hooks on a piece basis can become an attractive home industry. Despite all the flies that tyers tie, there is an ever-growing market for flies of quality. Far be it for us to say that fly-tying is the answer to the U.S. trade deficit or domestic unemployment, but tying flies can be of help. We were reminded of this recently when a New York City crafts teacher of the retarded went ape when he saw us tying flies. We didn't take notes of exactly what he said during his euphoria, but the essence of it was this: "I can't tell you how difficult it is for me to train a minority kid for a factory job. Employers are leery, especially if the kid is retarded. But if he or she can learn to tie flies—and I have some kids who have the patience and skill—this means that with an initial expenditure of only fifty or a hundred dollars for tools and materials, they can set up shop on their own and make a decent living as long as the quality is there. This is a godsend."

• Fly-tying is prompting some enthusiasts, such as Ted Niemeyer, who is profiled in Chapter 10, to take a closer look at natural materials and make better use of them. Some of the most shopworn or moth-eaten may have value. Recycle all the way by letting your mind have free rein.

• Fly-tying has made many of us look deeper into the anatomy, ecology and behavior of invertebrates. In the first volume, we devoted special sections to the overlooked insect orders of Trichoptera and Odonata. Since then, caddis have come into their own with publication of Larry Solomon and Eric Leiser's book, and in this second volume of the *Almanac* we give considerable space to the Plecoptera, stoneflies. The Plecoptera are a tremendously important order, and we offer here, so far as we can ascertain, the most information about stoneflies ever presented in any angling book. Indeed, given the plethora of Plecoptera information, there may be some readers who will accuse us of overkill, what with Stephen Hitchcock's detailed essay, glossary and references, but then there are nuts, God bless them, who can never read enough for fear of missing some insight into nature that they deem valuable. From our point of view, we can never have enough information about stoneflies, and we suspect that the material presented here will prompt at least one or two books on the Plecoptera, as was the case with the first *Almanac*'s emphasis on the Trichoptera.

We hope that this second volume of *The Fly-Tyer's Almanac* will provide pleasure, thought and inspiration. As before, we look forward to receiving criticisms, suggestions and ideas from you on how to make the third volume of the *Almanac*, scheduled for publication in late 1980, even better.

We would like to thank Ron Winch and Dick Mrstik for their help with photographs for this book, and we would like to extend our appreciation to Ed Burlingame, Pat Pennington, Janet Baker and Ruth Pickholtz of Lippincott. A final thanks to Nick Lyons, formerly of Crown and now on his own, for putting us in good hands.

ROBERT H. BOYLE
DAVE WHITLOCK

I. Stoneflies

1. The Super-Segmented Swannundaze Stonefly Nymph
by FRANK JOHNSON

Driving a truck for a living has its advantages. You get around.

Tying flies for fishing also has its advantages. You can create exactly what you feel is the right combination in order to take more and larger trout.

I agree with the generalization that it requires only a few given patterns to fool most of the trout. But I think you'll agree with me that all fly-tyers worth their salt eventually succumb to a disease known as "collectivitis." We gather much more than we'll ever use. The current trend, in fact, has taken us out of the realm of natural materials and into sundry synthetics found in department stores, five-and-dimes and hobby shops. Nearly all the items "discovered" and used were never created, nor are they manufactured, for fly-tying. But somehow we come up with a new pattern or fly out of the bins of the various plastics, mylars, polys and similar synthetics.

Only a season ago I discovered such a new synthetic. It is a plastic lacing called Swannundaze. What it does that no other synthetic has accomplished is form the bodies of such flies as stonefly nymphs and caddis larva.

Does it really make a difference? I can only tell you that Bob Greenwald, a fishing buddy of mine for many years, tried it last season on the Beaverkill, the Willowemoc and the big Delaware, in addition to a number of smaller streams. Results? Frankly, I wouldn't be surprised if the fly using this material were outlawed.

I'm going to illustrate the tying of one stonefly. However, don't stop there. Experiment on your own and try your own innovations. What really makes this material so unique is that it is a very flat oval, having just the proper amount of shoulder at the edges for a natural effect. It is not hard, like monofilament. In other words, it has "give" to it, much like the natural insect. And it is not flat, like latex, thus allowing for easier formation of the abdomen. If for any reason you desire to stretch the material for an even flatter and narrower effect, this can be accomplished by the simple expedient of stretching it under hot water and pulling. Once wound as a body, it will take any type of ribbing. Thread, ostrich, peacock herl and the like will conveniently fall into the natural groove formed when the material is wound, connected.

Swannundaze comes in over twenty colors. Many of them are solid opaque, but certain ones in clear, amber, olive, brown and black are manufactured as translucents. You can achieve any color combination desired. If it is not available as is, you have only to wrap the clear translucent over a proper shade of floss (which has been lacquered with clear cement) and allow the color to bleed through.

Frankly, there seems to be no end to the variety, style and color of the bodies that can be made from this marvelous material. I'm just surprised that no one "discovered" it sooner.

The Swannundaze Nymph (Amber) (Sizes 6 to 12)

Hook:	Mustad 79580
Tying thread:	dark-brown Monocord
Tail:	two dark-brown narrow-edge goose fibers
Underbody:	two strips of 80-pound test monofilament on sides of shank covered with amber fur
Body:	translucent brown Swannundaze nymph material
Rib:	dark-brown Monocord
Thorax:	amber fur (or Seal-ex or Fly-Rite)
Wing case:	ring-necked pheasant church-window feathers
Antennae:	dark-brown narrow-edge goose fibers
Legs:	brown partridge hackle or substitute

1. Clamp a No. 10 hook in your vise. Spiral brown Monocord thread onto the shank terminating at the bend. Because most natural stoneflies have a very flat appearance, I prepare the underbody by lashing a short strip of 80-pound test monofilament to each side of the hook shank. The tip end of an old fly line will work equally well. In fact, I've used a section of fly line for our photographs. When you use fly line or monofilament, the fly rides on a more even keel. (If you are of the school that prefers to weight the nymph itself, by all means use lead wire instead of the mono.) The monofilament should be cut at an angle at both ends so that it tapers neatly to the shank. Use a liberal amount of head cement on the thread windings that have lashed the monofilament in place.

Snip two fibers from the narrow edge of a dark-brown goose pointer quill and tie them in for the tails. They should flare outward at a slight angle. At this time the dark-brown Monocord thread is tied in just behind the tail. It will be used to form the rib of the fly later.

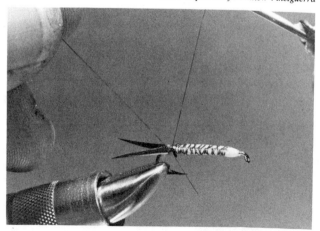

Photo sequence by Matthew Vinciguerra

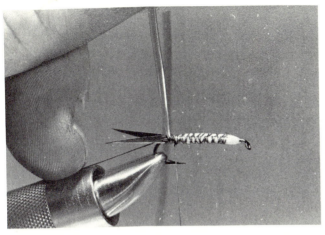

2. We're now ready to tie in the Swannundaze nymph material. First, however, it must be prepared. With a pair of scissors, trim the end that is to be tied to the shank to a fine point. This will allow for a natural and gradual taper when it is wound. Having properly trimmed the tip end, tie it in also just behind the tail.

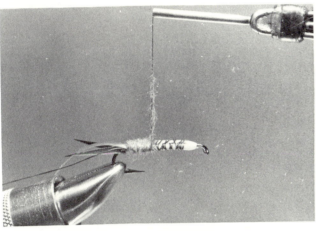

3. The bulk of the underbody is now formed in the conventional manner, using either fur or one of the synthetics of the proper shade. Fly-Rite in an amber shade is a good and easily dubbed synthetic material.

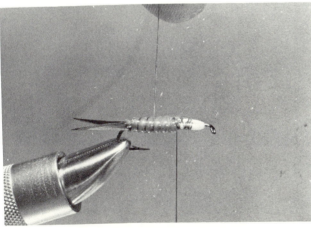

4. Once the underbody has been completed, the Swannundaze material is wound forward to the thread. The plastic lacing should extend one turn of material past the center of the hook shank. It should be well secured with thread and head lacquer applied to the windings. At this point, the dark-brown Monocord is wound forward. You will notice that it falls very easily into the grooves of the plastic lacing.

Incidentally, should you desire to tie a stonefly or a caddis larva having gills, the winding of peacock herl, ostrich herl or hackle through these grooves presents no problem. For additional security, with this type of ribbing it is recommended that the grooves be lined with a touch of head cement.

5. Once the rib has been wound forward through the grooves, secure it with your thread and snip the excess. You now have to spin some more amber fur onto your thread and partially build the thorax.

6. On a male ring-necked pheasant, there are a number of feathers on the upper back of the bird that have an appearance not unlike that of church windows.

Pluck two of these feathers from the skin and prepare them. The tip ends should be squared off with a pair of scissors, and both sections should be lightly lacquered with vinyl cement. Tie in the first church-window feather. Now build the rest of your thorax with amber fur over the base of the church-window feather.

7. We're now ready for the partridge "legs." If you cannot obtain any partridge, use woodcock, hen chicken body or any other suitable substitute. Cut a V-shaped notch in the feather proper and slip it over the hook shank so the fibers protrude downward, forming the legs. Now tie in your second church-window feather. It should cover half the exposed area of the first church-window feather.

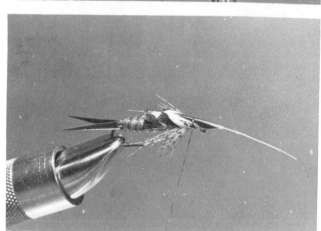

8. Snip two more fibers from the narrow edge of a dark-brown goose quill and tie them in so that they extend out past the eye of the hook. Whip-finish and apply a coat of head lacquer to both the windings and the wing-case feather. The Swannundaze Stonefly Nymph is complete.

2. Dave's Stoneflies
by DAVE WHITLOCK

A lot of years have gone by since I first began tying stonefly nymphs for myself and for Bud Lilly's in West Yellowstone, and when Bob Boyle suggested that we feature stoneflies in the second *Almanac* I was quick to agree. The order Plecoptera is a very important one for trout, especially in the West.

One thing I've learned over the years is that there is always something new to learn, even after tying and fishing stonefly nymphs for years. My nymphs have always been soft, fuzzy and light colored. Not until last year did I learn exactly why they worked better than the hard, dark nymphs many tyers favor.

Stoneflies are a treat for any trout, but some stoneflies are more of a treat than others. There are intervals in the one- to four-year life cycles of stoneflies when the nymphs must shed their outer covering or cuticle to grow. Before the new cuticle hardens and darkens, the nymph is much lighter in color, very soft and just about helpless. That's what I learned a year and a half ago, and that's exactly why a trout, if given the choice, will take the soft, juicy nymph over the nymph that hasn't shed.

Like any tyer, I'm always seeking to improve my patterns. Here is my latest Soft Stonefly Nymph. Fish it deep dead drift any time of the year you can, so it rolls right on the coarsely rubbled bottom riffle. Choice of color pattern to suggest a particular species is optional. The pattern I'm using as an example will imitate most larger brown to dark-brown stones.

Dave's Soft Stonefly Nymph

Hook:	Mustad 79868 or 9049, sizes 2 to 8
Tying thread:	CSE single-strand orange nylon floss
Body weight:	lead wire size of hook's wire
Tail and antennae:	boar hair
Rib:	CSE copper or gold rib wire
Body dubbing:	blend of orange and amber Seal-ex and African goat

Back, wing cases	
and top of head:	brown rayon Swiss Straw ribbon
Gills:	cream ostrich herl
Legs:	church-window feather from ring-necked pheasant's back, dyed light gold
Cement:	Pliobond and 5-minute epoxy

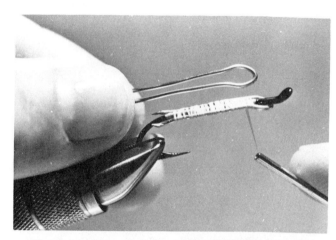

1. Place hook in vise jaws so that point and barb are not covered. Attach tying thread just behind loop eye wire and overwrap shank's full length to bend. Form a long loop with a piece of lead wire roughly the same size or a little larger than hook wire. Put loop over and under the hook eye and hold it just behind the eye. With tying thread, carefully lash lead loop down along sides of hook shank. With scissors, taper and trim off lead at hook's bend.

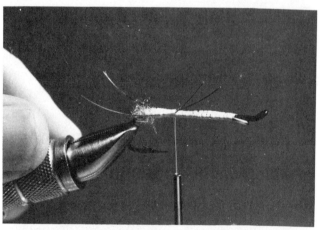

2. Mix a very small drop of 5-minute epoxy and paint shank and lead with it. Allow to set ten minutes. (You can do a dozen or more hooks to this point and then apply epoxy if you prefer to save time.) With tying thread, spin a small bunch of dubbing over the lead wraps at hook's bend. Select a pair of boar bristles and tie one to each side of the hook shank at the butt area. Tails should be one third the length of the hook shank and very widely separated. Tie on a 4- to 5-inch section of Swiss Straw just on top of butt. Make it about 40 percent wider than the body's base. Place end in spring material clip.

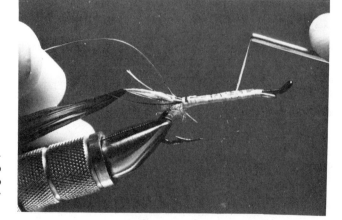

3. Just immediately in front and to the side, tie on a 4-inch piece of rib wire. Place its end in the material clip also. Paint body base with Pliobond to cement tail, rib and Swiss Straw and form a sticky underbase for body dubbing.

4–5. Abdomen: First, spin dubbing on thread and wrap it over rear half of hook shank to form a soft dubbed body. Second, remove Swiss Straw and pull forward down over top of abdomen and tie down also at mid-shank. With rib wire, carefully rib abdomen so that a distinct segmented effect is effected. Tie off rib at mid-shank and trim excess of rib wire, but leave excess Swiss Straw intact and attached.

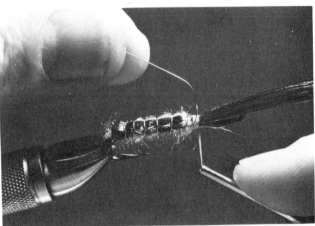

6. Legs: Place a pheasant feather on top of hook shank, dull side up. Attach two ostrich herl at mid-shank. Put a small amount of Pliobond around front half of hook shank. With same dubbing, wrap a soft, loose thorax up to end of lead loop. Now overwrap dubbed thorax with ostrich herl. Cut away excess herl tips. This completes thorax and gills.

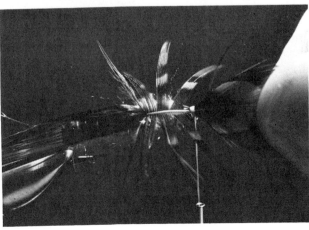

7. With left thumb and index finger, tease back pheasant feather fibers as you pull feather stem by tip forward and down over thorax. Tie down tip and cut away excess tip. Study photo carefully for correct leg position over thorax.

8. Make a fold in Swiss Straw ribbon with bodkin needle to form back wing case and tie down just immediately in front of thorax-leg area. Push it down close to body with index finger and adjust its length before securing it tightly with several thread wraps. Now make front wing case with a second fold and tie down. Leave Swiss Straw excess intact for forming top of head.

9. Select a matched pair of boar bristles and tie one to each side of hook shank just behind the eye. They should be approximately one half to two thirds the length of hook shank. Cut away excess and paint area with Pliobond. Over the area just behind hook eye, spin and dub a small ball of dubbing blend. Next, pull Swiss Straw down over top of dubbed head and tie down just behind hook eye. Cut away excess Swiss Straw.

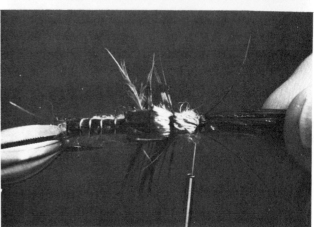

10. Whip-finish head and coat thread wraps with Pliobond. Remove from vise and put a slight arching bend in the hook shank to simulate a stonefly nymph's shape when not holding to rocks.

Note: After the nymph becomes wet, the rayon Swiss Straw swells and softens even more to simulate the soft, helpless stonefly nymph. This same combination of materials can also be used to simulate the mayfly, damselfly and dragonfly soft nymphs.

The most vulnerable period of the adult stonefly's brief life occurs when the egg-laden females flutter drunkenly back to the water to oviposit. To design a good-looking, durable and high-floating imitation, I've taken ideas from the half-dozen most effective adult patterns and added a few of my own.

The size and color pattern must be altered to match particular hatches in various areas. I've chosen the golden stone pattern for Western hatches.

Dave's Adult Egg-Laying Stonefly

Hook:	Mustad 90240 or 94831, sizes 12 to 2
Tying thread:	CSE single-strand nylon floss, orange or yellow
Rib:	grizzly hackle, dyed gold
Body:	elk rump hair, dyed pale yellow-gold
Underwing:	gold deer hair
Wing:	Microweb wing material colored brown and gold with felt pens
Head and collar:	light dun-gray northern deer, dyed Rit gold
Cement:	Pliobond

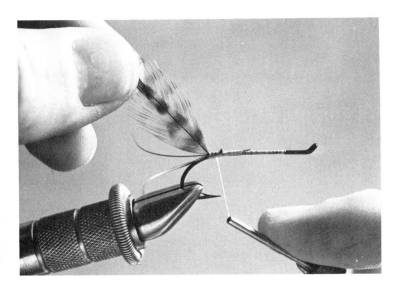

1. Place hook in vise so that point and barb are not covered by jaws. This absolutely prevents any possible damage to hook regardless of vise jaw or tyer's abuse. Attach tying thread just behind eye and overwrap entire shank length. Select a matched pair of boar bristles or small stripped brown hackle stems, and tie to sides of hook shank so that they extend back three fourths the length of hook shank and flare out to right and left. These give critical support to floating fly. At hook's bend, tie on a dry-fly saddle hackle that is approximately one size smaller than hook size. Return tying thread to front one fourth of hook shank and coat shank with Pliobond.

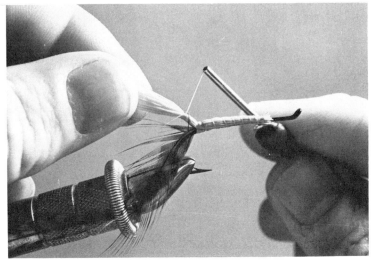

2. From a long-haired piece of elk or caribou rump, cut a bunch of hairs approximately the size of a wooden match. Tie butt ends to and around hook shank one third the shank distance behind eye. Pull hair back and carefully but firmly rib with thread back to hook's bend. At bend, take two or three tight wraps to anchor hair solidly to shank. Coat tied-down hair lightly with Pliobond. Now pick up tails and hair ends and wrap thread over both past hook's bend one fourth a shank's length. Tighten thread with two or three wraps to hold hair and tails together. Pull hair tip back toward hook eye and tie back down over bend to form an egg-sac extended butt. Be careful here not to mess up hackle for rib.

3. At this point, bring thread back up to front of body base. Now pull hair tips forward and equally around hook shank, tying them down in front. Trim off excess of tips and put a light coat of Pliobond over elk-hair body and egg-sac extension. Before it dries, reposition tails to proper flare. When Pliobond becomes tacky, rib body with saddle hackle. Cut away excess tip.

4. Cut a small bunch of gold deer hair, clean fuzz out of it and straighten tips. Size and tie it to top of shank directly over end of elk-hair body, *not in front of it*. Allow tips to flare slightly, and neatly trim away any butts. Underwing length should extend back to tail's length. Put a small amount of Pliobond on tie-down area and allow to become tacky before putting wing over it.

5. With felt-point waterproof pens, color Polyweb material light-brown and gold. After it dries, fold material and cut a wing from it with scissors. Make sure you cut a "neck" in the wing so that it will just fit over the top and side of body. Wing's length on fly should extend just to or slightly past tails and about twice the width of the body. Place neck of wing over the tacky Pliobond underwing-body area. Fit it carefully so that it lies fairly flat over top of body. Carefully wrap it down without using great pressure or it will deform the base and slip forward—a no-no! After wing is secure, advance thread to area in front of wing, behind hook eye.

6. Select a matched pair of light-brown boar bristles and tie them to sides of hook shank directly behind hook eye. They should be two thirds the length of hook shank and flaring out to sides. Pliobond tie-down area. From gold deer hair, cut a bunch of hair approximately ¼ inch in diameter. Remove fuzz and shorts. Straighten in hair aligner. Remove and trim *butts* until hair length is approximately one and one third that of hook shank. Hold hair so that squared butt ends are directly in line with end of wing base–body area. Carefully tie them down tightly here. Advance thread to just behind hook eye. Now pull tips of deer hair backward, down around hook shank, over and past hook eye. Make three or four very tight thread wraps around hair, right at hook eye. Coat this area with Pliobond.

7. Move thread back to the wing-body neck. Bend and pull hair tips back and around hook shank to form a neat head as you overwrap deer hair with several very tight turns of thread *just in front* of the wing-body base.

Head finish: Put a whip finish on this collar wrap and cut away excess thread. Make sure antennae are still in proper position. Now coat head and thread neck with a light coat of Pliobond. After all Pliobond is completely dry, dip or spray fly with Scotchgard to waterproof and enhance shape durability.

Special notes: This design can be slightly modified to better accommodate heavy or smooth water surfaces by the amount of hackle rib, underwing, and deer-hair head and collar you use. If you trim off bottom hackle and collar, the fly will ride much lower and flatter to the surface. So, when tying, consider these alternatives, and this design will serve you in all water situations.

II. Mayflies

3. Tarcher Nymphs and Flies
by KEN IWAMASA

The most consistently successful fly fishermen are as adept at dry-fly methods as they are at nymphing, and if all things were created equal, most fly fishermen of sound mind and body would avoid nymphing like the plague and be happiest just to fish with dry flies.

But let's face it, all things are not created equal, just different, and nymphing is here to stay because it produces trout in numbers and sizes that would stagger the imagination. Admittedly, no one can take the abomination out of casting weighted nymphs, but something has been done to help eliminate snags, the next most persistent frustration of nymphing. Testimony to the effectiveness of nymphing on trout and big trout is beyond reproach, and snags and losing flies have, indeed, become a way of life and not a state of mind for the successful fly fisher.

As nymphs and other submerged patterns are normally fished deep, often bounced off the stream bottom, a layman's inspection of the normal pattern reveals the primary reason for most snags and hang-ups—the point of the hook faces the stream bed and provides the initial and fatal contact with anything near the bottom. Snag.

Tarcher patterns, named after a frequent angling companion, invert this down-hook relationship, thus allowing the nymph to be effective in holes and runs that would normally deplete an entire nymph collection. These patterns run relatively free of most common snags because the hook faces the surface and not the bottom. This inversion takes place by wrapping lead wire around the foremost curve of the English bait hook and tying the pattern up-hook, thereby shifting the balance and causing the hook to ride upside down.

All favorite patterns can be tied in the Tarcher manner, and this unorthodox configuration makes sense to anyone who has ever watched nymphs swim. The curved shape mimics the up-and-down abdomen movement of the subimago in motion, and the bend and point of the hook become a more realistic and logical extension of the abdomen area than the normal straight-line down-hook patterns. Tarcher patterns are a little more difficult to assemble, but they have been proved effective in all weighted nymph situations and are worth the extra time and effort to produce them. However, not all conditions require weighted patterns. During a hatch, especially of Ephemerella species, patterns tied in the conventional down-hook manner with the English bait hook have also been effective when finished in the upstream dry-fly method, or with medium to larger emerger patterns worked in a quartering and downstream approach.

The Tarcher up-hook concept can also be adapted to the Swisher Richards Wiggle Nymph, but extreme care must be taken to secure the connecting loop to the eye area of the foresection. Also note that the final step calls for removing the bend of the hook from the foresection of the Wiggle Nymph and thus eliminating the down-hook point of contact.

For the fly fisherman who does not tie his own, and there are some, the Tarcher patterns are available from Creative Anglers in Boulder, Colorado.

Tarcher Nymph

Hook:	Mustad 37160 or English bait hook, sizes 6 through 20

(Editor's note: *This hook model is two to three times larger than a standard Mustad hook of the same size designation. Thus, 37160 size 16 equals 94840 size 10.*)

Tying thread:	Herb Howard's prewaxed 6/0 color to match nymph's underside
Body weight:	Buss lead fuse wire sized to equal hook's wire diameter (copper wire may be substituted)
Body material:	Fly-Rite, Seal-ex or natural fur dubbing to match nymph's underside
Wing case:	Swiss Straw or turkey-wing quill section to match nymph's top or dorsal side
Rib:	small gold wire or size 18 gold oval tinsel
Tail:	three fibers from a soft bird hackle, or three herl tips from an ostrich plume, colored to match nymph's tail
Legs:	soft, mottled, marked bird body feather such as grouse, partridge or pheasant
Body cement:	Pliobond
Head cement:	Laggie's Clear Head Cement

Photo sequence by Michael C. Simon

1. Clamp hook in vise, bend down, as is normally done with a standard hook. Do not enclose hook's point and barb in vise jaws. Attach tying thread at mid-shank and wrap shank back to bend. Wrap lead wire over thread base back to bend and trim off excess. Crisscross thread over and between lead wraps to secure lead wraps further.

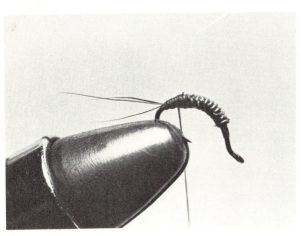

2. Tie tails just on the hook's bend. Tails should be two thirds the length of hook shank. Use three for mayfly nymphs; two, well separated, for stonefly nymphs. After tails are secured and spaced accordingly, attach rib material at tail connection point with hook. Overcoat wraps, lead and shank with Pliobond cement.

3. Just before Pliobond dries, wrap abdomen area and rear half of hook shank with dubbing, and overwrap abdomen with rib in opposite wrap direction. Tie off rib and trim away excess. Remove hook from vise and carefully invert it, and replace it upside down in vise jaws.

4. Attach wing case directly in front of abdomen—on top as hook sits in jaws. Place loose end of wing material in material clip and dub one fourth of exposed shank with dubbing. Tie legs, feather top first, to hook shank, then spin more dubbing onto shank to complete the thicker abdomen up to just behind hook eye, leaving enough space to tie down legs, feather, wing case and head finish.

5. Either bend feather down over top of thorax or wrap it around thorax twice, advancing toward eye. Tie down and trim away excess. Remove wing-case section from material clip and pull forward, shaping a modest-size wing case as you tie it down over top of thorax-head area. Trim away excess wing case. With tying thread, form a neat thread head or dubbing head and whip-finish.

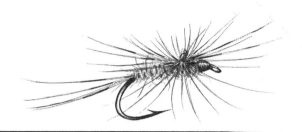

4. Mini-Spinners
by DEL BEDINOTTI

It is mid-July. As darkness approaches, you take up a position to watch and wait for a rise of trout. Your chosen waiting place is below a riffle where the current slows down enough so you'll be able to assess the location of your fly in relation to the forthcoming rises. Then, just as you're barely able to spot the rise forms, you begin casting. They don't take your No. 14 Light Cahill, even though there are a few large cream-colored naturals on the water. Your partner is slightly downstream, and you glance to see if his rod is bowed. Nothing doing. They're really tattooing out there now, so you keep pitching, even changing flies once as the failing light permits. Not even a refusal. Your partner calls nervously, "What the hell do they want? I don't know what fly to try next!"

It's too dark to change flies again, so you retire to the bank with your partner, shaking your heads in disbelief. You finally conclude that the trout were nymphing and thus wouldn't touch a dry. Evenings like this repeat themselves from early July right through to the end of the season. You try nymphs, but they don't work either, which is about what you had expected.

The above scene was typical of my vexation for many summer evenings along the classic Battenkill in upstate New York. It took nearly a week the year Bill Dorato and I finally figured it out. The answer: tiny spent spinners (or imagos, as the entomologists prefer to call them). At first Bill and I thought the fish were nymphing, but if nymphs were hatching close enough to the surface to cause such a large rise of trout, then where were the duns? What happens is that as darkness approaches, the dry-fly man sets up well below a riffle in slower currents where he can see to operate easily. Thus he never sees the thousands of spinners rising and falling in their nuptial dance over the riffs. Having completed their mission in life, the spinners fall to the surface and die. They then float half or fully spent down the feeding lane in droves, and this triggers the phenomenal rise of trout that you see each evening. Keep in mind that these spinners are small, have translucent wings and tiny bodies and are therefore most difficult to see in the fading light. Couple this with the fact that they are flowing out in the feed lane and you are standing back at least a short cast away, and this adds up to the reason that you seldom see them.

Bill and I discovered this one evening by sacrificing our fishing and wading right out to where the rises were in greatest evidence. We ruined our chances for fishing that evening, but as we played our flashlights on the water, we were amazed at the numbers of tiny red-brown-bodied spinners that were coming down. We came away quite elated and eager to start winding silk.

Our first imitations consisted of a Poly Body with radially tied hackle wings, variant-style. We then clipped off the bottom fibers, allowing the fly to float low in the water. These ties met with mediocre success. Although this style of winging worked for the larger imago imitations, such as the Hendrickson, we felt that the tiny ones were too buoyant and thus not floating low enough in the film in the manner of the natural. For this reason, we abandoned the use of Poly Bodies. I might add that I was happy to do this, as I feel our tying materials are becoming too synthetic; I much prefer using organic materials whenever possible.

We substituted a stripped quill for the body, but we were still perplexed about the winging method. No matter how much of the bottom hackle barbs we trimmed off, there was always enough fuzz left to prevent the fly from floating in the film. We knew that the body of the natural floated in and through the surface film and was therefore directly visible to the trout from below, as Vincent Marinaro revealed in his monumental and inimitable *A Modern Dry Fly Code*.

What we sought was a spinner imitation that allowed the wings to rest on top of the body, thus permitting the body to break through the surface film. Inasmuch as the fish sees the body directly, we tried to duplicate the body as exactly as possible. The stripped quill, when tied properly, offers the ideal segmented effect. And to our joy, the quill body allowed us to tie the wings just where we wanted them—above the body.

After winding the quill on for the body, I leave the quill butt standing upright instead of trimming off the excess at the thorax. I then tie in one tiny hackle and wind it parachute-fashion around the quill butt. The hackle is then tied off, the excess quill butt just above the hackle is cut off, and a tiny drop of lacquer is placed in the center of the hackle. The result is a spinner imitation that has worked more consistently than anything to date, and consistency, to me, is the measure of success in dry-fly fishing.

The hackle must be small, yet give off a great deal of sparkle when held up to light, not unlike the wings of the natural imago. I might add that this style of tying works equally well for the larger spinner imitations. It floats and floats and takes quite a lot of abuse, which is another important factor, what with the all-too-brief flurry of spinner activity that usually occurs.

This style of imitation works beautifully for spent-caddis imitations as well, with the hackle usually mixed brown and grizzly. It has always amazed me that very little has been written about spent-caddis imitations. Most writers report only on the newly hatched caddis. In late May and June, toward evening, you've seen millions of caddis flies winging upstream at about head level. I love to see this, as one is nearly assured of some fine sport to the spent caddis "spinners." I say spinner because these spent caddis come down the current not in a tent-winged fashion but spread-eagled. I have found trout very selective to these spents.

An alternative method of tying parachute when a fur body (caddis imitation) is desired is to tie the fur body and then tie in the hackle but do not cut the stems. Rather, position them upright and wind the hackle horizontally around its stems. After tying off the hackle tips, bring both hackle butts forward and tie off, thus securing the parachute wraps. (This cannot be done with the smaller quill-bodied fly because the quill is too stiff to bring forward.)

In tying the female caenis, I like to substitute clear horsehair for the stripped quill to obtain maximum abdominal translucence. (Note in photo that hook shank is visible under the horsehair.) This best imitates the female spinner's abdomen, which becomes translucent upon extrusion of her eggs. A wisp of black fur serves as the thorax, whereas with the red mini-spinner the olive tying thread serves as a thorax. The overall appearance of the imitation should be of a sparsely tied nature.

Quill body colors should vary with the natural to be imitated. A sample guide follows:

Natural spinner	*Body quill*
Baetis	Red-brown
Paraleptophlebia adoptiva	Red-brown
Pseudocloeon anoka	Dark olive
Caenis	Black (male); white or clear horsehair (female)

The Mini-Spinner

Hook:	20 to 28 dry fly
Tying thread:	prewaxed olive
Tail:	three olive fibers
Body:	stripped reddish-brown quill
Hackle:	any dun that emits a sparkle when held up to light

The Spent Caddis

Hook:	16 to 22 dry fly
Tying thread:	prewaxed olive
Tail:	grizzly tied short
Body:	olive and sandy rabbit fur (mask)
Hackle:	brown and grizzly mixed

Photo sequence by Dick Talleur

1. Place hook in vise with maximum amount of hook exposed. Start thread at thorax area and tie in three stiff hackle barbs at thorax. Wind back toward bend of hook, keeping barbs in place with left hand.

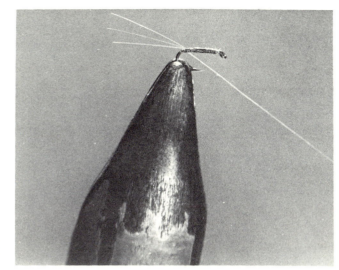

2. Bring thread around behind and under tail fibers and pull slightly; tails will flare. When you adjust thread tension, tails will assume desired flared position.

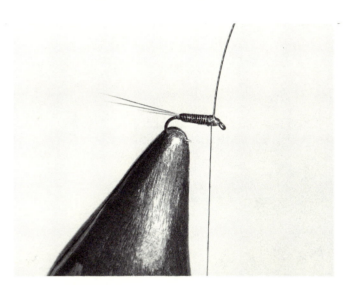

3. Tie in stripped hackle quill and wind forward to thorax area. Put a drop of lacquer along the quill body and base of tails.

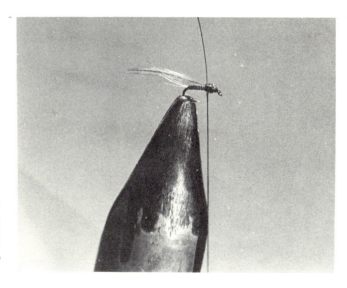

4. Using the tying thread, position the butt of the quill perpendicular to top of the hook shank. Sparse dubbing can be added for a thorax; however, tying thread serves the purpose also. Do not cut quill butt. Tie in appropriate-size hackle (which emits sparkle when held up to light) as close to quill butt as possible, shiny side up.

5. Wind hackle around quill butt parachute-fashion and tie off hackle tips at eye of hook. Whip-finish.

6. Clip excess quill butt close to hackle and put a tiny drop of lacquer in center of hackle. This will prevent hackle from riding up quill butt.

7. A completed size 24 red mini-spinner.

8. A completed size 18 caddis spinner in which hackle was wound parachute-fashion around its butt stems.

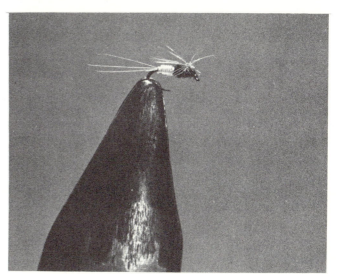

9. A completed female Caenis spinner. Clear horsehair is substituted for the stripped quill to obtain maximum abdominal translucence.

5. The XT System Mayflies
by R. K. (RAY) DOLLING

The fly-tyer who steps into the treacherous waters of dry-fly ideology had best be shod in the best of studded, felt-soled waders lest he be upended in the torrent of new concepts introduced in the past decade. Yet this surge of innovation is not without foundation. The establishment of the many "no-kill" or "catch-and-release" trout waters has greatly magnified the intelligence of our quarry, so new designs are constantly needed as old favorites become less and less productive. And this is all to the good, even though we protest loudly because of already overstuffed fishing vests.

Apologies aside, just what has the XT system to offer? Most surface mayfly imitations share a common shortcoming having nothing to do with dressings per se but rather the too-heavy foundation on which they rest—namely, the hook. Dry flies larger than size 16 float poorly, only for short periods and only in relatively quiet water. They must be changed frequently during our often brief hatch periods, a decidedly time-consuming handicap when trout are rising.

Since small flies float well, why not tie all sizes on small hooks, thereby gaining the benefits of better flotation, balance and lifelike behavior? Fine, but how? The XT system allows the tyer to build his fly—wing, body and tail—and attach it later to any desired hook in one or two simple operations. A technique had to be found for constructing a fly without the foundation afforded by the shank of a hook. I discovered it quite by accident whiling away a sullen winter afternoon five years ago. Since I experiment widely in fly-tying methods, I'd taken to testing various operations by tying on a darning needle clamped in the vise. This allowed my messes to be slid off and discarded without my having to remove dressings laboriously from hooks with a razor blade. That day I lashed some deer hair to the needle, and on sliding it from its support I was amazed to find it did not collapse! Thus was born a simple method for making durable and flexible extended bodies. The body stays intact because of the elastic nature of the deer hair under the pressure of its overlying windings. When the tiny mandrel is removed, the spongy hair refills the space evacuated and thereby keeps the body together. The key to a new system of "off-hook" imitations had been found. Let's turn now to the job of simulating the mayfly via the XT method.

The adult mayfly both begins and ends its short life at the water's surface, where it is most vulnerable to feeding trout. I firmly believe that mimicking the shape and attitude of the insect during its characteristic surface phases is of prime importance. Look at my photographs to see how the natural appears.

The first phase is the emergent dun. After reaching the surface from an upstream riffle, the nymph is faced with breaking through the overlying surface tension and molting. Lying flush in the surface film, it displays an elongated, streamlined form.

Once free of the casing, the wings pop open suddenly and the upright dun is born. It then rests on the surface for a varying length of time, depending on the weather and the time of day.

After flying to streamside foliage, it molts to the spinner stage, mates, lays its eggs and returns to the surface, often in an upright position. Weakened and near death, it gradually collapses to the spent-wing phase.

As the sequence photos show, all three phases—emergent, upright and spent—can be tied from one basic module, by attaching it to hooks in three distinct configurations. Paying close attention to size, proportions and color, the angler has at his disposal an exquisitely practical system for tying reasonable facsimiles of adult mayflies. You can tie Baetis olives on up to giant Hexagenias—and all on nothing larger than a size 16!

No special tools are required to tie XTs other than the mini-mandrels that provide temporary tying support. For flies a half inch long or larger, you can use a No. 9 embroidery needle, but for smaller sizes finer wire is required, or else the bodies will be too slack. I like the fine pins used for mounting dried insect specimens. For wings and bodies you'll need a supply of fine-quality deer hair. The best is found around the neck and throat of young whitetails. Small pieces can be dyed and/or bleached to yield a range of colors. To bleach hair to a light shade, wash hair thoroughly in detergent, rinse, then immerse in hydrogen peroxide (hair bleach) for a couple of hours. The hair can then be tinted with common household dyes. I use fine polypropylene for dubbing over bodies, and large neck hackle fibers for tails, but other possibilities are endless. For emergers I use regular shank dry-fly hooks; for duns and spinners, 5X shorts; both styles in sizes 16, 18 and 20.

The only supplier I know for short-shank (5X) hooks down to size 20, Mustad 94825 (which I use a great deal), is E. Hille, P.O. Box 996, Williamsport, Pennsylvania 17701. Fine insect pins can be obtained from Angling Specialties, Box 97, Ancaster, Ontario, Canada, or from scientific supply houses.

XT tyers, go forth and multiply.

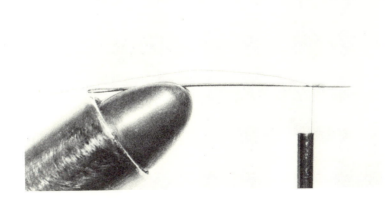

1. Mandrel and thread: Clamp a small embroidery needle in the vise. Attach fine prewaxed thread near the point. Allow free end of thread to trail to the rear, or secure it in a material clip. Don't cut it off. It performs an important function.

2. Wing and body: Tie in a small bunch of even-ended deer hair. The amount will vary, depending on the size and bushiness of the fly desired. Retain your grasp on the hair butts while lashing them down firmly to the needle. Continue winding closely until the end of the body you want is reached. The body should usually be the same length as the wing.

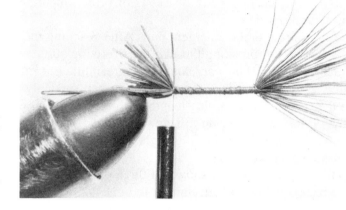

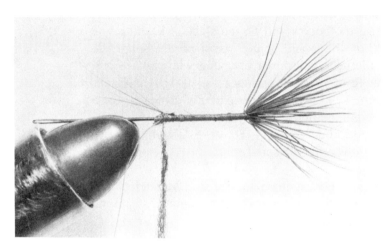

3. Tailing and spinning the dubbing: Trim excess hair butts closely, taking care not to clip tying thread or the free end. Tie in tails to suit the natural. Spin poly dubbing on tying thread. If planning an emerger, match coloration of nymph.

4. Dubbing the body: Take one turn of dubbed thread; then bring free end forward and wind dubbing over it and the body. Pull free end tight after every couple of turns. This prevents windings from slipping off the body during use. When dubbing reaches base of wing, cut off free end of thread and half-hitch or whip-finish.

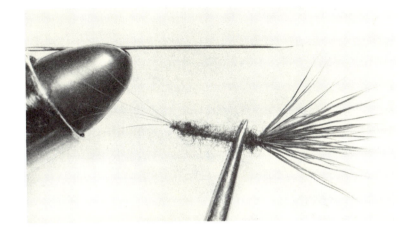

5. Basic module: Grasp body firmly with thumb and forefinger and slide it off the front of the needle. This module can now serve as the basis of three mayfly phases.

6. Attaching emergent dun: Remove needle and clamp a small dry-fly hook in the vise. Start thread at rear and then cover shank forward to eye. Take module from step 5, reverse it and tie it in by the tips just behind hook eye. Trim off tips. Hair that will represent the folded wings of the dun should equal the length of the hook shank. Apply dubbing to match underside of emerging dun (lighter in tone than that of nymph case).

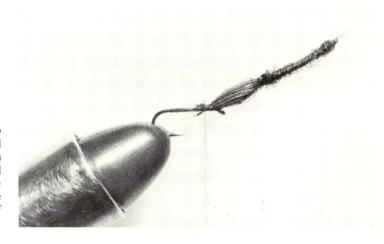

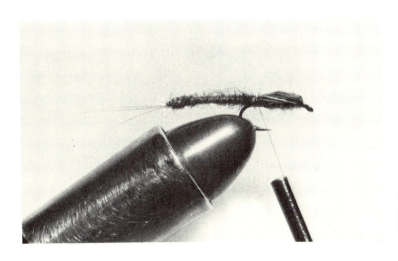

7. Emergent dun: Wind dubbed thread to a point directly above hook point. Remove any excess dubbing. Fold fly back over shank. Tie down behind wing, and whip-finish.

8. Attaching upright dun and spinner: Clamp a short shank hook in the vise and attach tying thread in center. Take module from step 5 and tie it to the hook over the base of the wing. You will see the hair flare if you do this properly. (Don't tie the first few turns over the body because the resultant upright wing will not stay that way during use.) Now wind front of body down tight. Hold body to prevent it from twirling around. Spin a little body dubbing on tying thread again, and cover the windings, working back to wing base.

9. Upright dun/spinner: Push hair tips well back and with undubbed thread wind several turns to form a buttress in front of the wing until it stands up perpendicular to the hook shank, flared out in a semicircle. Add a little dubbing in front of wing, then whip-finish.

10. Spent spinner: After completing step 8, divide hair evenly on both sides. (If you want a sparse wing, clip out some of the center fibers.) Wind tying thread in figure-eight fashion around wings until they lie flush. Spin dubbing on thread and figure-eight again to cover windings and build up a thorax. Whip-finish.

6. Skip's Inverta Dun
by LAYTON B. (SKIP) JAMES

Practically every set of fly-tying instructions begins with the words "clamp hook in vise." That first step is so automatic for most of us that we do it almost unconsciously. The position of a hook in a vise determines the outcome of our tying effort. We ignore hook position while we diligently study the use of feathers and fur. Picture a mayfly dun in your mind's eye for a moment, and then tell me what its primary features are. The abdomen sweeping up gracefully, ending in two or three slender tails; the wings glistening in the sun, sloping rearward over the body; six almost invisible legs, two extending before the fly. . . . Now imagine how a hook could be superimposed on that mental image so that it would most nearly conform to the silhouette of the natural. I think you will have the idea for what I call the Inverta Dun.

The development of this style of tying was actually an exercise in the use of materials. I wanted to see whether I could produce a more lifelike imitation by altering only the hook position. The techniques used in the construction of this fly, with the exception of the extended abdomen, are the same as those used in a standard dry fly. Although I was pleased with the original flies that I tied, several defects were immediately obvious. For one, the fly did not land properly, but use of a smaller hackle and clump wing helped. Then splaying the hackle out in front of the fly and cutting some fibers underneath the fly added to stability on the water. Soft wings, either as a clump or divided, are necessary. Quill wings are stiff and cause the fly to spin wildly when casting. What began as an almost artistic experiment in February turned out to be a useful imitation in May.

The Inverta Dun is not a fast-water pattern because it drowns easily. But its still-water effectiveness is superlative. Make sure you fish it on a very light leader tippet, no matter what size fly you happen to be using. I can tie imitations in the Inverta Dun style from size 10 to size 18, but next season I am going to restrict it to imitations of slow-water mayflies in small sizes only.

Inverta Sulphur Dun

Hook:	4X short-shank, turned-up tapered eye, extra-fine wire, size 16
Tying thread:	Danville's or Herb Howard's yellow
Tail:	wood duck flank fibers
Base of abdomen extension:	nylon monofilament, .015-inch diameter
Dubbing for abdomen and body:	golden olive Fly-Rite or Spectrum
Wing:	lightly barred mallard flank
Legs:	palest dun rooster hackle, size 18
Adhesives:	Flyhead cement

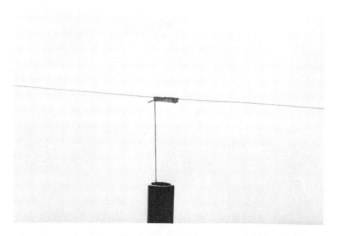

1. Abdomen extension: Stretch mono between jaws of your regular vise and some other handy fixture—say, a second vise. Anchor thread about 3 inches from vise and wrap along the mono a distance equal to the shank length of the hook you plan to use. To prevent mono from twisting, hold thread as shown.

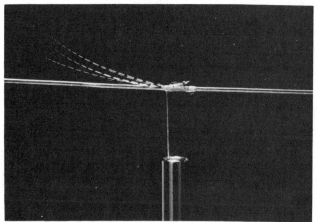

2. Abdomen extension, tails: Select three fibers of wood duck flank feather and tie in as shown. Make sure all three curve in the same direction. Tails should be the same length as the natural.

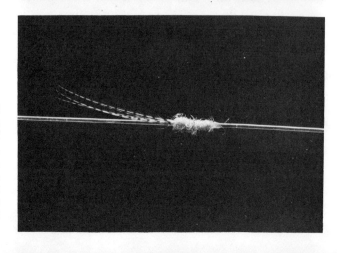

3. Abdomen extension, dubbing: Twist small amount of Fly-Rite or Spectrum onto your thread. Dub back to point at which you anchored thread on mono. Tie off with half hitches, and add a drop a cement for security. Now cut off excess thread and remove mono from vise. Cut mono under the place where tails meet dubbing, and again in front of the extension, leaving enough bare mono to bind to hook. (*Note:* When tying Inverta Duns in quantity, tie several abdomen extensions at once and cut them off as you need them.)

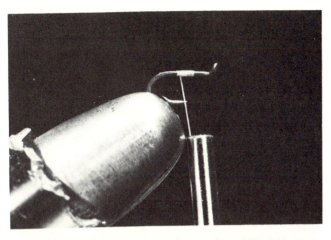

4. Body: Insert hook in vise and cover middle third of shank with thread.

5. Body, adding extension: Bind abdomen extension to top of hook shank. Make sure tail fibers point downward and that you wrap mono to hook slightly around the bend, as shown.

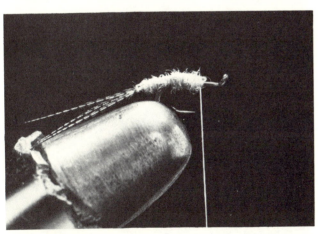

6. Body, dubbing: Add another pinch of dubbing to your thread and wind over shank and mono, blending with dubbing on extension. Dub back to point at which you anchored thread on hook.

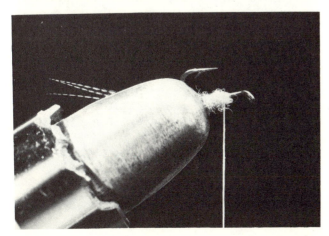

7. Body: Now take incomplete fly and invert it in vise. You will clamp both the mono of the abdomen extension and hook bend in the vise.

8. Wing: Now prepare a clump of lightly barred mallard flank fibers and bind to hook, tips pointing toward tail. Secure them in an upright position by taking several turns behind the clump while holding it erect with your fingers.

9. Legs: Tie in a single light-dun hackle feather by butt on side of fly, as shown. Hackle fibers should be shorter than wing. Make sure dull side of hackle is facing you.

10. Legs: Wind three turns of hackle, in front and behind the wing clump, thorax-style. Tie off and clip excess hackle.

11. Head: Finish with a small neat head and a drop of cement. After head cement dries spray Inverta Dun with Scotchgard to enhance durability and waterproofing.

7. The L&L Mayfly
by HANK LEONHARD and BILL LUZARDO

We began experimenting with new mayfly patterns because traditional patterns lacked realism. Our slant-tank observations showed that although some of the traditional patterns had one or more characteristics of the living insect, none of them, in our opinion, bore sufficient resemblance to a real mayfly before and after it enters the trout's window of visibility.

When a living mayfly lands on the water, its feet (and sometimes the thorax) exert pressure on the surface and cause saucerlike depressions. From below, these depressions look like inverted saucers that catch and reflect light. We concluded that proper simulation of a mayfly's legs were of paramount importance in devising a realistic pattern.

We looked for a material that was buoyant, durable, easy to work with and readily available. We chose deer hair. By tying a small bunch on top of the hook shank and dividing it into two equal sections, we created the effect we sought. The legs originate from the thorax position, and since only a few deer hairs actually touch the surface, they produce the saucerlike depressions or dimples of the natural. The deer-hair legs also help float the fly exceptionally well.

To be effectively represented, the wings cannot be obscured by hackle. We had to find a winging material that met the prerequisites of height, breadth and flatness established by Vincent Marinaro in *A Modern Dry Fly Code*. The wing, Marinaro writes, "is the part that a trout sees first, for it must be remembered that the wing is visible before the body of the insect comes into the window." We experimented with various feathers. None of them met our requirements, so we developed our own new winging material, Microweb. The wings can be cut to an identical shape each time, and the color of the natural wing can be duplicated with waterproof marking pens. Microweb is strong, and it has elasticity. When cast, the wings "give" and then return to their original position. This flexing prevents the fly from twisting. Microweb is inexpensive, and it can be bought from Barry and Sandy Beck at Cahill House, RD 2, Benton, Pennsylvania 17814.

For the body (abdomen and thorax), we use natural furs from mink, beaver or otter. These furs dub and compress easily and add immensely to the buoyancy of the finished fly.

We put great effort and concern into the tails. To simulate the tails with anything less than absolutely perfect tailing material in size and shape would be somewhat criminal, and so we chose Russian wild boar bristles. Our extended body fly has two (three when the species warrants) bristles tied on top of the shank. One third of the body of the fly is then dubbed up and onto the bristles so that the rear part of the abdomen and the tails curve upward and off the water surface. The bristles are naturally curved, strong and somewhat translucent.

For our extended body, we use a 3X fine, 1X long hook, three sizes smaller than usually recommended. The Light Cahill is usually tied on a size 12 hook, but we use a size 18. This allows for delicate presentation as the fly literally floats to the surface.

Our standard body fly uses boar bristles for the tails, but the fly is tied on a standard hook, though still 3X fine. We do not wind the dubbing up and onto the tails. Instead, we tie the dubbing onto the shank only, and end the dubbing at the bend of the hook.

Our fishing experience shows that L&L Mayflies are not only effective when trout are rising to a hatch but that they can raise fish when no hatch is on. They are dry flies to fish over sophisticated trout, but please, for the sake of the fish, pinch down the barbs on the hooks before using.

The L&L Mayfly, Extended Body

Hook:	3X fine, 1X long, three sizes smaller than usual
Thread:	Herb Howard 7/0
Tails:	two or three (depending on mayfly species) Russian wild boar bristles
Legs:	small bunch of deer hair
Body (abdomen and thorax):	mink, beaver or otter dubbing, dyed or mixed to match mayfly species
Wings:	Microweb cut to shape, colored with waterproof pen to match mayfly species

---

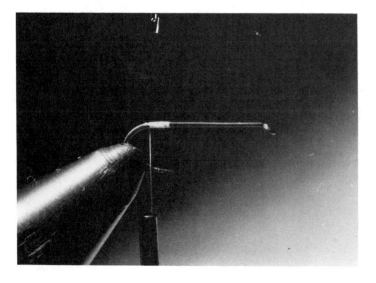

1. Attach thread to hook shank near bend of hook.

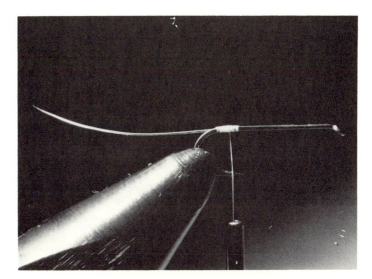

2. Hold one bristle of wild boar along shank with left hand and secure tightly with tying thread. Length of bristle should be slightly longer than length of hook shank.

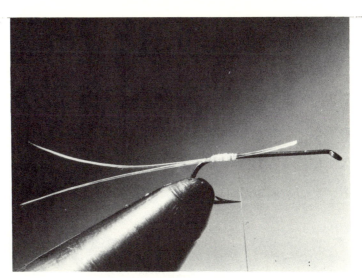

3. Secure second bristle to shank. Tie down bristle butts and cut off excess.

4. Bring thread to position directly above point of hook. Clip small bunch of deer hair and place in tamper. Tap well to ensure that all tips are equal. Hold bunch of deer hair on top of hook shank with left hand, with tips of deer hair facing over eye of hook. Secure with three or four turns of tying thread directly over point of hook. Without releasing deer hair from your left hand, raise butts slightly and clip with scissors. Clip at an angle to provide a tapered body.

5. With left hand, pick up deer-hair tips, holding upright. Take several turns of tying thread in front of deer hair. Deer hair should stand straight up. Part deer hair into two equal portions and spread to sides. Should look like a half circle from the front.

6. Return thread to rear of deer hair. Create a dubbing loop there.

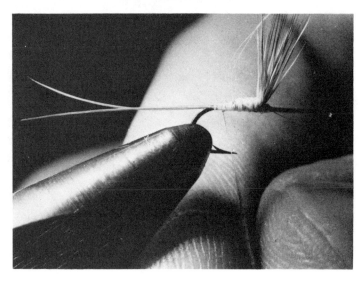

7. Continue with thread to rear of hook. Attach dubbing to tying thread, leaving enough exposed thread near hook to allow for spiral up tails.

8. Wind thread up and around both tails (with exposed part of thread that has no dubbing) to a point equal to one third the length of hook shank. At this point, exposed thread should be used and dubbing should be ready to wind down tails.

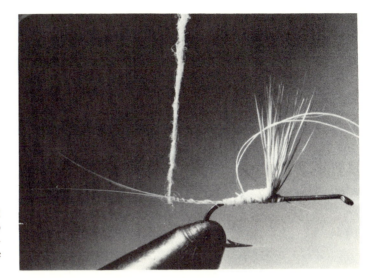

9. Wind dubbed thread around tails back to hook and then forward almost to eye. Place dubbing on previously made loop.

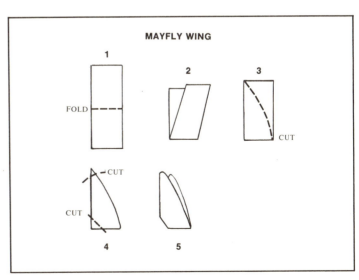

10. Cut wings, using diagram as an example. Height of wing should be the same as length of hook shank. Lay dubbed loop between wings and bring wing down on top of body through deer hair. Secure dubbed loop with tying thread and cut off surplus. Secure.

47

11. Put more dubbing on tying thread. Wind dubbed thread around base of wing (on outside), going first around the far side, and return on the near side (near you). Form head of fly and whip-finish. Apply drop of varnish to head and to inside portion of wing at base.

III. Caddis

8. The L&L Caddis
by HANK LEONHARD and BILL LUZARDO

The L&L Caddis was the next logical step for us after the development of our realistic mayfly. After all, the entire country is caddis conscious. It seemed simple enough. Just apply the same principles and use the same materials as were successful for our mayfly. Deer hair for legs, fur dubbing for the body and Microweb for the wings. There was no reason it shouldn't work. We were wrong. Tied in the tent-wing fashion of the caddis fly, our imitation just wouldn't land right side up every time.

To overcome this problem, we tied in the wing in a number of different ways while still trying to maintain the tent-wing shape of the caddis. Each time, we came up with a blank. The fly wouldn't land right side up 100 percent of the time. What seemed like a simple tie turned into a nightmare. Tied in tent-wing fashion on top of the hook shank, the fly looked to us like the real caddis. But did it look like a caddis to the trout? By accident one day while casting another variation into the bathtub (good exercise for overcoming the winter blues), we thought we'd found the answer to our problem. We decided to put it to the ultimate test—what did it look like through a slant tank? We hurriedly set up the slant tank, and while one of us cast the fly into the tank (we have been called various strange names when seen doing this), the other watched to see how many times it landed upright and what it looked like through the trout's window.

A cry of success from the face beneath the slant tank put an end to all the fruitless hours spent casting into that tiny little box. "Come look at this!" was the exclamation.

We finally saw the wing as we had seen it a thousand times before—on the real insect as it entered the window in our slant tank. We marveled at how alike our Microweb wing and the actual caddis wing looked. When finally our attention was placed on the imitation floating on the water, we noticed our imitation was floating upside down. The wing that looked so lifelike from below was actually inverted on the water's surface.

Rushing to the vise, we hastily constructed the caddis with the wing tied in upside down. We added some antennae, as our research proved this a very prominent feature on the real caddis as it enters the trout's window of visibility. Back we went to the slant tank. One of us cast, and the other gazed into the water from below. We finally had our L&L Caddis. It landed right side up each and every time. It had the same characteristics as the actual insect before, during and after it had entered the trout's cone of vision. The deer hair actually looked like the legs of the caddis and created the necessary saucerlike depressions. The wing was the most surprising element. It looked so much like that of the real insect, we were astonished. It had the requirements of "height and breadth and flatness." We were on the right track. Now if only the trout agreed.

We tied several dozen. Some we sent to Barry Beck to test on his property on the legendary Fishing Creek. The others we tested on our local waters. Our tests proved the fly was effective. Barry called to say the fly was equally effective there. We tied several dozen more, and off we went to Pennsylvania to Fishing Creek. We needed to fish a river not too well known to us, and the creek had a population of super-selective brown trout. With Barry as our host, we enjoyed excellent results fishing our new L&L Caddis. It succeeded in fooling the most finicky of fish. We fished for several days and continued to have success. Our stay ended, but Barry promised us he would continue to test our new caddis during the year.

We made many trips to test our new fly. They all proved successful. Barry called a number of times to remark on his success with the L&L Caddis.

Our most difficult job was in convincing everyone that our unusual-looking caddis actually looked realistic to the trout. From the surface (not as the trout sees it), it does look unusual. It does break away from traditional caddis-tying techniques. But if anyone has seen the actual caddis from below, before, during and after it enters a trout's window, they too will quickly agree that traditional ties are far from realistic.

We wish to share our findings with all, and hope we have added a step toward the development of the ultimate fly that will produce a fish every time it is cast.

The L&L Caddis

Hook:	Orvis Partridge Supreme 1XL 3X fine
Tying thread:	Herb Howard's prewaxed—color to match caddis wing
Legs:	short deer hair, such as found on deer mask, legs or summer hides
Wings:	Microweb wing material
Antennae:	stiff barred guard hair or duck flank fibers
Cements:	varnish and contact cement
Finish:	Scotchgard

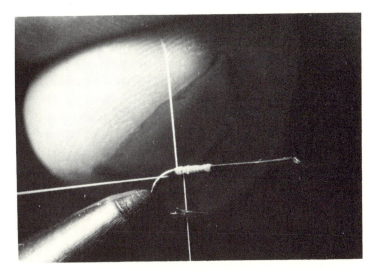

1. Attach tying thread to hook shank at bend (use 3X fine, 1X long). Form dubbing loop.

2. Bring tying thread to position on hook shank directly over point of hook. Clip small bunch of deer hair and place in tamper. Tap on tabletop to ensure all tips are equal. Hold bunch of deer hair on top of hook shank with left hand. Tips of deer hair should face forward and just past eye of hook. Secure with three or four turns of tying thread directly over point of hook. Without releasing deer hair from your left hand, raise the butts slightly and clip with scissors. Clip at an angle to provide a tapered body.

3. With left hand, pick up deer-hair tips—holding upright. Take several turns of tying thread in front of deer hair. Deer hair should stand straight up. Part deer hair into two equal portions and spread to sides.

4. Bring tying thread to rear of hook. Attach dubbing to tying thread and build uniform body to front of deer hair and almost to eye.

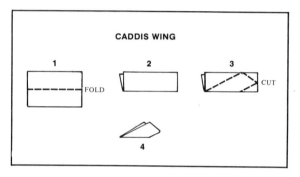

5. Place dubbing on previously made loop. Cut wings from Microweb, using diagram as example. Height of wing should be about the same as the distance between hook point and hook shank. Lay dubbed loop between wings and bring wing down on top of body through deer hair. Secure dubbed loop with tying thread and cut off surplus.

6. Attach antennae (made of wood duck or similar barred material, equal to length of body) and build up head with dubbed tying thread. Whip-finish behind head and apply head cement. Place drop of varnish to top of wing where it meets body to secure.

9. A Quartet of New Adult Caddis

Here are four very fine new adult caddis from four of the country's more innovative fly-tyers.

1. Poly Caddis by Gary Borger. A super all-round emerging, fluttering, egg-laying pattern. We've had countless rave reports on this neat new caddis. Gary is a fine entomologist, and his Poly Caddis reflects his special ability to understand and match aquatic insects. Gary says it is also a quite effective mayfly emerger pattern.

Hook:	Mustad 94833 or Orvis Supreme, sizes 8 to 20
Tying thread:	Herb Howard's prewaxed Flymaster
Body:	Andra Spectrum or extra-fine Fly-Rite
Hackle:	Dry-fly grade color of caddis legs
Wing:	polywing yarn
Coating:	Scotchgard

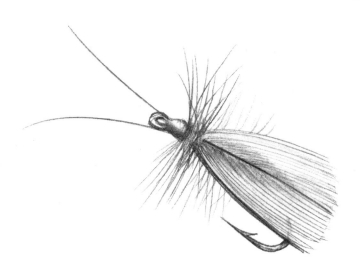

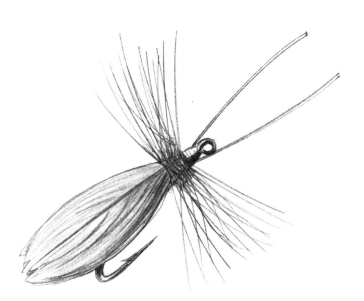

2. Buchner Caddis by Jay Buchner. Jay, who is profiled with his wife, Kathy, in Chapter 11, improvised this new resting and egg-laying adult caddis in response to Howard West's request that he and several other top tyers work up new patterns using complete skins of cock and hen chickens. The antennae are made by extending the stripped stems of two cock body feathers past the head.

Hook:	Mustad 94840, sizes 8 to 20
Tying thread:	Herb Howard's prewaxed Flymaster
Body:	two sections of cock tail feather wound like herl to form a body and ribbed with very small gold or copper wire
Wings:	two cock chicken body feathers with stems up to wing size stripped. Try to pick right and left feathers from full skin. Coat each feather with vinyl cement or Tuffilm. Stroke each a time or two just before they dry to compact the feathers.
Hackle:	one extra-long dry-fly hackle
Antennae:	wing feather stems extended over and past hook eye, separated and flared right and left

3. Lawson Caddis by Mike Lawson. Mike's caddis best simulates a fluttering or resting adult. This is another Howard West full-skin project.

Hook:	Orvis Premium, sizes 8 to 22
Tying thread:	Herb Howard's prewaxed Flymaster
Body:	Andra Spectrum
Wing:	two hen hackle or cock body feathers laid flat on top of hook, side by side
Antennae:	two spade hackle fibers
Coating:	Scotchgard

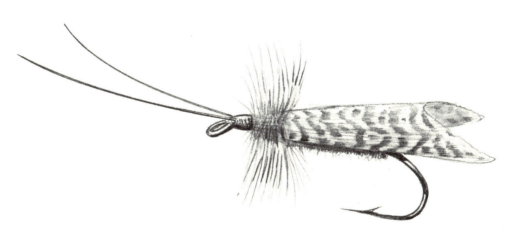

4. Hunter Caddis by Bill Hunter. This neat, beautiful adult caddis really is effective as a resting or twitched adult. Bill says it is one of his very best season-long fish catchers.

Hook:	Mustad 94840 or 94833, sizes 12 to 20
Tying thread:	Herb Howard's prewaxed Flymaster
Body:	Andra Spectrum or beaver belly
Hackle:	grizzly dry fly
Wing:	mallard or wood duck short barred flank feather coated with Tuffilm or vinyl cement and trimmed to caddis tent shape
Antennae:	two fine wild-boar hairs
Coating:	Scotchgard

All four caddis should be tied to match color of hatching insect's body, legs and wing color patterns.

IV. Fly-Tyers East and West

10. East: Ted Niemeyer
by ROBERT H. BOYLE

After fishing the Beaverkill one day, Ted Niemeyer walked into the bar of the Antrim Lodge in Roscoe and ordered a shot of gin. He got the shot and poured the gin into a medicinal vial to preserve a March brown he had captured on the wing. The bartender was so flabbergasted he gave Niemeyer the drink on the house.

Collecting and studying insects is a passion with Niemeyer. He is also an extraordinarily thoughtful student of materials, as readers of his fly-tying column in *Fly Fisherman* can attest. "Ted has first rummaging rights here at the Rivergate," says Eric Leiser. "Whenever I get a batch of materials, he goes through it, and I mean he goes through it. He'll go through goose feathers one by one, looking for something that might interest him. He'll use things I'd throw out, and I never fail to learn something from him. He and Poul Jorgensen have a little running game they play. Recently Jorgensen was tying at a Trout Forum, and he showed Ted a color photo of a salmon fly. 'Nice picture, but a horrible fly,' said Ted. Poul then picked up the stuff he had clipped or discarded and handed it to Ted, saying, 'Here's the garbage you tie with.' Ted took this junk, tied a beautiful nymph and handed it back to Poul."

I first saw a couple of Niemeyer's flies in 1966 at the Angler's Cove in Manhattan, run by Bob and Gladys Zwirz. One was an ultra-realistic stonefly nymph, and the other was a magnificent no-hackle mayfly with an extended body and six incredibly natural legs made from the belly hairs of a javelina. I was so dazzled that I sought out Niemeyer and did a column on him and his ties for *Sports Illustrated*.

To my mind, Niemeyer is as fine a tyer of realistic flies as anyone in the world. He is able to capture the spirit of the living insect with innovative use of materials and strict economy of movement. There are no waste motions in a Niemeyer tie. The fly is reduced to its essence by almost magical sleight-of-hand. As meticulous as Niemeyer is, he is not arrogant or dogmatic.

"I prefer the realistic," he says, "but I can't advise this for others because of the time involved and the lack of availability on the market of some of the materials I use."

Now forty-nine, Niemeyer works in Manhattan as an airline account executive and lives in Connecticut. He was raised in Seattle and studied architecture at the University of Washington. Until the age of thirteen, he was a bait fisherman. Then one day while he was fishing the Skykomish River to no avail with salmon eggs, he ran into a fly fisherman who was taking fish consistently. "I was so impressed that I went back home and started tying flies," he recalls. "Roy Patrick gave me a hand." For years he tied standard patterns, but, ever the perfectionist, he thought nothing of taking several hours to tie what he wanted to be the perfect Royal Coachman.

One night in 1964 in the midst of a winter tying session at home, he decided to tie some realistic mayflies without hackle. "I got disgusted tying standard patterns," he says. "There's great satisfaction in tying an old standard dry fly, and the old patterns work. But doesn't it get tiresome if you're always driving the same old car? I'm one of those people who are eager to see if something new won't fool the fish."

At first it took Niemeyer up to four hours to tie a realistic mayfly, but after he cut that to twenty-five minutes, he embarked on realistic stonefly nymphs. "Then I got involved with caddis, freshwater shrimp and crayfish," he says. "Then the damselfly and dragonfly. I was going to exact—I mean *exact*—imitation then. Then I got into spinner flies, damn difficult because of the fineness and texture of the materials I had to resort to. My tails came out of the base of stubble of picked-over mallard wing. They are fine, translucent and shimmer in the light. They are as fine as human hair but tough as a quill. You find what you need if you study *every* feather and fiber that comes off an animal or a bird."

For all this, Niemeyer was dissatisfied. Looking back, he says, "I was going too far. The flies were too realistic, too stiff. Realism is motion as well as design, so now I had to find materials that would impart motion. For instance, take beaver or muskrat. If you look at the guard hairs under a microscope, you'll find they're flat, not round, where they come out of the skin. Tie them in forward to buck the current as the legs on a nymph, and they act as paddles. Speaking of nymphs, many people doing realistic imitations make the mistake of giving them a glossy finish. The living nymph is glossy because it's just come out of the stream and has a coating of water that makes it look shiny. But in nature, under the water, the nymph is not shiny. I stay away from glossy tones. I use satin-finish varnish and glues."

Asked what attributes he regards as keys in fly-tying, Niemeyer says, "This might sound strange coming from me, but simplicity is critical. The pattern may be complex, but the tying procedure should be the simplest and most productive possible. Watch the way people handle thread. I see people winding on thread to move the thread, and they're doing some of the damnedest manipulations. There are tyers who do the wings on a dry fly and then continue the thread to the bend. Why? What they should do is hold the tailing material on top of the hook shank behind the wings and bind in the tail as they go down the shank. Halfway down the shank, dub your body material onto your silk. Now continue the thread to the bend, and then when you start your first turn coming back, you start winding on your dubbing." But how does a tyer gauge where to apply the dubbing to the thread so that it will begin winding just as it starts back up the shank? "Easy," says Niemeyer. "I only use silk and no wax. I use the moisture in my fingers to dub, and I can slide the dubbing up and down so it's exactly in the right position."

What tyers have influenced Niemeyer? "Jim Leisenring, for one," he says. "The blending of his materials and color tone and texture are very delicate and beautiful. He knew how to blend his feather with his fur and his hair. And all this was done and conceived with an eye to

Ted Niemeyer

proportion. Charlie DeFeo is another. He taught me the practicality of materials and how the most obscure materials can be utilized in fly design.

"I like Walt Dette for his precision and proportion in general. I've studied the head on a Dette fly for an hour through a microscope. I was intrigued by the fact that the head nearly didn't exist before it disappeared. I didn't understand how the hackle stem was secured with so few turns. I learned that two or three turns of whip finish was all that was necessary if done properly.

"I've studied Preston Jennings and Jack Atherton's flies closely under a microscope, Jennings for his color and material blending, and Atherton for delicacy and balance. Ernie St. Clair was a fine tyer. He was an exact hard-bodied imitation man in nymphs, and his nymph profile was closest to exact as anyone's I've ever seen. Mike Roche, another nymph man, was another influence on me. One fly that I've seen that has had as much impact on me is a Pryce-Tannatt salmon fly. The layering of wings made it one unit. It was sent to Charlie DeFeo in exchange for a wood duck skin.

"But you know, out there in this country there is a whole forestful of young superior tyers, kids from twelve to twenty. I've seen some masters in the raw. There are some great young tyers, and that to me is the most encouraging thing I've seen about tying. It has nothing to do with the style. It has to do with intensity. They're doing it in depth as an art, not as something just to slap on for the fish."

Niemeyer prefers to tie with natural materials, but recently he became interested in Swannundaze after Leiser showed him this new synthetic (see Chapter 1). Here is Ted's hellgrammite.

59

Niemeyer's Swannundaze Hellgrammite

Hook:	Mustad 9675A or 79580, sizes 2, 4 and 6
Tying thread:	size 4/0, waxed or unwaxed
Tail:	Canada goose primary flight quills and dun-colored marabou
Underbody:	four-ply rayon or silk floss and two plated brass pins
Abdomen:	translucent black Swannundaze
Gills:	dun-colored marabou
Thorax:	turkey marabou (soft furlike base from turkey body feathers
Legs:	Canada goose or turkey primary flight quills
Cases:	black duck breast feather
Antennae:	two dark porcupine guard hairs
Eyes:	two porcupine or horse hairs

Photo sequence by Matthew Vinciguerra

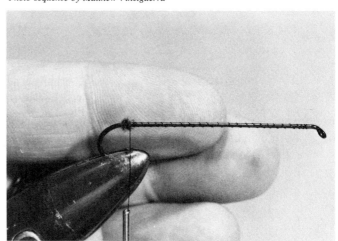

1. Tails on nymphs will seldom spread and hold in proper position unless some support is added. Form a small fur ball on the hook shank where tails are to be secured.

2. Very effective and lifelike tails can be had from the Canada goose primary flight quill feathers. Select the short stiff side of the quill.

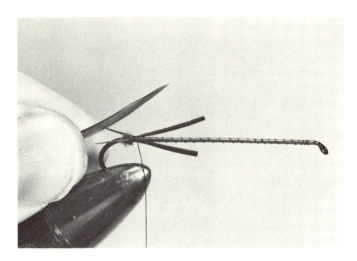

3. Position tails properly with firm turns of tying thread around tailing material and close up against fur ball. Taper the end of the Swannundaze and bind it firmly to the hook shank.

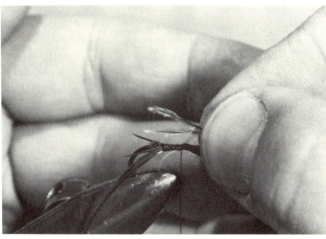

4. Select a good-quality dun ostrich plume for gills and place two of these fiber tips extending ⅛ inch over the tails.

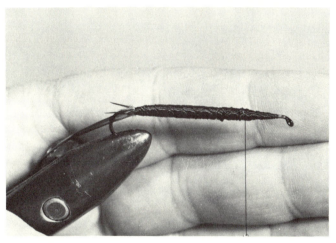

5. Thick floss provides a firm cushion on which the outer layer of materials is positioned. Keep this underbody smooth and free of lumps.

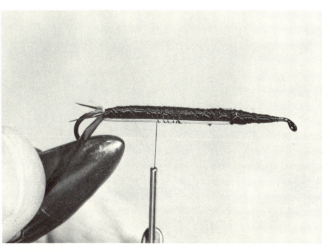

6. A pin (with head removed) is positioned on each side of the abdomen/thorax. They provide form and rigidity for the heavy exterior materials that follow.

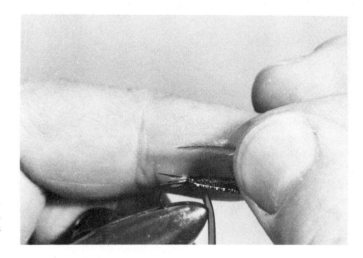

7. The challenge now is to complete successive turns of Swannundaze material as you set individual gills in place. Match near-side and far-side gills for thickness and length.

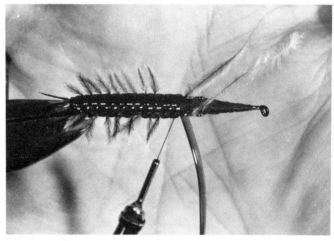

8. Keeping tension on the Swannundaze is essential to keep gills from slipping out of position. Although fragile, the gills provide a substantial amount of this imitation's underwater action.

9. Turkey marabou is a very desirable material for use in the thorax area. Its marabou-like action is important to the fly's effectiveness. Spin it on the tying thread as you would fur.

10. It is cheap, so use plenty. It compacts well and will provide a fine base for all the additional materials that are to be added. Color tone and size of the legging material is matched to the semicompleted fly.

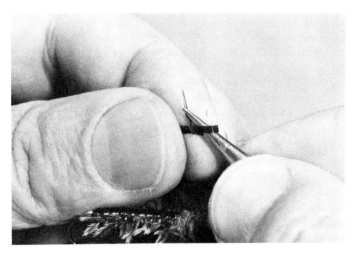

11. To form each leg, place a simple knot in the individual turkey quill fiber with fine-pointed tweezers. Granted, a little practice helps.

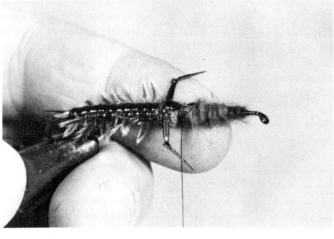

12. Keeping legs in position and secure against slippage can best be done with a series of tight figure eights with thread over their bases. Additional security can be had by bending leg butt back and binding it down again.

13. The cases are simple rectangular sections of varnished black duck breast feathers (stem left in). They can be glued and their stems tied into position.

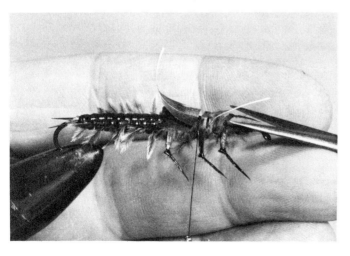

14. It is very important to trim all excess materials properly. Taper your cuts whenever possible.

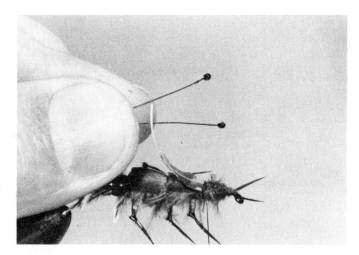

15. Antennae are secured along each side of head, their lengths adjusted by pulling on each butt of hair. Head case is in position, to be pulled forward over the top later. Eyes shown are made by knotting porcupine guard hairs, cutting the knot close and dipping the knot in dark spar varnish. Four to six dippings are necessary.

16. Extend the eyes, right and left, and secure the butts with figure-eight wrappings of the tying thread. Pull on butt of each hair to position eye. Bend these butts 90 degrees and secure them again so eye cannot pull loose.

17. It is important to have the center stem in wing and head cases. Otherwise it would be very difficult to bind cases down securely enough to hold them in place. Small applications of spar varnish on the final head knot will seep into the materials and finish the fly nicely. There is only one correct way to fish this imitation: *on the bottom!*

11. West: The Buchners
by DAVE WHITLOCK

A number of fly-tyers were to work at the first annual Jackson Hole Guide and 3M Scientific Anglers Youth Fly-fishing Clinic. Lefty Kreh and Paul Brunn were among them, and before the clinic began, Fred and Elizabeth McCabe gave a big milk-can stew dinner party at their Bar EW Ranch so everyone could get acquainted. There I was introduced to Jay and Kathy Buchner, and then I worked with Jay in the clinic. After it was over, Lefty Kreh and I floated the Snake River in Jay's boat.

Before we pushed off, Jay handed each of us a half dozen of his favorite Snake River dry flies. I found myself staring at six of the most beautiful Humpies, Royal Wulffs and Joe's Hoppers I had ever seen. "Who tied these flies?" I asked. Jay answered nonchalantly that he and Kathy had. I thought he was kidding me.

It turned out the Buchners had indeed tied the flies, and from that moment on I've admired these two young, attractive people who look as though they had been cast by Hollywood for their outdoor roles.

Jay and Kathy met and married in Jackson, Wyoming, but both grew up elsewhere. Jay was born and raised in Maquoketa, Iowa, and enjoyed hunting and fishing. His Michigan grandfather fostered Jay's love and development of fly-tying and fly-fishing. His grandfather died in 1957, but Jay still feels he had the single most important influence on his life and career. I can certainly understand this, as I also was blessed with a grandfather who left me rich with his legacy of the outdoors.

After high school Jay studied pharmacy and zoology in college. On a falconry trip to Wyoming, he fell in love with the West and moved to Laramie to attend the University of Wyoming. He worked as a buck fence builder in the summer, but after failing to find winter work he started tying flies in Jackson. He had tied lots of flies and jigs for friends and family but had never cranked out dozens of one pattern as he did that winter for Jack Dennis. Jay started with dry gray hackle yellows for $2.25 per dozen and tied sixty dozen. That doesn't figure out to much cash, but he managed to get through the winter. His next order was for Royal Wulffs, and he mastered the pattern well enough in three days, according to Randy Berry, who helped Jay get started.

When trout season opened, Jay began to do some guiding, as well as expanding his tying work to Jim Poor's Irresistibles. He specialized in Western patterns, such as Humpies, Hoppers, Muddlers, Wulffs, Matukas and Bucktails. Between summer and fall guiding and all-year fly-tying, Jay found a life he loved.

Kathy, a blue-eyed blonde, was born in Price, Utah, and moved to Jackson in June 1971 after completing a B.S. in journalism. Kathy's family are also avid outdoor lovers. At the age of eight she started fly-fishing with her father in the Uinta Mountains of Utah.

Kathy met Jay the first day she was in Jackson. Sensing that he might be a lady's man, she played the part of a selective trout. She wound up a year and a half later as Jay's best catch!

Kathy worked for the Jackson Hole *Guide* the first six months of their marriage, but Jay's work fascinated her and soon she resigned from the newspaper and began working with Jay as his full-time tying and guiding partner.

Kathy says it took her about six months of tying to please Jay with her work. At first she tied simple patterns and then moved on to more complicated hair-wing Western dry flies such as the Humpy. In 1973 they stopped tying flies for area sporting goods stores and started their own mail-order business, High Country Flies. At first they sold super-premium flies at giveaway prices, but they since have raised their prices to a more realistic level. Yet I still feel their Western patterns are worth twice what they charge. Anyone who sees or uses their flies agrees they are works of art; in fact, they are in great demand by collectors. Recently Len Bearden at the Millpond in California began offering limited-edition selections of their original ties.

Jay and Kathy usually tie, process mail orders and guide clients together. They enjoy their life and work so much that they seldom argue. Their partnership is based on building, working and sharing success. Their guiding and fishing hones their perspectives for tying days. They see how the flies cast, fish and endure wear. They see what is right with them and what is wrong, what is needed, effective or unnecessary. This is the finest experience any tyer can ask for to reach the absolute peak of perfection, and it seems to be the common denominator behind all great fly-tyers past and present. I know of no better innovator of all aspects of fly-tying than Jay. In fact, Jay is atypical of most professional fly-tyers in that he continues to research and innovate, a trait more common to master amateurs than order-laden professionals. Jay always had something new on his mind, in his vise or at the end of his latest cast.

Jay suggests that a youngster start tying as soon as possible after learning to fly-fish. He cautions teenage fly-tyers to not burn themselves out by tying too much initially, especially for sale. There is a big demand for good tyers, but if tyers want to go professional, they should specialize in designs and patterns that they like to tie and know most about. A budding tyer should not worry initially about quantity, but just work very hard on quality. It is the quality, not the quantity, that assures a demand for flies. Jay advises youngsters to be patient and get experience. In other words, "get your act together" before you expose yourself and your name to the public. Most full-time, high-production professionals last about eight to ten years. Usually then they must either expand into a larger operation with other tyers or use their reputation and experience to open up new areas of work such as lecturing, writing or consulting.

The Buchners plan to continue High Country Flies, limit their guiding and do more writing and lecturing on fly-tying and fly-fishing. Kathy particularly wants to write and has published some feature articles. They are close friends with Bonnie and René Harrop, Mike and Sheralee Lawson, and Don and Mary Hathaway, three other talented professional fly-tying couples in the Wyoming-Idaho area.

Three fall seasons ago, Jay and Kathy invited my wife, Joan, and me to enjoy a busman's holiday of floating and fishing. We floated and waded all day down a beautiful river backdropped by the Tetons and a vivid blue September sky. We traded boats and rowing turns and caught beautiful wild cutthroats all day. At lunch Kathy and Jay broiled trout and fried potatoes spiced with onions over an aspen and alderwood fire while Joan cut up a fresh salad. I opened cold beers and snapped pictures. The sun was almost touching the Tetons when Jay raised a 22-inch cutthroat from a boulder-strewn run on one of Kathy's fluorescent green-bodied Humpies. She waded out and stood by his side with the net to land and release his prize. Not thirty minutes later, he did her the honors as she got a 20-incher from a willow overhang on a Hopper that Jay had tied just the day before.

THE HUMPY by Kathy Buchner

(Editor's note: *I asked Kathy to write about her best fly, the Humpy, as she, in my opinion, is the foremost tyer today of this unique Western pattern. The Humpy is extremely difficult to tie right, even for the accomplished tyer, yet Kathy has developed her own methods that make it quite easy to do. Although the Humpy is not a new fly pattern, it is enjoying a new wave of popularity not only in the West but all across America. This is because it is being tied in much smaller sizes and in many new body-wing-hackle patterns. It is also an outstanding salmon and smallmouth bass dry fly. D.W.*)

The Humpy was the second or third fly I learned to tie. Since Jay already knew all the little tricks to tying Humpies, I learned them at the very beginning. Consequently, this fly seemed very easy to me and became my favorite fly to tie. I just assumed that the Humpy would be an easy fly for everyone else, too.

However, the first time I demonstrated tying the Humpy, I was astonished to learn how many people hate tying this fly and consider it to be very difficult. The reason, I found, is that most people have not had the benefit of having someone show them how to tie the Humpy. They have simply read the "pattern" in a book and seen a picture of the completed fly, or they have looked at one tied by someone else and tried to copy it.

The look of surprise and then delight on their faces as they watched me tie this pattern told me that the simple techniques I had taken for granted from the beginning were not common knowledge at all. And I began to see just how difficult this fly would be without the benefit of these few tricks.

I hope that the following instructions and photos will help make tying the Humpy easier and more fun for you.

The Humpy

Hook:	7957B (most common sizes are 10 to 18)
Tying thread:	3/0 mono for sizes 10 to 14, 6/0 mono for sizes 16 to 18; any color you want for the underbelly of the fly; single strand fluorescent floss
Tail:	stiff moose body hair
Body and wings:	mule deer or elk body hair
Hackle:	grizzly and brown, saddles first choice

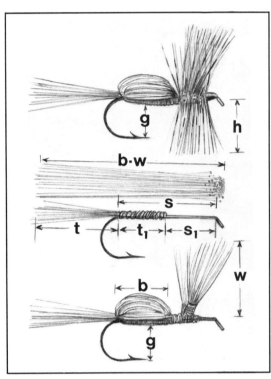

Humpy Proportions Diagram

g: gape of hook (known factor)
h: hackle length
w: wing length
t: tail length
b: body length
s: shank length (known factor)
$b \cdot w$: length of body and wing hair
t_1: tail tiedown area

$h = 1\frac{1}{2}g$
$w = 2g$
$t = s$
$b \cdot w = 2s$
$t_1 = \frac{1}{2}s$
$s_1 = \frac{1}{2}s$
$b = \frac{1}{2}s$

1. One of the major problems tyers have with the Humpy is getting the proportions of the fly correct—that is, the tail, body and wing lengths. *The key to the whole thing is the length of the tail. If the tail is the right length, everything else will come out right.*

The tail is measured, as with most dry flies, to be the same length as the hook shank (from the eye of the hook to the beginning of the bend of the hook). That is, the tail extends beyond the bend of the hook the same length as the hook shank. It is important that the tail material be long enough so that it is tied down in the *middle* of the hook shank. It is helpful in measuring the tail to mark the length of the hook shank on your scissors.

2. In preparing the clump of hair for the Humpy body and wings, it is important to remove as much of the fuzz and short hairs as possible. The tips of some deer or elk hair are naturally even enough, but most are not. If not, align the tips in a hair evener before measuring.

The deer or elk body hair that forms the body (hump) and wings is then measured to equal the length of the tail and hook shank combined. Hold the clump of hair over the hook, lining up the tips (ends) of the hair with the end of the tail, and then position the fingers to hold the hair just at the eye of the hook. Clip the butt ends of the hair off right at the fingers.

3. Another common problem people have with the Humpy is keeping the body and wing hair from rolling around the hook shank while tying it down. Here's how to cure that problem.

Keeping a tight hold on the clump of hair you have just measured and clipped, move the hair back to the *middle* of the hook shank. It will be tied down just over the tail. First make a few loose wraps of thread around the hair and hook shank. Then tighten the thread, pulling *straight down* on the bobbin.

Then move the fingers back, holding the hair *up off the hook shank* and away from the tail as you wrap the thread back toward the bend of the hook. Once the hair is securely tied down, continue to wrap the hair until it is completely covered with thread. The thread, of course, forms the "underbelly" color of the Humpy.

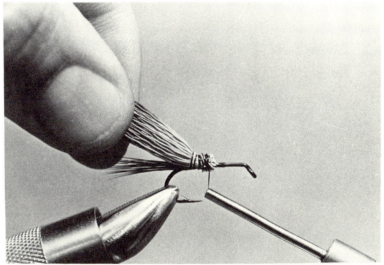

4. Now grasp the tips of the body hair and fold the hair forward. Smooth the hair and adjust it at the fold so that it is even on either side of the hook. Holding the hair tips tightly with the right hand *up off the hook shank,* make two or three loose wraps of thread just in front of the ledge formed by the body and tail hair at the middle of the hook shank. Still holding the tips of the hair up, pull the thread tight, pulling the bobbin straight down. This procedure keeps the body hair from rolling around under the belly of the fly.

Many people have told me that they have trouble separating the body hair from the tail hair as they fold the body hair forward. This problem is eliminated if the tail and body hair have been measured correctly, because the body hair extends beyond the tail, allowing you to grasp it alone. Furthermore, if the body hair is tied down correctly in a compact clump *on top* of the hook shank, it is less likely to get mixed up with the tail.

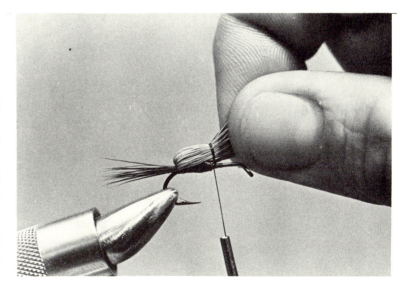

5. Once the hair is tied securely, continue wrapping forward slightly with the thread to form a small "platform" between the body and wings. Obviously, this also moves the wings forward. The wings should be just slightly behind center of the front half of the hook shank.

When the wings are in the proper position, hold the hair up and back and wrap the thread ten or twelve times in front of the wings to help stand them up. Then divide the wings evenly and wrap with figure eights to separate them. Also wrap the base of each wing two or three times. End with the thread back of the wings.

6. If you have measured the tail correctly, measured the body/wing hair correctly, based on the length of the tail and hook shank, and positioned the wings correctly, the wings will be exactly the right length—that is, the same length or slightly shorter than the hackle (one and a half to two hook gaps).

Since Humpies are designed to be high-floating flies, we like them heavily hackled. We use a grizzly and brown saddle hackle, with two wraps of each behind the wings and three or four wraps in front of the wings. This, of course, requires rather long hackles. The hackle is tied in with the dull, or concave, side of the feathers facing forward.

Complete the fly with a whip finish and apply a coat of Laggie's head cement or varnish.

Summary: 1. Measure tail; tie in middle of hook shank.
2. Clean, even, and measure body/wing hair.
3. Tie in middle of hook shank.
4. Fold over body hair.
5. Make platform for hackle and divide wings.
6. Wrap hackle and whip-finish.

THE JAY DAVE'S HOPPER by Jay Buchner

(Editor's note: *A couple of seasons ago, Jay showed me a kicker-legged hopper he was tying and fishing with great success. After I got back to Oklahoma I kept thinking about Jay's hopper with legs, so I put a half dozen live hoppers in one of my aquariums. I was amazed that the hopper legs from a fish's-eye view were as important as the wing silhouette of a mayfly in the total look of the live hopper. So I wrote Jay and suggested he tie up some legged Dave's Hoppers and try them before the hopper season was over that fall. He did, and they worked like magic on big cutthroat and brown trout.*

I consider this to be the best grasshopper pattern ever devised. It can be tied in all sizes from 16 to 1/0 in many color variations to match local hoppers in sizes and shapes. It is also a superb cricket and katydid design tied in the appropriate colors and body silhouette. Tie it with either a small or a large head to better accommodate the water it is fished in. Remember, grasshoppers do not float high but lie nearly submerged in the surface film. D.W.)

The Jay Dave's Hopper

Hook:	TDE 2XL—Mustad 94831 or 9671 or Herter 3029T, sizes 2 through 16
Tying thread:	Herb Howard's prewaxed 6/0, color to match wing and head or white
Tail:	red or blue short stiff natural deer hair
Body:	cream or yellow orlon or polypropylene yarn
Rib:	light-brown or grizzly hackle
Underwing:	light-yellow or gray deer body hair
Wing:	speckled turkey or peacock wing quill sprayed with Tuffilm (Microweb wing material colored appropriately is a good substitute for natural feather)
Legs:	golden pheasant tail feather or similar marked long-fiber feather
Collar:	well-grizzled short mule or whitetail deer hair
Head:	coarse mule or whitetail deer body hair
Cement:	Tuffilm spray, Pliobond and rod varnish

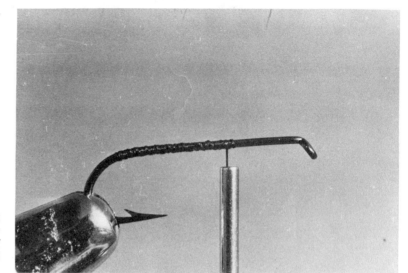

1. Place hook horizontally in vise jaws so that point and barb are exposed. Tighten jaws firmly, but not very tight. Attach tying thread and wrap rear two thirds of shank with thread, finishing at front portion of wrapped shank.

2. Cut a small bunch of tail hair and align tips with hair aligner to form tail. Trim butts to equal length of hook shank. Tie hair to shank just at front and on top of thread-wrapped area. Hold deer hair with thumb and index finger and wrap hair firmly—but not tightly—down to shank as you keep it *on top* of shank. *Do not* use so much thread pressure as to flare hair; tail should be compact and extend one third to one half the length of shank past hook's bend. Return thread to front portion of tail wrap.

3. Body (a): Cut a strand of body yarn several inches long. Attach its tip to front wrap area, and spiral-wrap it with thread down on top of the hook back to bend. There, make several wraps to well anchor yarn to hook.

4. Body (b): Form a short extended butt with looped yarn and tie down to hook's bend. Attach hackle for rib at this point also, but under shank. Coat material-covered shank with Pliobond.

5. Body (c): Spiral-wrap shank with body yarn to form body, stopping tying off and trimming excess just at front end of wrapped hook shank. *Do not extend body onto front third of hook shank!*

6. Body rib (a): Spiral hackle over body to form rib. Tie off and trim excess at front of body, but again *not over front third of hook shank.*

7. Body rib (b): Trim hackle fiber to about one to one half the gape of hook in length, except on top of body. Here, trim off hackle flush with body.

8. Underwing: Cut a bunch of deer hair equal in thickness to diameter of body. Align tips and trim at butts so that hair is equal in length to hook shank. Attach underwing hair to top front of body by tying down just ends of butts, firmly but not so tightly as to flare the hair. Make sure you hold hair *on top of body!* Put a small drop of Pliobond on tie-down area.

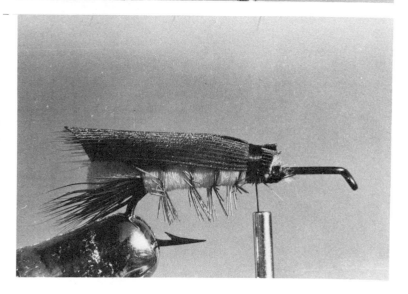

9. Wing: Select a quill section or piece of Microweb that is approximately two to two and a half widths of the body underwing. It should be at least as long or longer than hook shank. Carefully tie butt end down over front end on top of underwing, again using just firm thread pressure to avoid flaring distortion of under- and main wing.

(Editor's note: *Wing can be trimmed to length and shape before tying in, but I recommend this be done after all fly-tying is completed to match more perfectly the wing length and shape with the overall leg, body and head dimensions. D.W.*)

10. Jumping legs for hopper:
a. Place feather in fly-tying vise as shown. Stem may have to be flattened with pliers.

b. From right side of feather, select a section of feather fibers of the desired width (wider for larger flies) and hold them horizontal with the left hand.

c. Using forceps (curved are best) held in right hand, insert tips between feather fibers and left hand. (Insert forceps into space above left hand and under feather fibers.) This is the important step.

d. Holding fibers in left hand, bring left hand to the left (if the hands are properly crossed in previous step, there is no other place to go with left hand).

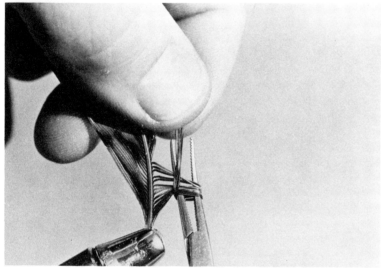

e. Bring tips up with left hand to now-open forceps jaws. Forceps should now be circled by feather fibers.

f. Close forceps on fibers and pull down through loop.

g. Before tightening knot, you can move it around to the proper position on the fibers. After knot is tightened and leg is put into proper angle, place a small drop of Pliobond on knot joint.

h. To do other side of the feather, turn feather around in vise, or just reverse hand positions.

(Editor's note: *After legs are formed and joint-cemented, a coat of Tuffilm or thinned head cement greatly increases durability of legs. I recommend that you knot up several dozen pairs of legs at a time, of whatever sizes you will need, to save time and ensure consistency. D.W.*)

11. Jumping-leg attachment: Coat sides of wing-body base with contact cement. Do same with inside of each kicker-leg base. Attach each leg to *side* of wing-body base. Wrap thread just firmly, not tightly! Set and angle legs about 10 to 15 degrees over horizontal wing plane.

(Editor's note: step-wing and wing finish: *At this point, it is most efficient to half-hitch off thread and set fly aside and tie to this stage other Jay Dave's Hoppers needed. This step-tying greatly enhances efficiency and reduces complication of this pattern. If step-tying is done, paint each hopper wing with thinned rod varnish before you begin collar and head. After they dry, trim wings to length and shape. Reattach thread on bare third of shank to finish fly. D.W.*)

12. Collar: For the first time, tying thread is advanced from wing-body area to front third of hook shank.

   (Editor's note: *The tyer who is not an accomplished deer-hair flarer could change to a larger, stronger thread to do this job. D.W.*)

Cut a bunch of collar deer hair approximately the diameter of the wing-body base. Clean out underfur with a comb or toothbrush. Align tips in a hair stacker. Trim bases so that hair is approximately equal to shank length. With hair tip extending back toward tail, hold hair horizontal with body. Wrap thread around hair bunch so that tips extend back just as far as hook's barb. With two loose wraps around hair and hook shank, begin a third but much tighter wrap to spin and flare hair equally around bare hook shank. Make two or three additional tight wraps around collar hair and shank in exactly the same area to anchor hair firmly to hook shank. This is exactly the procedure used to tie a Muddler Minnow collar.

   Advance thread forward in front of collar hair. With thumb and index finger, even collar hair around shank. Now push it firmly back against base of wing-body area of hook shank. Make two or three tight thread wraps up against base of this hair collar.

13. Head: Cut a little larger bunch of deer hair for head and clean it of underfur. Trim off tips and, using deer hair, wrap and flare bunch onto hook. If head does not completely occupy most of bare shank, add a second bunch and flare. Again, use the same procedure used to form a Muddler Minnow head. Advance thread forward to hook eye and push and pack head hair very tightly against collar hair base! This will give you a small area to finish head off.

14. Tie-off: With thread, close off hook-eye loop junction and whip-finish. Cut away thread. Inspect head for uniformity and pull hair even if head appears to be lopsided.

   Head finish: With sharp curved or straight-blade scissors or razor blade, trim head down to match body-wing diameter, or leave it a little larger. Trim bottom of head very close to hook shank to keep hook point and gape better exposed for hooking. Collar tips are not trimmed off except on top and bottom. Leave tips mostly on sides for best flotation and crawling-leg simulation. Head and collar are trimmed accordingly to best fish the type of water it is to be used in.

   Finish: Clipped head should receive a drop of thin rod varnish or head cement. After this and other cements are dry, spray-coat entire fly with Scotchgard to enhance durability and waterproofing. For heavy, rough water rub the clipped head with Musclin paste, Gink or Dilly wax to make it stay up.

   (Editor's note: *Billy Munn of Bridgeport, Texas, has a wonderful method he uses to finish the Hopper head. Billy soaks the untrimmed deer-hair head with* very thinned, clear, fast-dry head cement. *After it dries, it has become just slightly stiffened and fixed, so that it can be trimmed much smoother and with far less effort with a razor blade or sharp scissors. D.W.*)

V. Saltwater Flies

12. Lew Jewett's Blue Crab
by LEW JEWETT

(Editor's note: *The Jewett's Blue Crab is a very fine example of the new trend in saltwater fly-tying. The fly closely simulates a blue crab in size, color and action. It is easy to tie, and the materials are available and inexpensive. Moreover, it is durable and casts well. And with some color modifications, Jewett's Blue Crab could also easily imitate other species of crabs. D.W.*)

Wherever blue crabs are found in salt or brackish water, they are a favorite food for many fish. The permit, for example, considers the blue crab a prime morsel. Bait fishermen seldom fish permit successfully with any bait other than a live crab. Several years ago, I started experimenting with a variety of ties to imitate the blue crab, and the pattern that finally evolved was tested this past year in the Florida Keys and the Sea of Cortez with excellent results. Permit, a prized trophy for the saltwater fly fisherman, relish this Blue Crab fly.

Lew Jewett's Blue Crab

Hook:	Wright & McGill 66S 1/0, 2/0, 3/0
Tying thread:	Creative Sports single-strand nylon floss (white or yellow)
Body weight: (optional)	lead fuse wire six to ten wraps on hook shank just in front of mid-hook shank
Underbody: (crab belly)	five to six yellow-gold feathers from back of a golden pheasant skin, or five to six mallard flank feathers dyed pale golden-yellow

Crab body: (crab back)	fifteen pale-blue-and-brindle metallic feathers from a cock ring-necked pheasant's back. Try to select ones that have a bronze tip on them (lowest blue-brindle feathers)
Cement:	Pliobond rubber cement for feather bases tie-downs, 5-minute epoxy for head finish, or Al Price's head cement
Snag guard: (optional)	hard, colorless nylon monofilament of .021- to .024-inch diameter

Photo sequence by Ron Winch

1. Hook and thread: Place hook deep into vise standard jaws, or use magnum jaws or Hunter's HMH vise. Attach tying thread to front portion of hook shank. Coat wraps with Pliobond. Keel hook can be substituted for 66S hook if desired.

Underbody (belly): Tie five to six golden-yellow pheasant feathers or dyed mallard flank feathers very close to hook eye on *underside* of hook shank. The hook may be inverted to make it easier to tie in these feathers. Try to get a fanlike spread on these feathers and make them extend one shank length past the hook bend. The spread is accomplished by tying each stem butt at an angle to the hook shank. Clip away any excess stems and cement tie-down area.

2. Crab body (left side of back): Considerable time and effort can be saved if you will join the three to five blue-brindle pheasant groups together with Pliobond before they are placed in the three back positions of left, right and center. Simply put a small amount of Pliobond on the bases and, when it becomes tacky, stack the five feathers together and press the bases together and let dry. Be careful to use only a small amount of Pliobond just at the very bases so as not to ruin feathers' shape and texture.

The wide oval crab shape is created first by taking five of the stacked blue pheasant feathers and tying them to the *left top side* of the hook shank at one time. Feather stem butts are angled across top of hook shank, pointing to the right; tips extended back and to the left. Be careful to keep this group and next groups horizontal (flat) to the hook shank to assure the wide flat shape of a blue crab. Also make sure you crowd the hook eye with these tie-downs, leaving just a very short space for final head whip-finish. Apply a small amount of Pliobond to tie-down area.

3. Crab body (right side of back): Take second stack of five pheasant feathers and place them across top of hook shank in the same horizontal plane just behind the hook-eye position, except stem butts are angled from right side to left side and feather tips then point to angle right of hook shank. Carefully wrap down with thread, keeping them together, flat and horizontal with hook shank. After second bunch is secure and trimmed, apply a drop of Pliobond to tie down. Check position of both bunches, which should now be in the same position on right and left top side of hook shank.

4. Crab body (top of back): Place third bunch of brindle-blue pheasant feathers directly over the top, straight down the hook shank, hold firmly in position, and carefully wrap and tighten them to top of hook just behind the hook eye. Add more Pliobond and make final flat position adjustment with fingers.

5. Crab blades: Take two identical jungle cock blades and set them on either far side back to effect an edge of the fly. They should not extend past the end of the brindle-blue back feathers. Make sure they, too, are set and tied in flat—not offset or angled. Those edges can also be done with orange grizzly hackle tips, cree hackle tips or orange bucktail.

Crab finish: After all feathers are set, carefully whip-finish head with tying thread. Mix small amount of 5-minute epoxy or Al Price's head cement and coat head and just into the bases of feather bases.

13. The Bally Hoo Tail Streamer
by MIKE PRAZNOVSKY, JR.

One day I started thinking big. Big about what? About going to the offshore reefs and trying my luck against some bigger fish than I had been used to catching. My fly-fishing experience had all been backcountry-style, fishing in water sometimes six inches to six feet in depth.

I looked around for some patterns I could tie to fish with. I looked at all the standard patterns, but none was to my liking. I began trying something I called the Bally Hoo fly.

I showed this Bally Hoo fly to John Donnell, who is a local Orvis dealer and an avid saltwater fly fisherman. John and I discussed the possibilities of this pattern. I gave John a few to field-test. About two weeks and a couple of fishing trips later, John and I sat down and compared notes. We both agreed about one thing: the fly looked good in the water but was very difficult to cast. The nylon would mat while false-casting. Temporarily I went back to my backcountry fishing, and the Bally Hoo was put off to the side.

Later I had a chance to visit a friend of mine, Lefty Kreh, who was in town doing some promotional work at a local rod shop. I showed Lefty this fly and told him the problems I was experiencing. Lefty looked at it and suggested that I glue the tail together at the very end. We talked for a while; then I beat a straight path home for the glue.

At first I could not decide if it would work. It should work; Lefty had said it would. The fly looked funny sitting there in the vise with a little glued stub at the tip of the tail. The real proof was in the casting and appearance in the water. The nearest canal was to be the testing water. The casting was perfect, and in the water the fly looked even better than before. I called John and told him of my trials and success.

Later that night, I had a flashback about something Lefty had said that day. Lefty had told of the days when fish would accept most any pattern fished, but now the fish have become more educated and are not so easily fooled by patterns that do not simulate the fish they prey upon, and new patterns would have to resemble the real thing more and more. My Bally Hoo looked somewhat like the real thing but was not perfect. When I took a closer look at a real bally hoo and my fly, things stuck out that were lacking on the fly: a reddish-orange spot on the tip of the beak, also eyes and a tail.

The spot and eyes were easy to copy, but a *tail?* I started looking for ways to turn the stub end into a tail. It took about two days of testing. Then at last I had a tail that looked real.

How about fish? Does it really catch fish? I started throwing this fly at anything that swims. Dolphin, cobia, amberjack and kingfish have fallen victim to the fly. It works especially well with barracuda. I have found it best to make a long cast to known barracuda hangouts. Put the fly rod between your legs and use a fast two-handed retrieve. The fast retrieve drives barracuda up the wall. You have to be careful when doing this; if not, you may lose a good rod and reel.

A good friend of mine, Bob White of Fort Myers, Florida, saw a couple of flies in my fly box. He liked what he saw and told me he was going to take a couple home to try. Bob called back to report limited success and a few problems. He caught snook, but the fly sank too fast.

I converted a sinker to a floater by removing the thread head and replacing it with cork. I went snook fishing soon after the conversion to try the floater out. We anchored the boat upcurrent and started casting across the current. The fly would drift back under the bridge. I slowly swept my fly rod back and forth with small six-inch retrieves, giving the fly a look of a baitfish playing in the current of the bridge. The fly worked so well I got my limit of four snook in one hour.

I sent Bob the floating Bally Hoo and told him about my luck. Bob has used this floater very well on snook, tarpon and jack. Ladyfish and some big trout (weakfish) have been fooled by it, too.

The Bally Hoo Tail Streamer

Hook:	WMC 254 CA, sizes 1/0 to 5/0
Tying thread:	clear mono, size A white, lime floss
Body:	green over white nylon, 6½ to 7 inches
Mylar:	silver and blue $1/16$-inch wide
Eyes:	red, white, blue enamel (painted)
Cheek:	reddish-orange enamel (painted)
Cement:	fast- and slow-setting epoxy
	(*Note:* Because of the size and teeth of the fish that this fly attracts, I use no head cement. Instead, I use two different kinds of clear epoxy. The first is slow-drying (about two hours). The second is fast-drying (about five minutes). The first epoxy is used to hold the fly together; the second is used for the finish over the painted heads.)
Variations:	body—green over yellow, blue over white; head—cork head for floater instead of size A thread

1. Wrap mono thread around hook and apply slow-drying epoxy. Tie white nylon at mid-shank back to underside of hook. Repeat with the green in same shank area on top. Use more white nylon than green (two thirds white, one third green). Both equal lengths. Add mylar to each side (two strips silver, one strip blue). Bring mylar back half the length of the fly. Try to use mylar strips that are free of curl.

2. Cover tie-down area with slow-drying epoxy and begin white size A thread. Form head and wrap shank up to eye of hook. Finish thread with a whip finish. Be sure at this point to wipe off any excess epoxy.

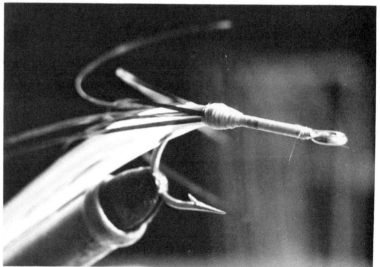

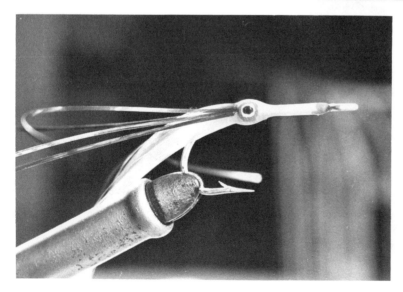

3. Cover head and shank with lime-green floss. Also use whip finish for floss. Paint eyes at the point where nylon butts are tied to shank and cheek band just behind hook eye. Cover head and shank of hook with fast-drying epoxy.

4. Comb nylon to straighten out fibers. Make sure white nylon strands are divided evenly between hook's bend to ensure conformity and balance in lower body. Tie a slip knot with tying thread and put it over body at hook's bend. Tighten down only snugly and slide back toward tail. When in place, snug knot tight. Make sure both green and white nylon are pulled back evenly together, *all slack out and not mixed,* before you tighten slip knot! With your thumb and forefinger, hold knot and fan nylon out to form tail.

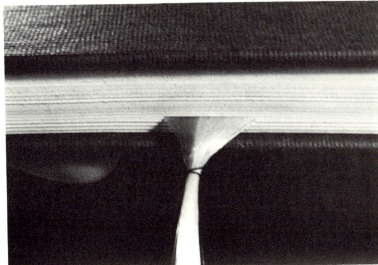

5. Place fanned-out portion of tail in a book or spring-loaded paper clamp to hold its shape. While in place, use fast-drying epoxy to keep its shape. Maintain tension on body to keep its wrist shape at tail.

6. Remove from book or clamp when epoxy has dried. Trim off knot and shape tail "V" with very sharp scissors.

For floater, follow tying steps for Bally Hoo Tail Streamer through step 3. Make a bullet-shaped cork or balsa head ¾ inch long and ⅜ inch in diameter.

Slot head and bore out to fit over hook shank and nylon butt of wings tie-down area. Fill slot with fast-drying epoxy and fit over hook.

After epoxy sets, paint floating head and nose with lime-green enamel. Overcoat it with clear epoxy to protect head and paint from premature wear.

Proceed to steps 4 and 5 of Bally Hoo Tail Streamer and form tail as described.

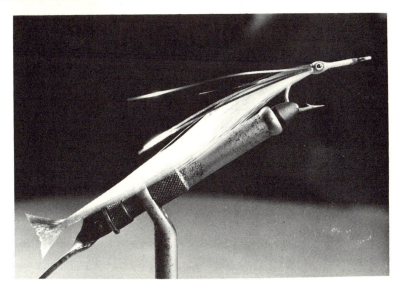

14. The Mono-Body Knot
by CAPTAIN RICK RUOFF

This knot is begun at the most forward portion of the desired mono-body (closest to the eye of the hook). A circle is made with the body material, which can be any type of colored or clear monofilament line. The flat mono provides an interesting body form, but it is very difficult to work with because of the amount of twist produced. The length of line in this circle corresponds to the length of the body desired. Experience wil be your best guide. Sixteen inches would be about right for a full size 2 streamer body. The smaller patterns seem to achieve best results with correspondingly lighter-weight mono lines. Small nymphs work out nicely with 6- to 8-pound test, while 10 to 15 will suffice for most situations. For the larger streamers, such as salmon and tarpon flies, I use a 20- to 30-pound-test mono, depending on length of body and size of hook.

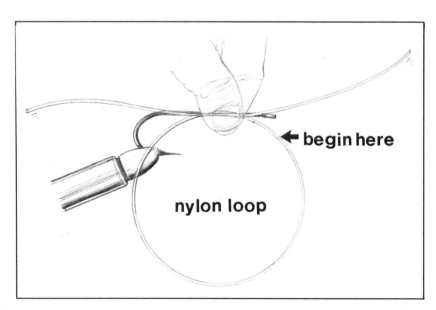

Illustration of first position of Mono-Body Knot, showing loop position, ends, and holding on hook.

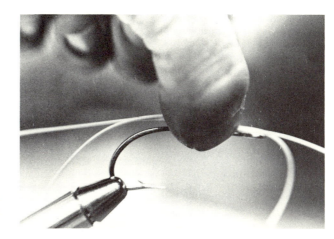

1. Form a loop with the nylon filament and place the crossing point of the two ends of the circle at the most forward portion of the body.

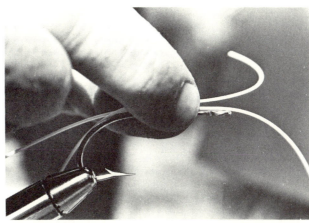

2. Ends should protrude approximately 2 inches past the eye and bend, respectively.

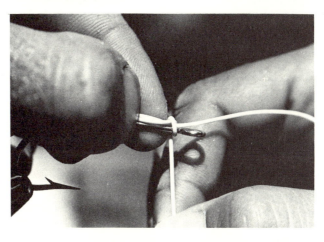

3. Pinch double line with thumb and forefinger closely to hook at desired body starting point.

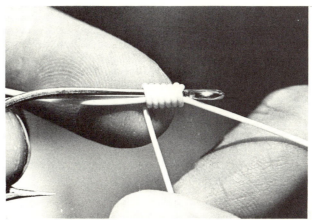

4. Grasp forward portion of loop and wrap closely and carefully back over double strands and continue until body is complete. Try to keep nylon strand straight along body as you wrap over it and body (hook shank). Make sure there are no gaps.

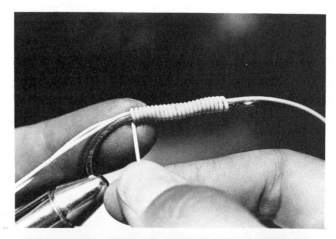

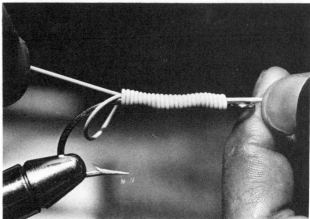

5. Squeeze remaining loop tightly against hook behind last wrap and pull the forward (protruding) end slowly. It requires a firm grasp, and the use of forceps or a small pair of pliers aids greatly. The loop is pulled inside the knot, and a tight, clean, compact fly body results that requires no further wrapping or tie-down. I generally grasp the posterior end and pull it snug also, just to eliminate any possible slippage. Clear cement or epoxy can be applied to enhance durability still further.

Now that we have completed the body, let's look at several useful additions. To achieve the most reflective finish possible, I always underwrap the area of the body with mylar or shiny aluminum foil. When the mono body is applied over this wrap, a very deep, scalelike reflective finish results. When clear, colorless nylon is dyed various colors, all sorts of colored flash bodies are possible. When you are wrapping long bodies on large flies or Keel hooks, the mono has a tendency to bind and break as the knot is pulled tight. To solve this problem, I rub a tiny dab of liquid soap on the area before the body is applied, and the knot will pull down very smoothly.

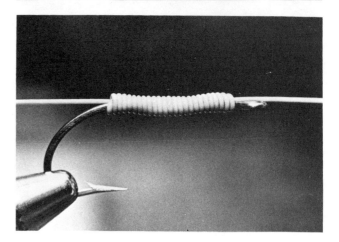

The mono-body is not a new invention. It has been used for a good many years by a few anglers in both fresh and salt water. This mono-body knot is simply a method whereby the body can be created more quickly and conveniently. It is certainly much more compact, because it is *completely self-contained* and *requires no tie-down of materials.* And if used on a "back-tied" fly, it forms a head/body that is very durable and attractive, with no head to lacquer or cement.

The new uses and applications of this body style are unlimited. It is a most successful nymph body because of its rugged construction and translucent appearance. In streamers the advantages are obvious in the distinctive scalelike finish and the myriad colors available in monofilament line. (No more chewed tinsel or piping bodies.) In the mono-body fly that I tie for some of the more dental denizens, such as mackerel and barracuda, I epoxy the body and base of the wing, creating an extremely long-lasting fly. And on occasions that call for high visibility, a fluorescent orange or yellow monofilament body will entice even the most myopic game fish. Here is a photograph of a finished fly.

VI. Unique Flies

15. Latex Roly-polies
by A. L. (TONY) SHUFFREY

American fly-tyers are much keener on new methods and materials than those here in the United Kingdom, and as one who always has an eye on new materials, I was fascinated by the articles on latex by Raleigh Boaze, Jr., and Bill Charles in the first volume of *The Fly-Tyer's Almanac*.

I soon obtained some liquid latex and tried coating my own sheets of dyed latex as described by Bill Charles. Those who have handled latex adhesive will know how any surplus on the spreader or your fingers can be rubbed off. In doing so, it rolls up into "worms." I realized that these looked just like fly bodies; that started me on my way, and I lost no time in using a "worm" to make a detached fly body. I have since developed a whole new field of techniques, and I am sure that more are to be found. I do not tie as much as roll, so I have called these flies Latex Roly-polies, no matter what species of aquatic life they imitate. In the United States, the name probably would be meaningless, but here roly-poly is the name of an old-fashioned country sweet or pudding made by spreading jam on a layer of suet pastry and rolling it up before baking. Recently I visited the put-and-take fishery at Avington, which has some very large rainbows, and a friend caught a 14-pound 11-ounce fish on a Roly-poly floating snail.

In the United Kingdom, there are two easily available latex adhesives, sold in hardware and handicraft stores in convenient 2-ounce tubes or 4- and 6-ounce jars under the names Copydex and Caratex.

The latex can be used either straight from the jar or with a little decanted into a separate small container and diluted with some water—say, 10 to 20 percent. A spare 135-millimeter film magazine container gives an ideal seal for storage. The dilution controls the thickness of the latex coating and in turn the diameter of the fly body.

Dip your finger or a strip of plastic, such as a plant pot label, into the latex and spread it on a piece of glass, Formica or other plastic surface as shown.

I use some square pieces of glass and smear patches of latex about 1 inch wide and 4 inches long, parallel to each of the four edges. I stand them on edge in a toast rack while they are drying.

When the latex is dry, after a quarter to a half hour, according to the thickness, one can start. The dried latex on the sheets of glass should be protected from dust.

The first trials were with the dried latex colored with a fiber pen and rolled up with the finger. But then I realized that ribs could be added by making parallel stripes with a fine fiber pen as shown in the next photo. Since then, I have rolled the bodies with all sorts of materials inside. Feather, fiber or hair can be included and left projecting for the tails of mayflies, nymphs, etc.

A most useful inclusion is a strip of metalized mylar or tinsel as a longitudinal core, also shown. This shows through and gives a translucence and brilliance.

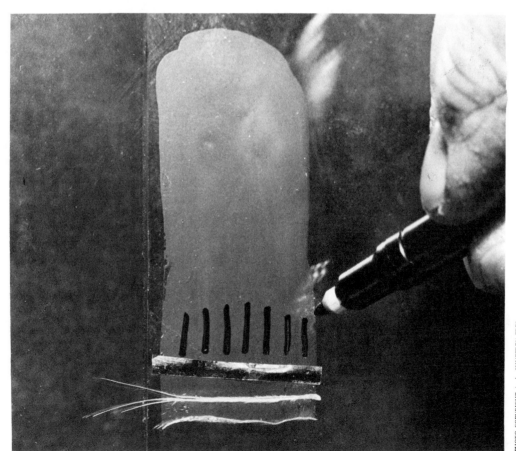

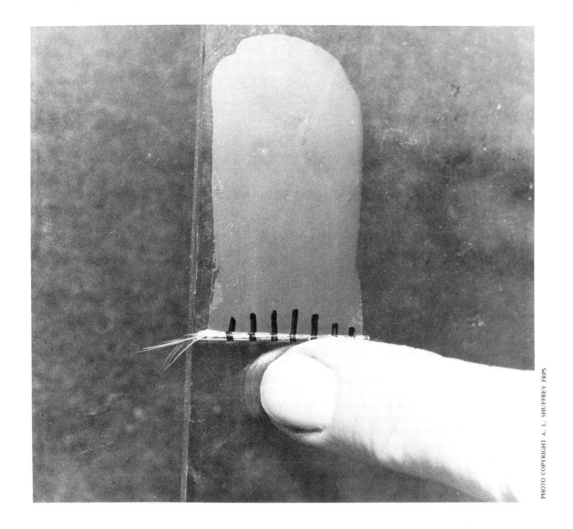

When you have rolled sufficient latex for the body, cut the latex with a knife or scalpel.

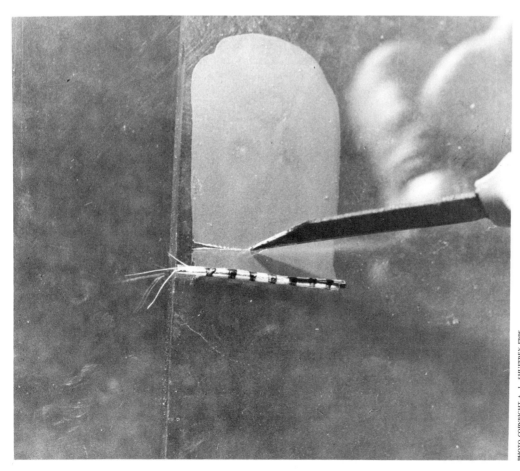

To speed marking the "ribs" on the latex, I have had some rubber stamps made. They work quite well, but I am still seeking a satisfactory quick-drying ink pad where the ink takes on the latex without tending to smudge.

Because the marking does not have to be waterproof, there is the possibility of marking in quite fine detail with a brush or fine fiber pen. Ribs or other marks need not be continued all around the body. Our principal mayfly, *Ephemera danica*, has distinct blotch marks on the upper side near the tail. These can be marked on the body using the felt pen before rolling the last convolutions of latex, as shown.

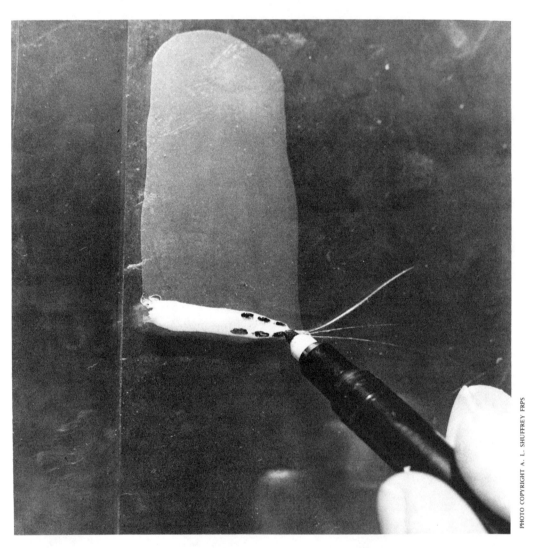

For the chironomid or midge pupae, usually called "buzzers" on English lakes, the striped rib and the glistening tinsel core are particularly suitable. The body can either be left detached or, for the hooked shape of the typical buzzer, the end of the latex body can be impaled on the hook like a worm. It is easier to put the point of the hook through the latex and slide it over the barb before tying in the thorax end, because if this is done afterward it is quite difficult to avoid kinks or twists in the body. When a fish is hooked, the tail end of the fly body slides up the hook, which is some advantage. The point of the hook should pierce the latex body parallel to its length, not across; it will then set more naturally on the hook.

Alternatively, tying silk can be taken down the hook to the bend, at the same time tying in appropriate tail fibers. Tie down the tail end of the latex body with the silk coincident with the last rib marking. Take a few turns around the hook shank only, until the silk is in line with the next rib mark. Make one or two turns around the latex body at this point. Continue winding alternately around the hook shank and then the successive rib marks until the thorax position is reached. If heavier silk is used for this purpose, it is not really necessary to make the inked rib markings on the latex.

Foam plastic encapsulated in the latex with felt pen tinting can be bound in wide-open turns to make most realistic floating snails. Small "worms" of rolled latex can be stuck on at the head end to give them eyes or "antennae."

Caddis pupae and shrimp bodies with lead-wire strips and metalized mylar centers without rib markings can be bound onto the hook with open turns to give a segmented effect. In the case of the shrimp, the body is tied down over a palmered hackle, which forms the legs.

Phantom nymphs can be made by tying long, thin, uncolored worms of latex as detached bodies. A few white hackle fibers can be rolled in at the tail end to form breathing gills. After binding to the hook with a slight bump at the head end, small black eyes can be marked on with a fine black waterproof fiber pen.

An assortment of Roly-polies is shown here.

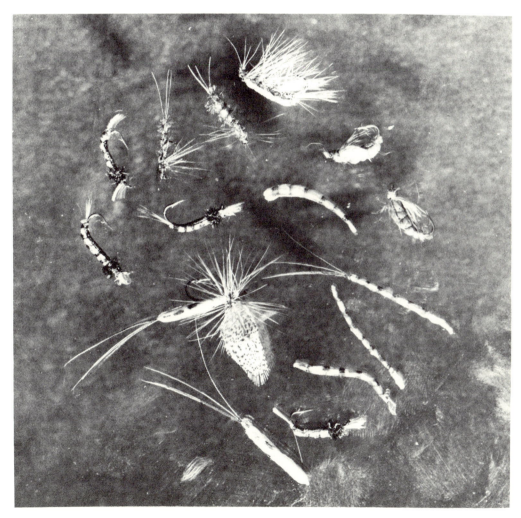

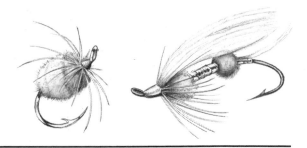

16. The Omelet Series for Steelhead, Salmon and Trout, *Part 1: Egg and Egg-Sperm Flies*

by DAVE WHITLOCK

Traditionally, fly-tying and fly-fishing have always emphasized matching or simulating aquatic and terrestrial insects, minnows and crustacea. Over the years, there has been only occasional interest in patterns that imitate fish eggs, egg-sac fry and very young swimming fry. Yet in many major fisheries, especially where salmon, steelhead, char and trout still have spawning runs, their eggs and fry are eagerly and regularly fed upon by most species present. This section offers patterns simulating eggs, egg sperm and fry.

When spawning fish pair and build their nest, this attracts other males, jacks of the species and resident fish. As the eggs are laid and fertilized and before they can drop into the coarse gravel pockets, many are eaten. As they incubate, they are often washed out by water turbulence and again may be eaten. When the eggs hatch, small helpless yolk-sac fry then emerge, and some are eaten when they expose themselves. As the yolk-sac fry develop, they become more active and developed physically. They move about, and some are eaten by resident fish. Later, when the yolk sac is completely used up, some swim-up fry are eaten as they school and feed in the streams or inlet lakes. These four stages represent a very important source of food to many fish, especially where natural reproduction is good.

Don Hathaway of McCall, Idaho, has created three special fry patterns, which he describes in Chapter 17, and I have rounded out the Omelet Series with the single-egg fly and the two-egg sperm fly. Neither pattern is totally new, but there are a great many fly-tyers today who are unfamiliar with them.

The Single-Egg Fly

This pattern simulates one or a small group of freshly laid trout, salmon or char eggs. It should be kept simple, in general size preparation and natural egg colors. Generally, colors run much brighter orange to red for sea-run fish to a pale orange or yellow for trout not feeding on crustacea in lakes or streams.

It should be fished slowly, tumbling right on the bottom, particularly below areas where spawning takes place.

Note: To imitate salmonid single-egg sizes accurately, please consider the following: eggs are smallest from small fish, largest from large fish. King salmon eggs average 6.5 to 7.5 millimeters; silver and sockeye, 5.5 to 6.5 millimeters; steelhead, 5 to 6 millimeters; rainbow and brown and brook, 3 to 4 millimeters.

Hook:	Wright & McGill Single Egg Salmo Hook No. 575 gold, sizes 8 to 12
Tying thread:	CSE single-strand nylon floss, fluorescent orange or pink
Weighting:	six or eight turns of small lead wire
Body:	medium or small chenille, either fluorescent orange, orange or light-orange
Hackle:	soft orange hackle from saddle or hen neck
Cement:	Al Price's clear head cement

1. Place hook in vise and attach thread. Overwrap shank with thread. If weighting the fly, place four to six turns of lead wire at mid-shank. Attach a 3- or 4-inch-length chenille to mid-shank with tying thread. Place a small amount of head cement on shank and lead.

2. Beginning at mid-shank point, build up by wrapping a pyramidlike design with the chenille until a round egg-shaped ball is formed the size to match a one- to three-egg clump. Tie off chenille wrap just behind fly's eye and trim off excess.

3. Attach a soft hackle, bright side out, just behind the hook eye, and make one or two turns around shank in front of body. Tie off excess and trim away excess. Often, two or more single-egg flies can be made with one hackle. Whip-finish head and paint it with a coat of Price's head cement.

Two-Egg-Sperm Fly

As far as I can learn, I originated this pattern some ten or twelve years ago for a dear friend of Dick Storts for his salmon and steelhead fishing trips to Alaska. Since its initial success I've refined it, and it has become an extremely effective and popular "egg-attractor" pattern for Pacific salmon, steelhead, rainbow, grayling, Arctic char and dollies. Some success has been reported even for Atlantic salmon. It is a much easier fly to fish effectively than the single- or clump-egg patterns because it does not always have to be fished on the nose of the egg feeders. The combination of white marabou, gold flash and fluorescent eggs seems irresistible.

Hook:	Mustad 3658-B or 9049, sizes 2 to 8
Tying thread:	Herb Howard's prewaxed Flymaster (fluorescent orange or red)
Body weight:	six to eight wraps of lead wire
Tag:	gold mylar (tinsel or thread)
Tail:	one golden pheasant crest feather
Body:	fluorescent chenille in orange, red, pink or green, with gold mylar tinsel
Wing:	white turkey marabou
Hackle:	one gold-orange or red-orange soft saddle hackle
Head:	fluorescent orange thread
Cement:	Al Price's head cement on body and head

1. Place hook in vise and attach tying thread just behind hook eye and overwrap shank's length. Wrap six to eight turns of lead wire mid-shank, approximately the size of hook's wire, to weight the body.

Just behind lead wraps, attach gold mylar tinsel. Wrap back to mid-bend and forward over first wraps to shank. Tie down tag and trim off excess. Just in front of bend and on top of hook shank, tie on a golden pheasant crest feather. Position it as the tail so the natural curve goes up and no longer than hook's bend. Trim excess.

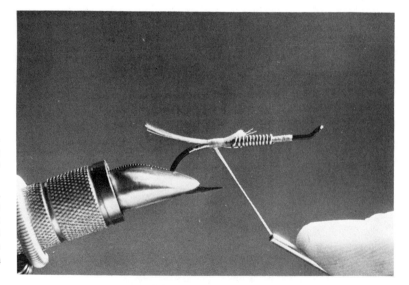

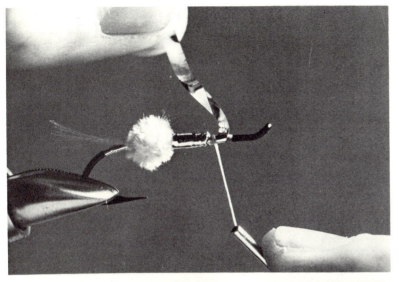

2. First egg body: Attach a 3- to 4-inch length of chenille to side of hook shank just behind lead wraps. Place a small amount of head cement over tie-down area and lead wraps. Wrap chenille in a pyramid order to form a small round ball just in front of tail. Trim excess chenille off.

   Body waist: Just in front of first egg, attach with tying thread a strip of gold mylar sheet or tinsel. Wrap it carefully and tightly up to and over lead wraps. Tie off just in front of lead wraps and trim away excess. This forms a neat gold waistband between first and second egg.

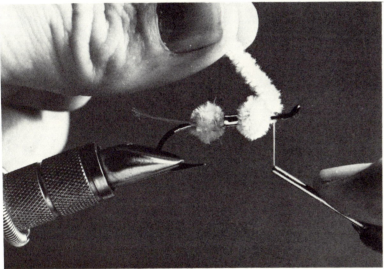

3. Second egg body: Attach another length of same chenille just in front of waist. Paint area with head cement and, before it dries, build a second egg with pyramided wraps. Tie off and trim away excess. Second egg should be just behind loop ends of hook eye, so that one fourth of shank is still exposed.

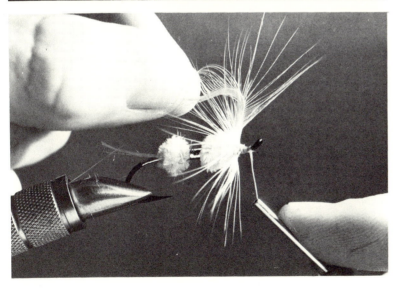

4. Hackle: Attach a soft, webby fluorescent orange saddle hackle, bright side out, just in front of second egg. Make one or two wraps only and tie down. Trim away excess—it can probably be used on another fly. Place a small amount of head cement to this area.

5. For the "wing" of sperm, select a very soft white turkey marabou feather and tie it over body and hackle so that it just extends to hook's bend and tail end. Try to position it so that it lies as close to the body as possible. Trim away excess.

6. Head and finish: Build a neat head with thread over the wing base and hackle tie-down without crowding hook's loop eye. Whip-finish and cut away thread. Paint with two coats of Price's head cement or 5-minute epoxy for a neat, durable, shiny head.

Note: The two eggs of body should match the natural egg size and color. However, at times much larger eggs in different colors, especially fluorescent green or yellow or red, seem more effective in high off-colored-water streams. Occasionally, fluorescent yellow or pink marabou wings are a second good variable.

17. The Omelet Series for Steelhead, Salmon and Trout, *Part 2: Fry Flies*
by DON HATHAWAY

Before moving to Idaho, I read every book I could find about the fish and waters of the state. A number of books dealt with trout and insect hatches, but there was next to nothing on sea-run fish. Only two authors seemed to deal with sea-run fish: Roderick Haig-Brown's books mentioned Idaho's once-abundant salmon and steelhead runs, and Trey Combs's *Steelhead Fly Fishing and Flies* spoke of the runs that are, I am happy to say, making a comeback.

Haig-Brown's *A River Never Sleeps* drew my special attention because of the many fry patterns and the author's knowledge of their effectiveness. While attending the Federation of Fly Fishermen's conclave in Jackson, Wyoming, I met Dave Whitlock for the first time. While we were talking about new ideas and techniques, we both decided to search for a fry pattern that would simulate the first swimming forms of the salmonids. Upon returning home, I tied up some experimental patterns and sent them to Dave, and as new patterns evolved we kept up our correspondence and exchange of ideas. The patterns here are effective, and they are as much Haig-Brown's and Dave's as they are mine. I also want to give a special thanks to Carl Ruhkala of Donnelly, Idaho, for his help in working on fry patterns.

Note: The colors of fry vary from area to area, so a little time spent researching the waters you plan to fish should provide you with the right information on coloration.

Fry Flies

Hook: Mustad 36890 (made of very strong and heavy wire, it requires no added weight)
Body: underbody, CSE mylar tinsel, 1/69th inch; overbody, heavy-duty size A nylon
Gills: CSE red mylar tinsel, but for free-swimming fry only
Throat: pink marabou next to the hook, orange and yellow marabou over the pink (use short fluff at bottom of feather—what you want is a short, compact

bunch that simulates the yolk-sac fry—and add smaller, thinner bunches for swim-up fry and fry)

Wing: Plymouth Rock body marabou dyed to body color of fry (salmonid fry are heavily parr marked, and barred marabou effectively imitates parr marks in looks and swimming movement in action)

Head: CSE olive heavy-duty size A nylon or Herb Howard's prewaxed olive (wrap on a large head: if you wish, you can saturate the head with cement and, when it is partially dry, flatten it on the sides with long-nose pliers)

Eyes: yellow and black paint

1. Tie in mylar tinsel behind eye. Wrap backward about halfway. Then tie in body nylon and continue wrapping tinsel to rear. Stop above hook point and wrap tinsel evenly back to end of eye. Take care to put all materials on same side as open end of looped eye to balance offset. Untwist body nylon and wrap on an even body to front. Tie in working nylon and tie off body. Tie throat marabou. Be sure to keep it short and full. On swim-up fry and fry you will want to add a longer bunch over this.

2. Tie in wing; use a good bunch of fluff for best results. The wing on sac fry should be no longer than a bend of hook; the wing on swim-up fry matches the length of the hook; the wing on fry should be one fourth longer than hook length.

3. Untwist nylon, bind down materials, and wrap on a large head. Saturate with cement. When partially dry, flatten on sides.

4. Apply eyes. The easiest way is to dip the flattened, rounded end of a small dowel, flathead nail or toothpick into yellow paint and touch lightly to each side of the head. When the yellow dries, use a *smaller* dowel, dip into black paint and apply to the center of the yellow on each side. I use Tester's paints and overcoat with Al Price's professional-quality head cement or 5-minute epoxy. Let dry. You're ready to go fishing.

The patterns in the following list are effective in the waters we fish.

Rainbow Fry

Sac Fry

    Hook: Mustad 36890, size 10
    Body: copper mylar tinsel under, yellow-amber nylon over
  Throat: pink marabou next to hook, orange marabou over
    Wing: light olive next to hook, dark olive over

Swim-up Fry

    Hook: Mustad 36890, size 8
    Body: copper mylar tinsel under, yellow-amber nylon over
  Throat: pink marabou next to hook, orange marabou over, a few olive fibers over this
    Wing: dark olive

Fry

    Hook: Mustad 36890, size 6
    Body: silver mylar tinsel under, pink nylon over
    Gills: red mylar tinsel
    Throat: bunch of olive marabou fibers half wing length, one thin golden pheasant crest on bottom
    Wing: dark olive, well barred

Brown Fry

Sac Fry

    Hook: Mustad 36890, size 10
    Body: copper mylar tinsel under, yellow-amber nylon over
    Throat: pink marabou next to hook, orange marabou over
    Wing: light golden next to hook, light olive over

Swim-up Fry

    Hook: Mustad 36890, size 8
    Body: copper mylar tinsel under, yellow-amber nylon over
    Throat: pink marabou next to hook, orange marabou over, a few light-golden fibers over this
    Wing: light-golden marabou next to hook, olive marabou over

Fry

    Hook: Mustad 36890, size 6
    Body: copper tinsel under, white nylon over
    Gills: red mylar tinsel
    Throat: light golden, with one thin golden pheasant crest feather on bottom to simulate belly of fry
    Wing: light golden under, dark olive over

Brook and Dolly Varden

Sac Fry

    Hook: Mustad 36890, size 10
    Body: copper mylar tinsel under, yellow-amber nylon over
    Throat: pink marabou next to hook, orange marabou over
    Wing: light-gold-brown marabou under, light olive over

Swim-up Fry

    Hook: Mustad 36890, size 8
    Body: copper mylar tinsel under, yellow amber over
    Throat: pink marabou next to hook, orange marabou over, a few light-olive fibers over this
    Wing: light-gold-brown marabou under, olive marabou over

Fry

    Hook: Mustad 36890, size 6
    Body: silver mylar tinsel under, white nylon over
    Gills: red mylar tinsel
    Throat: a few olive fibers
    Wing: dark olive, heavily barred

Coho and Cutthroat Fry

Sac Fry

    Hook: Mustad 36890, size 10
    Body: copper mylar tinsel under, yellow-amber nylon over
    Throat: pink marabou next to hook, orange marabou over
    Wing: light tan

Swim-up Fry

    Hook: Mustad 36890, size 8
    Body: copper mylar tinsel under, yellow-amber nylon over
    Throat: pink marabou next to hook, orange marabou over, a few light-tan fibers over this
    Wing: tan-brown

Fry:

    Hook: Mustad 36890, size 6
    Body: silver mylar tinsel
    Tail: orange marabou to simulate orange tail spot on fry (keep this short; do not go past bend of hook)
    Gills: red mylar tinsel
    Throat: small bunch of golden fibers and one thin golden pheasant crest feather on very bottom
    Wing: golden under, brown over

Sockeye and Kokanee Fry

Sac Fry

    Hook: Mustad 36890, size 10
    Body: copper mylar tinsel under, yellow-amber nylon over
    Throat: pink marabou next to hook, orange marabou over
    Wing: light olive

Swim-up Fry

    Hook: Mustad 36890, size 8
    Body: copper mylar tinsel under, yellow-amber nylon over
    Throat: pink marabou next to hook, orange marabou over, a few light-olive fibers over this
    Wing: light olive under, olive over

Fry

    Hook: Mustad 36890, size 6
    Body: silver mylar tinsel under, white nylon over
    Gills: red mylar tinsel
    Throat: light olive with one thin golden pheasant crest feather on bottom
    Wing: olive under, bright grass-green over

Chinook Salmon Fry

Sac Fry

    Hook: Mustad 36890, size 8
    Body: copper mylar tinsel under, yellow-amber nylon over
    Throat: pink marabou next to hook, orange marabou over
    Wing: light golden

Swim-up Fry

    Hook: Mustad 36890, size 6
    Body: copper mylar tinsel under, yellow-amber nylon over
    Throat: pink marabou next to hook, orange marabou over
    Wing: light golden next to hook, light olive over

Fry

    Hook: Mustad 36890, size 4
    Body: silver mylar tinsel under, pink nylon over
    Rib: about five turns of silver mylar tinsel
    Gills: red mylar tinsel
    Throat: orange marabou next to hook, light-olive marabou over, one thin golden pheasant crest feather on fry bottom
    Wing: golden marabou under, dark olive over

VII. Streamers

18. The Rabbit Muddler
by JOHN TIBBS

As in the case with most "new" developments in fly patterns, the Rabbit Muddler was the product of inspiration derived from two great styles of well-established fly patterns, one of well-known North American ancestry and one of lesser-known (in North America) New Zealand ancestry.

The Muddler Minnow/Spuddler/Marabou Muddler/Whitlock Sculpin style of dressing, originated by Don Gapen and developed and popularized by Dan Bailey and Dave Whitlock, needs no introduction to American fly-tyers. It has become almost as established as the Catskill school of dry-fly design.

On the other hand, although New Zealand's Matuka style of dressing feather-winged streamers has recently become popular in the United States, few American tyers are aware that feather-wing Matukas are regarded as passé by New Zealand fishermen, who now favor the rabbit Matuka style of dressing. The essence of this style of winging is the substitution of a narrow strip of V-shaped tanned rabbit (or other suitable fur) for the feather wings most commonly associated with the Matuka style.

Keith Draper, in his excellent book *Trout Flies in New Zealand* (quoted by permission of the publisher, A. H. and A. W. Reed [Wellington, 1971]), states in describing the Rabbit Fly:

> Here perhaps is the best fly of its type in this country. There are possibly more claimants to the invention of the Rabbit Fly than any other pattern, but the oldest supported claim I know of is that of Alan Duncum of Napier. He tells of the time in 1932 when he was fishing down the Waikato—about where Reid's Farm camping reserve is now. During a shower he sheltered under a bush with a Maori angler who had in his tobacco tin a large fly made with a dark hair wing and a red body. The Maori claimed it was a great night fly and Duncum—later anxious to try it—snipped some black rabbit fur and pelt from his wife's slippers. It was tied as a night fly and met with great success.

Flies tied from grey rabbit skins were tied with the same result, and today they are sold in their thousands. I myself consider the Rabbit Fly to be the best lure of its type when fishing for lake-run trout. The soft fur works and ripples with every nuance of current and the skin soon softens in the water.

There are several variations of the Rabbit Fly, but they are all based on using a strip of rabbit skin. The fly can be tied on as small as size 8 or even 10, and in this form of tie it makes a very good fly for smelting. Tied heavy the fly can be used as an imitation bully and to help enhance this appearance two cheeks of hen pheasant feathers can be tied in alongside the body. I can vouch for this method of tying and have taken many fish on it over the years.

Some anglers prefer the black rabbit for night and evening fishing but as anyone who has tied these flies will tell you, the rabbit fur is only black on the tips. The underfur is a pale blue or even almost white at times, so to make a really black "Rabbit" fly other furs are sometimes used. If you have any friends who make their living by trapping opossums ask them if they ever take any black cats. The feral cat is often taken by opossum trappers, which is a good thing, as these predators take a large toll of game and wild life. The skin of a black cat with its thick pelage of winter fur makes excellent flies, but remember that it is illegal to trade in them. Promise your trapper friend a nice trout in exchange for a cat skin.

With a rabbit skin several parts of the pelt will give a different colour. The fur varies from a black flecked with brown to a pale grey or even pure white if the skin has a good belly. For the body wool, chenille or seal's fur can be used. It makes little difference which is used, so long as the angler is happy with it. I prefer dyed seal's fur as it glistens so well in the sunlight. One often thinks that it could sometimes be small considerations such as these which induce a sulky trout to strike.

The Rabbit Fly was first introduced to me by my longtime friend and a superlative commercial fly-tyer, Colonel Joe King (USAF ret.) of Spokane, Washington, who makes an almost yearly pilgrimage to the fine trout fishing of New Zealand, particularly the Taupo region. The first time Joe gave me a sample of the original New Zealand pattern, in 1974, I was immediately struck by the thought of what a great improvement the dressing was over the wing-tangling and twisting problems associated with the otherwise excellent marabou feather style of streamer dressing. What a great Marabou Muddler this would make! I thought.

With this in mind, I proceeded to scour my supply of fly-tying materials to find every possible shade of tanned rabbit and muskrat and then set about tying an array of Rabbit Matuka Muddlers. The success of the pattern was immediate. Both large trout and bass seemed to relish its tantalizing pulsation in the water.

Since then, the pattern has been fished throughout the West, South America and New Zealand with consistent results. Big trout seem to love it, as do striped bass. Cam Sigler, a longtime fishing companion of the late Joe Brooks, returned from a trip to Wyoming's Green River in 1976 and told me that in five days of fishing on this great river, the Rabbit Muddler in a golden-tan color tied on a 1/0 hook proved to be the only pattern in his companions' fly boxes that would interest the big brass-sided browns. Soon thereafter, he found a large white dressing to be similarly successful for enticing the huge stripers of the Umpqua River in Oregon.

The more I fish with this wonderful material, the more I appreciate that it shouldn't be relegated to being only a streamer-fly wing material. My good friend and angling companion Dean Malencik further convinced me of this fact when I first gave him a Rabbit Muddler. Dean is a research chemist by profession, which no doubt contributes to his experimenting nature, so it was no great surprise when he soon showed me a selection of rabbit-winged steelhead flies. The potential for soft-winged steelhead flies is great, as was illustrated by the fine work of Darwin Atkin in the first volume of *The Fly-Tyer's Almanac*.

Perhaps the best recommendation that I can give for this great material in conclusion is to recommend that you try the Rabbit Muddler—I'm sure that you'll like it. But then, next time when you sit down to tie your own favorite wet-fly patterns, give it a try on them—that's what creative fly-tying is really all about.

The Rabbit Muddler

Hook:	Mustad-Viking 9672, sizes 2/0 to 8, or other heavy wire streamer, 3 to 6XL hook (hook in photos is Viellard Migeon 225519)
Tying thread:	white or black Monocord or Nymo, Herb Howard's fluorescent red for securing the mylar tubing
Body:	gold or silver mylar tubing ribbed with gold or silver medium-width oval tinsel (size 12) to match
Wing:	narrow V-shaped strip of tanned rabbit hide (or other suitable soft fur-bearing animal), tied in Matuka style
Collar:	well-marked even-tipped hair from a West Coast black-tailed deer or from the shoulder of a northern whitetail
Head:	clipped coarse body hair from mule deer or whitetail

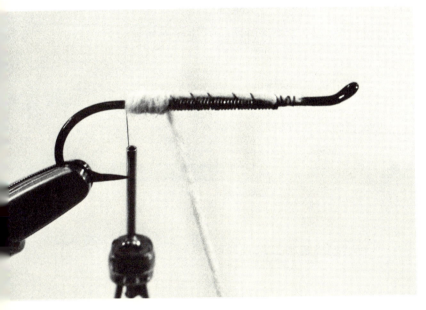

1. Cover shank of hook with twenty to thirty wraps of .020 fuse wire. Apply thin coat of head cement and then cover surface with a thin layer of yarn or floss while cement is still tacky. Be careful to leave plenty of space that is not built up for both the head of the fly and the point where tinsel is to be secured.

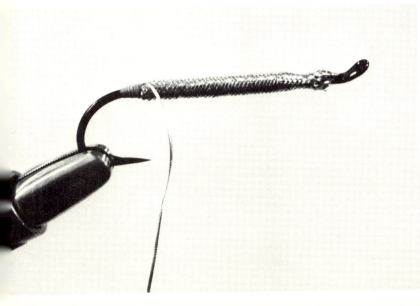

2. Cut a length of fine-diameter mylar tinsel tubing and slip it over hook eye, after first having attached fluorescent red thread near curve of hook. Push tubing all the way back along hook shank and secure loose ends with red tying thread. Cut off an 8-inch section of medium-width oval tinsel and secure with red thread so it protrudes from eye side rather than bend side of red butt that is being formed with the thread. Finish red butt off neatly with a whip-finish knot and apply two coats of head cement. While butt is drying, prepare wing as next described.

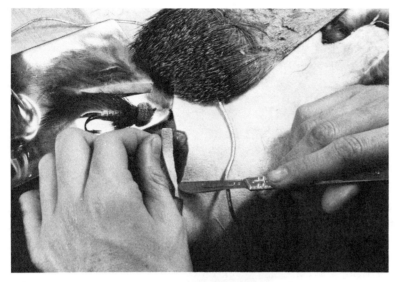

3. Obtain a tanned rabbit skin with fur color you wish to use. (I have been able to discover the following while searching through fly-tying supply shops and leathercraft supply shops: white, iron-blue dun, gray, grizzly gray, light and dark ginger, hare's-mask brown.)

Examine fur and note that hair fibers are longer in the center (back) of the skin and shorter near the sides (belly). For tying large flies, use fur from the center section. For small flies, use fur from the belly section.

Turn the hide skin side up and, using either a scalpel (preferred) or a single-edge razor blade, make a lengthwise incision *with the grain of the fur* in that area where the fur length is best suited for the size of your hook. Now cut a V-shaped section of hide that tapers from a width of approximately $5/16$ inch for large flies or $1/8$ inch for small flies. *Be careful to cut only the hide and not any of the fur.*

4. Returning to the tinsel-covered hook, attach Monocord or Nymo tying thread near eye of hook and secure loose ends of mylar tinsel.

Take V-shaped strip of rabbit and lay it on top of hook shank with a short section of the hide one third to one half the length of hook shank protruding out behind fluorescent red butt. Carefully stroke fur fibers forward to make a valley in the fur, exposing the skin at a point directly above point where oval tinsel is tied in.

Grasping oval tinsel with your hackle pliers, wind it over exposed valley of skin while maintaining firm tension on the fur's tip. Separate fur fibers into a new valley, $3/16$ inch forward of first wrap, and repeat. The separating procedure may more easily be facilitated by using the point of your scissors or a bodkin. The two most critical factors in applying fur wing material are to *be careful to not bind down bunches of fur with the tinsel* and to *maintain a constant firm pressure* with the tinsel *so the wing material will not slip.*

5. After winding tinsel up length of hook shank, tie it off at point where fly head is to begin. Then wrap two or three turns of thread over remaining protrusion of rabbit skin. Clip end of skin into blunt V-shaped point to facilitate forming smooth base for deer-hair head. Wrap multiple turns of thread to form a firm base and prepare to apply deer-hair collar.

6. With the aid of a stacker tool, prepare a good-sized bunch of well-marked even-tipped deer hair from a West Coast black-tailed deer or shoulder hair from a whitetail. Grasp bunch of hair by tips and, starting from bottom, gently distribute hair around circumference of hook shank so that hair tips extend ½ to 1 inch, depending on size of hook. Wrap three or four turns of tying thread around collar hair to secure it firmly; then fold butts of hair back to make it extend perpendicularly.

7. Select a coarse-fibered piece of mule deer or whitetail hair for forming characteristic Muddler clipped hair head. Cut off a good-sized bunch of hair and remove excess underfur. Tie it down approximately at its midlength. With some gentle help from your fingers, make sure hair spins all the way around hook shank so that it is evenly distributed.

8. Repeat this process until you reach eye of hook. Whip-finish head and proceed to trim until it assumes shape and size you prefer.

Preferred color combinations:
- white rabbit with silver tinsel
- iron-blue dun rabbit with silver tinsel
- grizzly-gray rabbit with silver tinsel
- grizzly gray dyed yellow with picric acid in cold water with silver tinsel
- golden-ginger rabbit with gold tinsel
- salt-and-pepper brown rabbit (cottontail) with gold tinsel
- Whitlock Sculpin tied with either golden-ginger or cottontail rabbit

19. The Kat's Meow
by DMITRI (MITYA) KOTYIK

Just before I submitted this article, Bob Boyle showed Eric Leiser of the Rivergate some of the weighted streamers I call the Kat's Meow.

"You're going to have this in the *Almanac?*" Leiser asked, startled.

"Sure," said Boyle.

"Well, you guys are going to catch hell because it's nothing but a jig," Leiser said with contempt.

"Wrong, Eric," Boyle said. "It's a weighted streamer. You can cast it easily on a fly rod. It's basically just the smallest ball of split shot pressed on a size ten hook. Some fly fishermen weight their streamers or nymphs and wets with lead wire, or they pinch a split shot on the leader. With the Kat's Meow, the split shot becomes the head of a minnow, part of the design."

Leiser scratched his head. "I don't know," he said.

"Here, take one," said Boyle. "Have two of them. They're barbless. They have to be because they catch so many fish."

"Thanks!" exclaimed Leiser. "I'll use them in the pond out back."

My brother Alyosha and I heard about this conversation later as we had dinner, a lovely chopped platter served up by Bob Boyle's wife. "Hey, Lyoshik, what do you think of what Eric Leiser had to say?" I asked.

"Mitya, it's the greatest streamer, lure, jig or whatever you want to call it," Lyoshik said, wiping his whiskers. "Any fly fisherman who uses split shot and criticizes this is nothing but a hypocrite. It's simply the Kat's Meow."

I agree with what Lyoshik had to say. If you don't like the Kat's Meow, don't use the split-shot head version; use the thread head tie described later. But if you want to get down to the fish, if you want to scrape the bottom, the Kat's Meow with the split-shot head is the answer. In fact, I will say this: If I had to fish with only one fly or streamer, or spoon, jig or plug, or any fly-casting, spinning or bait-casting lure you'd want to name, I would immediately choose the Kat's Meow. It has taken all kinds of fish, including species supposedly reluctant or unwilling to strike an artificial.

Here is how the Kat's Meow came about. Some years ago, I was intrigued by the runs of alewives and blueback herring that leave the Atlantic in the spring to spawn in coastal rivers. These herring—which, incidentally, belong to the same family of fish as the American shad—throng the Hudson River and its tributaries by the millions, and although they would follow a streamer or wet fly, I could not get them to strike. I needed to get down at least three feet in the strong current of the Croton River, and I needed something that was small and had some movement. I won't bore you with tales of my experimentation, but after some tinkering I finally came up with the split-shot Kat's Meow. I originally named it the Katyusha, the diminutive of Kathryn, the name of a splendid Russian lady who helped Lyoshik and me get fixed and established, but in time the name became shortened to the Kat, and it then became the Kat's Meow because it is just that, the best.

I am sure I sound immodest in saying this, but besides herring, the Kat's Meow has taken trout, largemouth and smallmouth bass, pickerel, assorted panfish, shad, bluefish, jack crevalles (in the murk of the Hudson River, believe it or not) and striped bass. The largest fish I've taken so far has been a 5-pound striper, and although it may seem odd that a 5-pound striper that had been gorging on minnows would take something as small as the Kat's Meow, it was like offering a fat person just one little piece of fudge. The fish couldn't resist it.

The Kat's Meow works where other flies or lures fail. Seth Rosenbaum of Queens, New York, says that several incidents stand out in his mind. He felt triumphant using it to catch some very wary largemouths that lurked around a lakeside dock refusing absolutely everything anyone else offered them, including worms; and that fall, while other fly fishermen were doing nothing on the Connequoit River on Long Island, he used the Kat's Meow to score on brook trout. "I couldn't keep them off the hook," Rosenbaum told me. "I'd simply let the Kat's Meow hop along the bottom." Finally Rosenbaum, who is an enthusiast of catching odd fish, told me that he uses the Kat's Meow to catch golden shiners.

For my own part, I have also caught a number of unusual species with the Kat's Meow. While in the Bahamas, for instance, I used it to catch pilchard, a species of sardine ordinarily taken only with a net.

Hook:	Mustad 94833, size 10, dry fly (I prefer the fine wire of a dry-fly hook to the thicker wire of the wet because it fits more easily into the slit in the split shot)
Head:	lead "B-B" split shot, lacquered white twice and with eyes of yellow iris and black pupil
Tying thread:	Herb Howard's (Danville) prewaxed white
Tail:	a dozen or so fibers from the feather of a wide hen hackle, plus four strands of fine silver mylar

---

Photo sequence by Ria

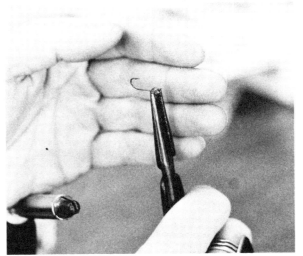

1. Squeeze split shot with needle-nose pliers. Insert hook shank in split shot so that hook will ride barb up and not snag on bottom.

2. Insert hook in vise and tie in fibers from a white hen hackle. The longer and webbier the fibers, the better the action. These hackle fibers are preferable to marabou, which can cling and wrap around bend of hook.

3. Tie in two strips of fine silver mylar at their midpoint, so you have four strands of mylar blending into the hackle fibers. Tie off and remove Kat's Meow from vise. Apply a coat of white lacquer to head and wrappings, let dry and lacquer again. Dab on iris by dipping flat end of a dowel into yellow lacquer and gently touching to each side of head. Dab pupil in middle of each iris with flat end of a smaller dowel dipped in black lacquer. Let dry, and then fish.

It should be evident to anyone that you are not restricted to white patterns. You can use any color you wish, although I have found white to be the most effective. You can mix colors or materials (bucktail, rabbit, you name it), and you can imitate bait fish à la Keith Fulsher's Thundercreek Series, Whitlock's Sculpin or the Muddler. You can imitate nymphs, and by using the ultra-small split shot from Pezon-Michel in France, you can tie Kat's Meow streamers to size 16, 18 or even 20 hooks. But be sure to make the hook barbless so as not to hurt the fish. Incidentally, for brown trout, I have found the Kat's Meow most effective when the head is simply lacquered red, without any eyes.

Finally, for those fly purists who think the use of a lead head smacks of spinning, I suggest the thread head Kat's Meow. The only difference is that, instead of pinching on a piece of split shot, you take a strand of "D" tying thread used for deer-hair bass bugs, wax it (I prefer Overton's Wonder Wax, a new product) and just tie it on the head of the hook over itself until it is ball-shaped. Then you secure the tying end of "D" thread with Herb Howard's fine prewaxed thread and use the Herb Howard thread to fill in any gaps on the head. Apply a clear lacquer (or fingernail polish) to this head after tying in the tails and mylar. It enhances the appearance when the regular colored lacquer is applied.

As my brother Lyoshik says, *"Vot chudnaya veshch!"*—What a wonderful thing!

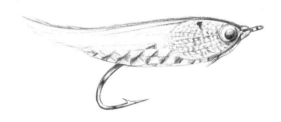

20. The Whitlock Prismatic Marabou Shad
by DAVE WHITLOCK

The various species of shad and herring throughout the United States are often devoured by game fish. Threadfin shad, gizzard shad, alewives and blueback herring all have a very definite deep, flat but streamlined flashy body. I've never really been satisfied with the looks and actions of streamer designs said to be patterned for these fish. In 1976 I thought I came pretty close to the right fly with my Matuka Marabou Minnow (*Fly Fisherman* magazine, vol. 7, no. 5) but there was just something it lacked when I watched it from underwater. In 1977 while in Michigan with Dick Smith of Rochester, I discovered (for myself) a new prismatic tape for dressing up flash on spoons, spinners and plugs. Dr. Dan Crockett had told me about it earlier at a Pere Marquette clinic, but I let it slip out of my mind. Seeing Prism-Lite in the Luhr Jensen display packages prompted me to purchase an assortment to test.

Later, Buz Ramsey, outside sales manager of Luhr Jensen, sent me a complete assortment of the tape. I did all sorts of things with it on bugs, on saltwater streamers and on streamer body wraps. Then one winter afternoon, while watching millions of chilled threadfin shad drift out of control down the White River where I live below Bullshoals Dam, it came to me. Their refractive silver-pearl metallic bodies could be perfectly matched if I used a sandwich of Prism-Lite pearl tape. Within a week, I had worked out the pattern and was testing the new fly in my aquariums and on White River rainbows. I matched it against my Matuka Marabou Minnow, and it was much more effective. The design will also work for nearly all the thin, deep-bodied fish and minnows. Just alter the color schemes and shapes to accommodate the imitation of your minnow. The Prismatic Shad is also a much easier, faster fly to tie than the Marabou Matuka.

Whitlock Prismatic Marabou Shad

        Hook: Any bright-tinned, nickel-plated or stainless-steel ringed-eye 3 to 6X long hook, sizes 3/0 to 8 (hook used in tying photos is Wright & McGill, 4X long nickel plated)

Tying thread: CSE fluorescent white single-strand nylon floss

Body weight (optional):	lead wire
Wings:	one or two white turkey marabou feathers
Body:	prismatic mylar tape, silver-pearl finish
Gills:	red feather fluff or red mylar tape
Cheeks:	two gray-barred mallard drake breast or flank feathers
Overwing:	three to six gray emu or ostrich herl and three peacock herl
Eyes:	doll eyes, or eyes painted with black and yellow enamel
Cements:	Laggie's Clear Gloss Cote and Clear Dow Corning rubber aquarium cement

1. Hook: Place hook firmly in tying vise and attach thread just behind eye. Overwrap all of shank back to bend and, returning, overlap to just behind hook eye. Do not coat wraps with cement. Select one or two white turkey marabou feathers and tie them down to top of hook shank without stripping stems. Feather tips should extend one full length of hook shank past hook's bend. Trim away excess marabou stems in front of tie-down. Coat tie-down area with a little head cement.

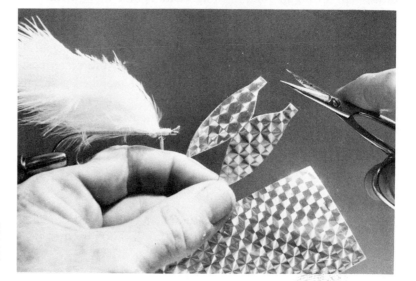

2. Body trim: Fold a piece of prismatic tape one and one third lengths of hook shank and trim to general shape shown before removing tape backing. Note small "neck" at front end of tape for tying to hook.

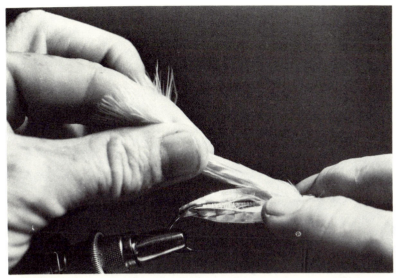

3. Body tape application: Carefully, from under hook shank, position tape with backing removed. (*Hint:* Practice this step without backing removed first.) Hold marabou wings as shown until tape is positioned and closed slightly from bottom to hook shank. Then carefully bring marabou stem down to hook shank and close tape on its lower half. Now, with tying thread, tie tape's neck to hook just behind eye. Study photos carefully for correct tape-marabou marriage.

4. Overwing: Select emu herl the length of marabou wing and tie arching down over top of marabou wing. Several strips of silver mylar can also be added for more action flash just as you add herl. Over emu herl, tie down three metallic green or bronze peacock herls. Try to use natural herl curve to cap marabou wing completely for a neat, compact shad-back shape.

117

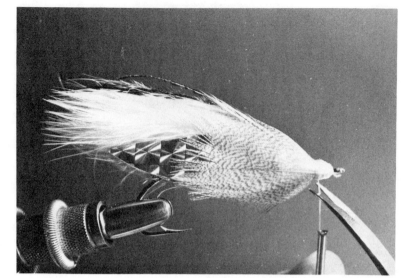

5. Gills: Place a small tuft of bright red fluff from a red saddle hackle's lower stem on the hook below and just behind hook eye. To form shad's head, take two barred mallard feathers and place each on sides of hook shank directly next to hook eye, bright sides out. Study photo carefully for size, position and length detail.

6. Head: Close up hook eye with tying thread; whip-finish and cut away tying thread. Do not apply any head cement yet.

Eyes: (A) Put a small gob of silicon rubber cement on each cheek feather directly behind thread head–*feather* junction. (B) Place plastic doll eyes into cement. Cement holds immediately, but you have several minutes to position eyes if they don't look right. While eyes are setting, you can mark shad gill plate spot and top of thread head with waterproof ink felt marker, as shown. After eyes are dry, coat thread head with two coats of Gloss Cote head cement.

Optional: If doll eyes are not available (see new materials chapter), you can paint eyes on by first coating a spot on the mallard feather with clear Gloss Cote. After it dries completely, paint a yellow iris, allow to dry, then paint a black pupil. After they are completely dry, overcoat them with another coat of Gloss Cote head cement. *Note:* Be very careful you do not allow excess head cement to ruin marabou feather.

VIII. Materials of the Art

21. Genetic Hackle
by HOWARD WEST

In years past, the fly-tyer who had half a dozen assorted necks was well prepared to tie most popular patterns. Today, fly-tying has evolved into a much more complex hobby. Increased awareness of aquatic entomology and the desire to match specific hatches as closely as possible have created a demand for very specialized materials.

Many of the animals that supplied traditional materials, such as jungle cock, seal and polar bear, are now endangered species, and these products are no longer readily available. Today's technology has created some satisfactory substitutes, such as imitation jungle cock eyes, Seal-Ex and FisHair. Gamecocks are also in critical danger of becoming scarce. Their populations are dwindling, not from environmental pressures but by being scientifically bred out of existence. Poultry science wizards are creating new, meatier breeds to replace the traditional birds that were the backbone of fly-tying. Tyers turned chicken raisers are striking back. Their selective breeding programs are producing special, genetically improved strains exclusively for tying. These birds consistently have feather quality that was formerly only a dream. Their natural sheen and vitality make dyed necks look drab and lifeless by comparison. The sheer luxury of being able to hackle a fly fully with one feather—and have a few turns left over—is a rich experience. This is why the new feathers are known as spoilers.

WHAT IS HACKLE?

Long ago, the expression "Getting your hackles up" became synonymous with being angry. Undoubtedly, this expression was coined at a cockfight. When a rooster prepares to fight, his neck feathers flare rigidly to form a protective ring around his head and throat. These long, stiff feathers are the hackle for which the fly-tyer is constantly searching.

To most tyers, hackle is the most important material, since it is used on nearly all wet- and dry-fly patterns. Stiff, resilient hackle is required on dry flies to support them on the surface in hopes of duplicating the floating natural. Conversely, wet flies require soft, water-absorbent hackle to help them sink and have a lifelike movement in the water. Dry-fly hackle comes from the narrow part of a mature rooster's neck near the head. Hen necks and rooster capes with soft, webby feathers are the sources for wet-fly hackle.

Rooster and hen necks are available from both overseas and domestic sources. The majority of imported necks come from India, China and the Philippines. Several of the larger supply houses send feather buyers there to purchase staggering quantities of necks. When these necks arrive in the United States, they are fumigated, sorted by color, graded for quality and sometimes dyed. Domestic sources have all but dried up, except for a handful of raisers who breed birds especially for the fly-tyer.

Foreign countries are able to supply necks in the desired colors because of their lack of modern technology, while almost nothing suitable for tying comes from our huge poultry industry. Our country is the world's leader in scientifically developing more efficient breeds that grow faster, lay more eggs and, of course, eat less food. As Murphy's Law would have it, even though poultry production is up, these "new improved" birds are unsuitable for fly-tying. The traditional breeds that were useful for fly-tying—the Rhode Island Red, Buff Cochin and Plymouth Rock—have been replaced by scientific strains with such romantic names as the Shaver Starcross 289 and the Garber GX 291. The majority of these new birds are a drab white color and would have soft, webby hackle even if allowed to grow to full feather maturity. In a modern poultry facility, most roosters are slaughtered before they are six months old, when they cease to make rapid weight gain in proportion to the amount of food they consume. They may never touch the ground or see the light of day. Their sole purpose is the economical conversion of feed into flesh for the table. The tremendous expense of highly specialized, totally automated buildings has made chicken farming uneconomical for all but the largest poultry raisers.

Senior tyers still talk about the days when a drive through the countryside replenished their supply of good-quality fly-tying capes. Roosters kept for propagation of the flock, and possibly to keep the farmer from oversleeping, were "king of the barnyard" and usually lived to an age when their hackles were prime for tying. Many a farmer laughed about selling a tough old rooster to the city slicker for two whole dollars! Today these farmyard flocks are no longer commonplace—in fact, most farmers buy their poultry and eggs at the supermarket like everyone else.

The same plight the domestic rooster is in has now begun to affect overseas suppliers. India, China and the Philippines have just begun to feel the influence of our scientific methods. The poultry science departments of many major universities have a surprisingly large number of students from foreign countries. The bottom line is that the traditional overseas sources of inexpensive necks will dry up. Feather importers have already seen a decrease in quality and availability of necks as a result of advanced poultry-raising practices. As technology marches on, native strains will be replaced or diluted by the modern "wonder birds." Cynicism aside, more productive breeds and efficient raising methods will help lessen food shortages in these countries. Inevitably, however, it will be a crippling blow to fly-tying material importers and the end for most of the native bird populations. In the past, these birds provided an ideal source of good, inexpensive hackle for fly-tyers. From each flock only the hardiest survived to be breeders in a hostile environment of fighting, disease and predators; thus, the native strains became very tough. Crossbreeds were the rule, adding vitality and giving the tyer colors like the red game variant, cock-y-bondhu, natural dun and a host of unusual "freak colors." In addition, the lack of refrigeration meant the birds were kept alive until needed, and as they matured, their hackle improved for tying. India, China and the Philippines will continue to be the major suppliers of hackle only until the new breeds replace or destroy the vitality of the native strains.

Clearly, the introduction of modern poultry strains will be the knockout punch to our import sources. But as Eric Leiser explains, "Another reason for the inferior quality of Indian rooster necks is the fact that there are many more companies in the fly-tying material business. There are just not enough good necks to go around. When I first ventured into the fly-tying material business in 1966, the very finest necks from India's leading exporter cost a maximum of forty-two cents, and B-grade capes were only fourteen cents. Today, top-quality Indian necks will cost the American buyer from a dollar-fifty to two dollars, and B-grade seventy-five cents. The price has gone up, but the quality has gone down.

"In a way, we are at fault for the higher prices. Prior to the seventies, few, if any, American buyers went to India. Thus, every U.S. importer had an equal chance. Since then, more and more buyers have been traveling to India to select their necks personally. At first, the American feather merchants were warmly welcomed. However, instead of concentrating in the distributing area, some buyers went so far as to visit the local poultry establishments. The result was that everyone connected with raising chickens soon got a good whiff of the American dollar, and the competition drove the prices higher and higher.

"Since fly-tying and fly-fishing are becoming increasingly popular and because the wild strain of Indian birds and those of other countries are becoming more diluted, prospects for the future look dim. Even though the inflated price of the import is still much lower than genetic birds, the value will no longer be there. I do believe there will come a day when most of our top-quality necks will come from enterprising domestic hackle raisers. Though there will always be some foreign barnyard stock (and some domestic farm birds) available, the halcyon days of being able to pick and choose a super-grade neck for two or three bucks are gone. And yet there is really no need for concern. Personally, I would rather tie flies with the genetically raised necks. I know what I'm going to get. It will be what I'm looking for. I can tie five times as many flies from one of those necks, compared to the Indian variety."

The decreasing supply of quality imported necks only partially explains the development of today's genetic hackle. The pioneers of feather farming tried to establish a personal source of scarce natural dun necks. Natural dun color is controlled by an elusive combination of genes, and the probability of getting any dun shade from a nonspecific mating is low. To further complicate things, dun-colored roosters usually have inferior-quality hackle and tend to be less hardy than other birds. When they do live long enough to breed, they rarely produce dun offspring. During the early development of modern American fly-tying, men such as Rube Cross, Harry Darbee and Andy Miner recognized these problems, and they developed their own strains of natural blue dun. More recently, the disappearance of the Plymouth Rock created a great demand for grizzly hackle. Henry Hoffman responded by raising the original Super Grizzly strain.

Today's genetic birds have been further evolved, primarily to meet the increasing demand for smaller hackle. The overall selection of imported necks has remained fairly consistent until recently, and they are still an economical source for some hackle. However, over the decades, the size of the average dry fly has decreased. In the early days of fly fishing, a size 12 was considered very small. Today, the average size is probably 16; but truly lucky is the tyer who finds an imported neck that will tie a size 16 properly. The increased knowledge and skill of the modern fly-tyer and his desire to match the hatch for hyperselective trout has created a great demand for hackle of all colors in the 16 to 24 range. Since finding a quality neck is difficult and getting

Henry Hoffman's Super Grizzly full skin.

the desired color shade nearly impossible, most avid tyers have developed the habit of buying a good-quality neck regardless of color, hoarding it until needed or perhaps trading it for a more desirable shade. Today, genetic feather raisers are beginning to offer super-quality necks in a full array of colors. Genetic birds offer the only consistent source of hackle for small flies.

JUDGING HACKLE

The importance of hackle size and color is easy to understand; however, the term "quality dry-fly hackle" deserves further explanation. A good dry fly requires hackle and tailing of sufficient stiffness to support it properly on the surface film. A superior-quality dry-fly feather gives the tyer a maximum number of stiff, web-free barbs. To evaluate its quality, hold the feather by the tip end and stroke the barbs toward the butt end several times. Once they are at a right angle to the center shaft, hold the feather up to the light for easy examination of the web pattern. Every feather has a portion of soft, webby barbs near its base. The barbs that are shiny, stiff and web-free snap back to their original position more quickly and persistently than those of the webby section. The ideal web pattern is one that sharply tapers off into web-free barbs. Hackles with a web pattern that gradually tapers toward the tip of the feather are acceptable, but usually will not support the fly as well; they also absorb water more readily. Therefore, the most critical measurement in evaluating the quality of a hackling feather is how many web-free barbs it has.

The second most important consideration in judging hackle is the degree of stiffness of the barbs. Although a feather may have a long web-free section, this is no guarantee that the barbs are stiff enough to support the fly properly. Many tyers determine the stiffness by lightly pressing against the ends of the barbs with the tip of the index finger. Those who lack the necessary finger sensitivity can gently push the barbules against the lower lip, which is sensitive enough to distinguish degrees of stiffness. The latter method has a drawback: you have to put up with the stares of onlookers if you do this in a public place. It has been said that some tyers aren't impressed unless the hackle is stiff enough to make their lips bleed!

Once the tyer has determined that a neck has a sufficient amount of stiff, web-free hackles, he or she must determine the range of hook sizes the neck will tie. The length of the hackle barbs determine what size fly can be tied; naturally, the longer the barbs, the larger the fly. The proper length of the barbs for any standard fly is one and one half times the hook gap. Hackle barbs that are not correct length for the hook size will cause the fly to ride at an unnatural angle, and the result is an improperly balanced fly.

Most tyers tend to use hackle that is one or two sizes too large for the hook they are using. It is so difficult to judge barb length without actually measuring it that even the best fly-tyers are sometimes fooled. For this very reason, many top commercial tyers presize their hackle before they begin tying. It is all too easy for the occasional fly-tyer to misjudge the size of the hackles on a neck and be disappointed when sitting down at the tying bench.

Many feel that the size of the neck determines the range of flies it will tie. Nothing could be more inaccurate. Just because a cape is small doesn't mean it will have hackle for small flies. Actually, the size of the neck is determined mainly by the size and type of the bird and the amount of shrinkage that occurs while the cape is drying. Most imported necks will do a good job on hook sizes 8 through 14, though two feathers are often needed. However, a neck that has good hackle for the 8s and 10s generally is weak in the smaller sizes, and one that ties 12 through 16 will usually have feathers that are too soft and webby for large flies. With the exception of the genetic birds, it is unusual to find a cape with high-quality hackle in both large and small sizes. By accurately measuring the largest and smallest usable feathers on a neck, its useful range can be determined. Most fly-tying suppliers sell pocket-size hackle gauges that make accurate measuring quick and easy.

Choosing a quality dry-fly neck is clearly an involved process: first finding a neck with a desirable color, then evaluating and gauging the feathers to make sure there are enough stiff, web-free hackles for the desired hook sizes. Getting exactly the right neck may not be too difficult if there is a well-stocked fly-fishing shop nearby. Those who buy their material by mail soon learn the value of dealing with a knowledgeable and dependable mail-order house. By and large, most fly-tying supply houses make a sincere effort to meet the tyer's needs. Unfortunately, everyone's idea of a medium-blue dun color or what constitutes a prime-grade neck is different. When requesting a special shade, it is always helpful to send a color sample if possible. The descriptions of hackle quality used by supply houses are so confusing and misleading that it would be ridiculous to attempt explaining them. In short, the best costs the most. However, one supplier's best may not equal another's second grade—"You pays your money, and you takes your chances." In the long run, it is beneficial to establish a buying relationship with a reputable house. Give the supplier as much information as possible with the order, and return anything that isn't right with a detailed explanation. Loyal tyers keep the established material houses in business year after year, and they usually go to any reasonable length to try to please their customers.

Neck prices follow the traditional economic law of supply and demand. The tremendous price increase for first-quality grizzly necks is a good example. The demand for these necks has increased in the last decade, simply by virtue of the dramatic growth in fly-tying and the increasingly limited supply. A really premium Plymouth Rock neck is darn hard to come by, and expensive if found. The reverse is true for imported brown necks because an overwhelming proportion of foreign birds are some shade of brown. A good-quality brown cape that will tie down to size 14 dries can be purchased for a relatively small expenditure of from $4 to $5. However, brown necks that will hackle size 16 and smaller flies are not so readily available. Quality in a neck, regardless of its color, will bring a substantially higher price. For the tyer whose forte is small flies, genetic hackle is the only recourse.

It is easy to understand how high-demand necks in short supply bring a premium price, but the difference in cost between a good-quality imported neck and a genetic neck is staggering. High demand is only a partial explanation for the impressive cost of genetic necks. Consider for a moment that imported necks are an otherwise useless by-product from a bird that is destined to be someone's dinner, while a genetic bird is bred and raised solely for its feathers. By our domestic culinary standards, the meat from a fully mature rooster is only slightly easier to chew than a rubber tire. For the foreign raisers, getting anything for the feathers is a bonus; to the genetic raiser, the feathers are everything.

USING FULL BODY SKINS

While a genetic neck fills the primary requirement of providing the finest available hackle, there is much more to a functional dry fly than just hackle. For this reason, many of the genetic raisers, including Ted Hebert and Henry Hoffman, completely skin out their best birds. These full body skins offer an almost unbelievable variety of material. For instance, few tyers realize that the best source for natural wing and tail material is the same bird that provided the hackle he or she uses. The color and silhouette of the wing is critical, and all too often the effectiveness of a genetically hackled fly is diminished by dyed wings and tails. Following the impressionistic tying theory, using natural wing and tail material produces an important broken-up color pattern. Art Flick says, "A tied fly, when held up to the light, has a 'shimmering' effect which I assume makes it look alive. You won't find this in any dyed feather I have seen."

When domestic birds are available, tyers use spade and saddle hackles for tailing. Spade feathers are located on the back and shoulders of the rooster, just above the saddle, and are easily recognized by their hard, shiny appearance. Because of the unavailability of full body skins, most modern tyers resort to using neck hackle for tailing. The best neck feathers for tailing are the throat hackles found on both sides of the neck. Although adequately stiff, all too often the

FULL SKIN FEATHER USES

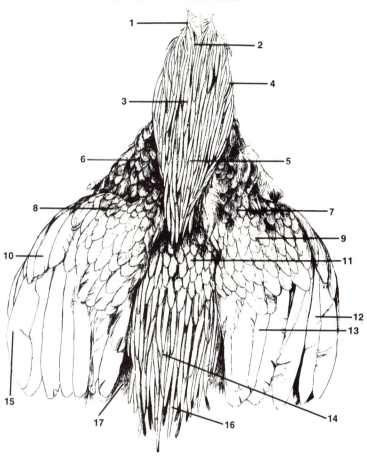

1. Comb (tip) hackle (sizes 28 to 20): Smallest hackle for midge adults, micro caddis, mayfly dry-fly hackling.
2. Nap hackle (sizes 18 to 14): All dry-fly hackling, bivisibles, hackle wings, wet and nymph fly hackle, small streamers. Hackle stems for tails, antennas and small quill bodies.
3. Mid-neck hackle (sizes 12 to 6): Large dry flies, large nymph and wet flies, cut wings, woolyworm hackles, fly tails. Stems for quill bodies, extended bodies.
4. Throat hackle (sizes 12 to 4): Dry-fly tails, adult caddis wings, spider and variant hackle, bass bug tails.
5. Neck butt hackle (sizes 6 to1/0 or larger): Large wet fly and nymph hackle, streamer wings, large woolyworm hackle, bass and saltwater bug tails, saltwater streamers, bass bug skirt hackle, bass bug tails.
6. Breast feathers and belly feathers: Dry-fly fan wings, cheek and shoulder for streamers, adult caddis cut wings, mayfly cut wings, mayfly spinner wings, bass bug wings, caddis pupa wings, wet and nymph hackle, soft hackle flies, matuka wings, nymph wing cases, terrestrial wings (jassids, etc.).
7. Spade hackle: Dry-fly tails, adult caddis wings, spiders, variants, bass bug tails, adult caddis antennas.
8. Shoulder feathers: Fan wings, no-hackle dun wings, upright mayfly cut wings, streamer cheeks, terrestrial wings, nymph wing cases.
9. Coverlets: Trimmed adult caddis tent wings, quill wings, bass fly fan wings.
10. Primary coverlets: Quill section wings for small wet and dry flies and caddis pupas. The leading edges good for small nymph antennas and tail material.
11. Tippet saddles: Small wide-wing streamers, matukas, wet-fly hackling, bass bug tailing, bonefish and permit fly wings. Also for spent dry-fly wings, damsel and dragonfly wings. Stem bases excellent for ribbing.
12. Primary wing quill: Quill section wings for wet and dry flies, caddis pupa wings and wings for no-hackle duns.
13. Secondary wing quills: When sprayed with Tuffilm they are excellent for adult caddis quill section tent wings, nymph wing cases and some wet fly wings. Quill stems from both primary and secondary feathers can be stripped off to make beautiful large quill bodies.
14. Saddles: Large western and salmon dry-fly hackling, Wulff dry flies, woolyworm palmering, fresh and saltwater streamer wings, bass bug tails and skirting, hackle palmering for such flies as bivisibles.
15. Leading edges of primary wing quills: Excellent tails and legs and antennas for nymphs. Quills excellent for quill bodies, antennas and tails.
16. Butt saddles: Large woolyworm palmering, saltwater and bass streamer wings and hackling, bass bug tails and skirting. Hackle quills excellent quill bodies.
17. Rump fluffs: Soft maraboulike feathers excellent for nymph gills, nymph tails, marabou streamer wings, woolyworm tails, marabou matuka wings, bass bug and moth wings and tails.

125

barbs of the throat hackle are too short to tail medium- to large-size dry flies properly. Longer, softer neck feathers must then be used, and more barbs are necessary to support the fly, as weak tails will cause the fly to roll to one side. Spade feathers make such ideal tailing because they are long and so stiff that only a few barbules are needed to support the fly properly, thus giving it a very delicate, lifelike appearance.

The use of both rooster and hen feathers for wings goes back to the origins of fly-tying. In recent decades, body-feather dry-fly wings have been promoted by such gifted tyers as Bill Blades and Poul Jorgensen. The natural color and shape make them ideal for realistic simulations of mayfly and caddis wings. Although they may appear very fragile, the natural webbiness of the body feathers ensures surprising durability. Whether this exacting detail is appreciated by the trout is open to discussion, but they sure look nice to the fisherman.

Because only necks have been available in recent years, the importance of genetic birds has affected only the dry-fly-tyer. Now that genetic full body skins have become more readily available, a host of new feather uses has been developed by creative tyers from across the country. As René Harrop puts it, "In my opinion, virtually every feather on the full skin has an ideal fly-tying use. The potential is limitless."

RAISING BIRDS

Raising roosters for tying is a very expensive and risky proposition. A genetic bird must be fed and cared for until it reaches full feather maturity, usually somewhere between ten and eighteen months, with twelve months being the average. Right off the top, a full-size rooster will require between $8 and $12 worth of standard chicken feed to keep it in good health for twelve months. Many feather farmers feed their birds special custom mix, which can easily double the feed cost. Adding further to the feeding expense are the large numbers of breeding stock kept year-round and the chickens that die from disease or predation. In order to get the desired number of roosters, more than twice that number of chicks must be raised to the point where hens and less desirable colors of roosters can be culled.

Disease is the number-one problem that the raiser faces. Unfortunately, there are numerous poultry ailments that can all but wipe out an entire flock. Disease problems are more critical for the feather raiser because he must keep his birds alive three or four times longer than the commercial poultry raiser. The necks from birds that die of disease before they are mature do not bring enough to cover the expense of the bird's feed because the feathers are soft and undeveloped. In order to ensure maximum yield from a flock, disease prevention is a necessity, and that means expensive medicine and technical ability. The raiser is constantly on the lookout for health problems in the flock and must have the knowledge and experience to recognize a potential outbreak. Birds that show early symptoms must be destroyed immediately. Most breeders destroy both the brothers and sisters of the diseased bird and the parents, ensuring that the disease carriers won't be bred into the next year's flock. This becomes a difficult task when it is a light-blue dun with promising-looking hackle quality. The effects of disease in the flock are hard on the raiser in terms of mental anguish over potential economic loss. A few drops of blood in the droppings or a lethargic bird with drooping wings means sleepless nights for the hackle farmer.

Second only to disease on the breeder's ulcer list is predation. Approximately 15 percent of a noncaged flock will be lost to predation. Every bird killed by a fox, owl, hawk, weasel, skunk, raccoon, cat, dog, mink, rat or bandit fly-tyer means money down the drain. Owls, weasels and raccoons are particularly devastating—they hit at night and will kill far more birds than they can possibly eat. A large owl can easily kill thirty adult birds in one night. There is no more pathetic sight for the hackle raiser than to open the chicken coop door some morning and see the floor littered with torn-up carcasses. Stray dogs are also a threat. Often they will kill or cripple as many birds as they can until stopped. If the dog belongs to an unfriendly neighbor, the situation can become unpleasant.

On the predictable side of a feather farmer's life is the work involved in keeping a flock fed, watered and properly housed. The labor necessary to maintain a large flock of genetic birds from chick to adult is awesome. Eight hundred birds, a rather modest quantity in the hackle business, consume about 200 pounds of feed and almost 100 pounds of water daily. Besides hauling and distributing feed and water, what goes in must come out—and that creates a lot more work!

Today's genetic raisers are of two minds on housing birds: Henry Hoffman and Bucky Metz cage birds individually, while Ted Hebert (as well as the late Andy Miner) believes in group ranging. Obviously, the cage method reduces predation losses, and it is possible for one man to take care of a large number of birds if automatic feeding and watering systems are used. Although cages and automated equipment remove some of the risk from hackle raising, they commit the raiser to a very large capital investment. In experiments with birds from the same breeding, the free-ranging birds were found to develop harder and shinier feathers with a better overall hackle quality than their caged brothers, though the yield from the caged group was higher and much more consistent. Ranged birds seem to benefit from a diet supplemented with the free choice of natural foods (insects, plants and so forth) and the exercise they get from foraging outside. Unfortunately, much of this exercise comes from fighting with each other. Unlike the mild-mannered, domesticated feed converters advertised in the poultry catalogs, the genetic heritage of the breeds raised for fly-tying has been heavily influenced by fighting gamecock crosses. Most of the fly-tying strains are not friendly pets but fierce competitors. I have seen ranged genetic birds attack dogs, cats and people. In fact, I had one bronze-white rooster that had it in for me so badly he would come from as far as a hundred feet to get a piece of me. Once his neck filled out, it was I who had a piece of him.

At any rate, the raiser who does not use cages has to contend with constant fighting. From the time they are young chicks, the pecking order is disputed and reorganized daily. Anyone who has seen a good cockfight knows that the feathers really fly. Excessive fighting can completely ruin a rooster's neck for fly-tying purposes. Fighting birds direct their attack on the area just behind the head, where size 14 to 18 hackles are located. To compound the problem further, the loser of a fight may be subject to a gang onslaught from lesser roosters, who painfully welcome him to the bottom of the pecking order. Despite numerous "tricks of the trade" to reduce fighting, it always takes a substantial toll.

Although roosters are the primary villains when it comes to feather pecking, hens can also cause serious damage. Art Flick points out, "Hens will peck the rooster's neck sufficiently to cut off the very tips of the hackles, and it is usually the smaller and more desirable hackles that are spoiled. The heck of it is, they don't cause noticeable damage as the roosters do, but it is mighty aggravating to purchase a neck only to find when you start tying that many of the hackle tips are missing."

HACKLE RAISERS

No matter what method of raising is chosen, the breeder has a sizable investment in every bird that survives long enough to see the skinner's blade. All the costs of hackle farming come up front, long before the skin or neck is sold. It is a gamble like any other type of farming. Despite the high cost of a genetic neck or full body skin, no one is getting rich raising birds for the fly-tyer. Bill Tobin of the Trout Brook Hackle Company offers this advice: "If you even play with the thought of raising hackle for profit, you'd better have a friendly brain surgeon open your head and rearrange your marbles!" Why, then, do these men continue to raise birds? For most of them, the real reason goes beyond the hope of someday making a big profit; a partial explanation is the tremendous feeling of pride and accomplishment in watching a chick develop into a prime rooster with hackle that would make any tyer drool. Hackle farming requires more than a large financial commitment; it takes total dedication, with a generous sprinkling of insanity. There is no vacation for the feather raiser—a long weekend means sixteen extra hours of mixing feed, skinning birds or shoveling you-know-what. With so much time spent caring for the flock, the raiser soon learns whether he loves or hates them. Once this point is reached, the die is cast, usually forever. For some it is cats, dogs or parakeets, but only a very few make it as hackle raisers. It would be a sad situation for the fly-tyer if hackle raisers became concerned only with making a good return on their investments of time and money.

Bill Tobin

Bill Tobin is the most outspoken and perhaps the most colorful of the feather farmers. Combining the talents of Hank Halstead and Charlie Willcox, Bill founded the Trout Brook Hackle Company. Although he is very proud of their birds, Bill is quick to admit they have done everything wrong that they could have. Further thwarting their progress has been an unusual amount of bad luck. As Tobin put it, "Think of at least two hundred of the most improbable things that can happen, and you'll be just nicely under way. To mention one, let me relate how a drunk decided the road wasn't wide enough, so he took out into the field a hundred yards from our chicken yard and flew—straight as an arrow—smack into a power pole. He snapped it clean as a whistle and stopped! So did the electrical source to our barn, and the incubators holding six hundred specially selected eggs which we had carefully noted to try to determine more specifically what came out of which breeding match-ups. Result? Two years of attempted research went to hell—no egg hatch from those incubators!"

It all started some fifteen years ago when Bill and his fishing partner made the "fatal" mistake of stopping at a local farm with a sign out front that said: FANCY CHICKENS FOR SALE. Bill walked away with four hens and the "greatest buff ginger the world has ever known." Soon after, fate added a strain of Plymouth Rocks and a few natural duns. Following a learn-as-you-go shotgun breeding program, Tobin found himself locked into the feather business. The Trout Brook Hackle Company currently produces strains of buff, light ginger, grizzly and nine varieties of blue dun.

Being "a hundred and twenty years old and on one foot," Bill's main function in the business is selecting breeders, grading capes and handling their sales. He is proud to point out that they don't have customers—all their purchasers are considered clients. Serious fly-tyers can write for Bill's annual list of available necks. His address is 4 North Church Street, Cortland, New York 13045. Better hurry—if Bill gets caught having one of his "real friendly chats" with his best grizzly rooster, Champ, you may have your letter rerouted to "Happydale Home"!

Andy Miner

Andy Miner was one of the major contributors to the development of today's genetic fly-tying breeds. Like many early hackle raisers, Miner was an avid fly-tyer who became involved out of his own desire for better-quality necks—especially those rare natural blue duns. He began raising chickens in 1954 with a setting of blue dun eggs from Harry Darbee. He also advertised for gamecocks and fancy varieties in a number of magazines for chicken hobbyists. He soon had birds from all over the country. Miner bred and crossbred these birds, keeping detailed records of the results of each experimental breeding. He read all the available books and articles of the day on different theories of feather color inheritance. However, little of the information was reliable, as most of the published ideas had not been scientifically proven. Much of Miner's early work was a painstaking process of trial and error, depending on his own previous experience and luck.

Through the years, Miner continued to improve his strain with experimental outcrosses that added vigor, feather quality and color. His records indicated that quality was by far the most important factor in selecting breeders. It took decades to make a substantial improvement in the quality of the feather, while color could be manipulated in a relatively short period of time. Proper selection of breeders meant the slow and tedious process of hackle-gauging all likely candidates. Even in the early years, Miner's criteria for breeders were almost unbelievable by anyone's standards. To be considered, a bird had to have 1¾ inches of size 12; he was looking for that much web-free hackle in a size 16! Although his primary interest was in raising natural blue duns, Miner also produced a large variety of other colors. Regardless of their color, all these birds shared one common trait: their long, slim, short-barbed, rapierlike hackles. The strong, dominant influence of this characteristic is especially evident today in the Hebert and Metz flocks for which Miner provided the foundation stock.

Andy Miner corresponded regularly with Darbee and other well-known bird enthusiasts. His meticulously kept records provided him with an invaluable reference for assisting others sharing his interest in raising birds for tying flies. He and Darbee became close friends, and over the years they often exchanged feathers and visits. In 1974 Darbee wrote: "I want to thank you for the magnificent neck and saddle you mailed me. I have never seen anything approaching it. The hackles are not only extremely long and narrow, but there are a great many barbs on the quill and they are stiff and beautiful. As soon as time allows, I will tie some flies and mail them to you. I intend to preserve the neck intact forever. Then when people come in to brag about the hackle they have, I can cool them pretty easily." That must have been some neck!

Miner not only supplied breeding stock to two newcomers to serious hackle raising but also information and encouragement. In 1973 he gave Ted Hebert a number of choice breeders to improve his flock. He also generously shared a great deal of the knowledge that made his bird-raising program so successful. A few years later, he supplied Robert ("Bucky") Metz with some eggs when Metz decided to enter the hackle business. This type of assistance was typical of the unselfish contributions Miner made over the years.

What is most remarkable is that with all the time, hard work and money he devoted to these special birds, he never sold a neck—any he didn't use were given to friends. Miner's dedication provided those currently in the hackle business with chickens that would have taken decades for even an expert poultry geneticist to produce. When asked if he would do it all over again he smiled and nodded yes, but he was also quick to point out, "I never added up how much it cost, because if I knew, I guess I'd have to quit!"

(Editor's note: *We learned with sorrow of the death of Andy Miner as this book was going to press.*)

Harry Darbee

It would be presumptuous of me to describe the contributions of Harry Darbee of Roscoe, New York, who became a pioneer hackle herder at the age of fifteen, more than fifty years ago.

Harry and his wife, Elsie, were the subject of a profile in the first volume of *The Fly-Tyer's Almanac,* and Harry has since written his autobiography, *Catskill Flytier*. In the chapter entitled "Running a Hackle Farm," he notes, "In the New York Public Library there are close to three thousand books on the subject of poultry. Only one of them is exclusively about chicken feathers—the effects of diet on color—and it is in Italian. This gives you some idea of our lack of knowledge on growing hackles." It also gives some insight into the perseverance of Harry Darbee, who has done so much to lay the foundations for hackle herders of the present day. Read *Catskill Flytier*. You'll love it.

Ted Hebert

Ted Hebert became interested in hackle raising in 1969. Soon the interest became a compulsion, and within a year he was in the feather-farming business. Disappointed with the results of breeding common domestic strains, he began looking for the "perfect" bird. The search ended in 1973 at Andy Miner's Blue Dun Farm. Through Andy's generous sharing of select breeding stock and his long years of experience, Ted was able to breed the superior hackle characteristic of the Miner strain into his own flock. Further enhancing the pedigree of his flock was a gift from Harry Darbee of a fine black rooster and a shipment of fertile eggs.

One would think that with this kind of start, Hebert should have had it made in the feather business. But having the right breeding stock is only one piece of the puzzle. Ted was a neophyte to the magnitude of diseases that could prey on his flock. His losses were heavy for the first few years; the problem was solved only with persistence and technical help from the poultry scientists at nearby Michigan State University.

With the threat of heavy disease losses minimized, Ted began to concentrate on the difficult problem of selective breeding. If the hackle-quality characteristics are lost from the strain, it means starting over again. Breeding to produce a desired color is relatively simple. However, when attempting to control both color and feather quality in the same breeding, it becomes very confusing, especially with blue dun and grizzly birds. Henry Hoffman has solved this problem in his barred rock strain, but no one as yet has developed a true color-reproducing strain of natural blue dun. By working closely with Andy Miner, Hebert continued to improve quality and color with frequent outcrosses to the Miner blue dun stock.

Although Hebert's major effort has been directed toward raising blue duns, he offers the most complete color selection available. In part, this is due to the large variety of crosses he uses to produce the various blue dun shades. As a by-product, he gets a predictable percentage of highly desirable "freak" colors like chocolate dun and badger dun fleck, as well as black and cream. He also breeds specifically for many shades of brown and furnace.

In response to the rapidly increasing demand for body, spade and wing feathers, the vast majority of Ted's genetic birds are fully skinned out. The skinning process is both time-consuming and expensive. As Ted puts it, "Separating the skin from an old rooster couldn't be any more difficult if it were glued on with epoxy; it takes a razor-sharp knife and a whole lot of tugging." Even though the full skins are expensive, Hebert's limited facilities are running at full production.

After eight years of devotion to his genetic hackle business, Hebert is now in too deep to quit without losing his shirt. He plans to build a large, automated rearing building to reduce the amount of hand labor and time he and his wife, Sue, spend caring for the flock. With more space and time, Ted plans on adding grizzly and badger strains, as well as going all out to perfect a true reproducing strain of blue duns.

Henry Hoffman

A small town in Oregon is the home of the Super Grizzlies and their obedient slave, Henry Hoffman. Feather farming requires dedication—and a lot of time. Having abandoned a normal career, Henry is totally devoted to his birds. Peak activity at the Hoffman Hackle Farm begins in the fall, when the roosters are prime for skinning, and doesn't let up until after the spring chick hatch is over. During this hectic six-month period, the normal weekday is twelve to sixteen hours long. By late spring, the pace slackens, and Henry can look forward to an "easy" eight to ten hours a day. Sounds unbelievable, doesn't it? Henry and his wife, Joyce, do all the feeding, watering, waste removal and skinning without the aid of automatic equipment or outside help. Last year, Henry was away from the farm for only four days, and that was spent promoting his necks at the Federation of Fly Fishermen's national conclave.

A onetime commercial fly-tyer, Henry became involved in hackle raising when he could no longer buy quality grizzly necks. By 1965, after many false leads and visits to dozens of chicken raisers, Hoffman found the base breeding stock he wanted. As Henry puts it, "I feel fortunate to have found these few birds, since all the ones I have seen since then seem to be declining in fly-tying qualities." It took five years of selective breeding and accurate record-keeping to develop his Super Grizzly strain. In 1970, he shook the fly-tying fraternity with the finest barred rock necks anyone had seen. His necks became so synonymous with quality that others began using the name Super Grizzly, but no other necks could match the short-barbed, daggerlike hackles of the Hoffman strain. Hoffman calculates that his top-grade necks have well over a thousand tyable hackles for sizes 6 through 24, plus feathers for streamer wings and other large flies. Approximately three hundred of the hackles are in the highly desirable 12 to 20 range.

One of Hoffman's prime roosters. Note the length of the saddle hackles.

The demand for Hoffman's necks soon outstripped his ability to supply, and he has never caught up. In fact, in his advertisements he states: "To maintain the quality and continued improvement of the stock, I raise only enough birds to supply present accounts (often coming up short), so please, no more dealer inquiries." In order to ensure that the demand stays high, he does not sell eggs or breeding stock.

Henry is constantly striving to develop his Super Grizzly strain further and to broaden his color selection. He now produces marketable quantities of light, medium and dark barred rock necks and full body skins, light barred cream and white necks. In the near future, tyers can look forward to brown, ginger, barred ginger, blue dun and barred dun. However, owing to his current caging facilities, the availability of these new colors will be limited.

Bucky Metz

The Metz Hatchery in Pennsylvania, known primarily for meat birds, has recently entered the hackle business. During the last thirty-nine years, they have been raising chicks for meat production operations. Their size, automated facilities and experience in growing large numbers of chickens was no doubt invaluable in helping Bucky contend with many of the problems that face newcomers to feather farming.

Bucky Metz went with George Harvey, a well-known fly-tyer, to visit Andy Miner in hopes of attaining breeding stock. Harvey, a longtime friend of Miner, considered his birds to be "the best-quality blue dun birds in the United States." In 1975, shortly after his visit to Andy's Blue Dun Farm, Metz wrote him that he was "so kind to give George and me some of your stock and me the initial inspiration to attempt such a project." Metz used the high-quality Miner strain to produce commercially a variety of blue dun shades and more common colors. From these birds, he was able to develop a very nice light ginger that has been well received and is currently in high demand. At present, Metz is working on having grizzly and barred dun necks in marketable quantities. The resources of the Metz Hatchery should allow Bucky to supply large numbers of birds to help satisfy the growing demand for quality hackle.

22. New Materials and Tools
by DAVE WHITLOCK

These are the good old days. Never has there been a time in flytying when so many materials and tools were available. Since the first *Almanac* was published, there has been almost a doubling in products to meet growing market demand. Don't let anyone tell you that the good old days were in the past. They're right now, and they may even get better.

FEATHERS

Sure, some old-timers will mourn about the dwindling supply of fine necks, but genetic hackle is here to stay, as Howard West has explained in the last chapter, and there have been new developments in bleaching and dyeing. The Photo-Plus necks from Fly Fisherman's Bookcase have excellent color and sheen, and the Kaufmann brothers of Streamborn Fly Shop are masters at bleaching grizzlies to barred creams and gingers and dyeing them to browns, olives, duns, etc. In my opinion, a Hoffman Super Grizzly bleached or dyed by Lance Kaufmann is much better than natural solid colors because of the barring. Dave Inks (formerly of Creative Sports) and Lance Kaufmann have also perfected the dyeing of fluorescent hackle. Steelhead, salmon and saltwater tyers will find great satisfaction in strung saddles and necks covering all the important blues, greens, olives, reds, oranges and yellows. My eyes water and my hands twitch when I see them in the daylight.

Saddle capes and full skins are becoming ever more available. A full skin gives you an incredible choice of perfectly sized, sorted and packaged hackle ready to pick and use. Full cock or hen skins offer great dollar value for the tyer. (See the diagram of a cock skin in Howard West's chapter for a handy guide to full utilization of a skin.)

Hen hackle is as scarce as or scarcer than cock hackle—or hen's teeth—but I expect the demand to be relieved when more full skins reach the market. Many of the body feathers are as good or better than the hen hackle we used to see.

All sorts of good things are happening with chickens. There are some bantam and game hens that have markings like partridge or pheasant. Bill Hunter of Hunter's Fly Shop gave me a couple of tricos hen skins that are better than partridge for soft-hackle wet flies or tailing and legging nymphs.

Strung white turkey marabou is available in several grades and sizes. It is most useful for any number of patterns. It comes dyed in a wide range of colors, or you can easily dye it any color you wish. The original stork marabou is now almost off the market, but I think turkey actually offers a superior and more versatile marabou.

Speckled turkey secondaries have all but disappeared from the world market. That's a shame, but the North American wild turkey has a similar feather.

HAIR AND FUR

Demand from the fashion trade for fox, bobcat, coyote and raccoon has sent the price for long furs out of sight. The more traditional tying furs—mink, rabbit, squirrel, beaver, muskrat, woodchuck and opossum—are in good supply.

I am very much taken by the African goat hair sold and distributed by Fireside Angler and Orvis. The hair is glassy, long enough for easy dubbing and can be dyed a great range of colors. It is an excellent substitute for seal or polar or brown bear underfur. Blended with other naturals or synthetics, it makes a beautiful lifelike body. By itself, it makes shaggy, shiny bodies.

Hair from bear, seal and wild game from Africa and South America is either scarce or illegal now. But hair from deer, moose, boar, squirrel and goat can do a nice job of substituting. Dave Inks has been working on bleaching and dyeing techniques to utilize more fully the ample supply of wild squirrel tails. Bleached and/or dyed, the tails are just what's needed to meet the increasing demand for hairwings in salmon, steelhead and streamer flies.

Hare's mask and ears are a staple for nymph and soft-hackle wet-fly-tyers, but here's a tip: squirrel *body* hair is better. That goes for gray and red fox squirrels, pine squirrels, ground squirrels and black phase squirrels. The hair is short and perfectly textured for body dubbing. In fact, I prefer squirrel body hair over all other naturals for dubbing nymphs. Try it and you'll see what I mean.

Wild boar and domestic pig bristles are ideal for making antennae, tails and extended bodies. Bristle is very durable, has a beautiful taper and a natural sheen. The L&L Mayfly and my two stoneflies in this book show how it can be used.

Northern White-tailed Deer Hair

The single best tying material we have is deer hair. It's available, prices are reasonable and it has versatility. All in all, deer hair is a tremendous bargain. The best of all comes from the northern whitetail. Material dealers offer it in natural dun brown, natural white and dyed colors, but you're missing out if you don't pick up a full hide when you get the chance. The hair from different parts of the body can be used for a wide variety of purposes, as explained here.

1. Masks and Ears: Dark grizzled gray and black short, stiff hair. Hairwings for caddis, comparaduns, irresistibles, etc., and tails for dry flies.

2. Front Legs: Short, fine-textured hair from light tan to grizzled gray and brown. Excellent for caddis wings and tails.

3. Mane and Neck: Stiff, medium to short hair, very coarse and wiry. Grizzled black, gray and dun brown. White on throat. Good for hairwing on Wulffs, humpies and caddis. Excellent tailing and muddler minnow collars. Hairwings and tails for small bass bugs.

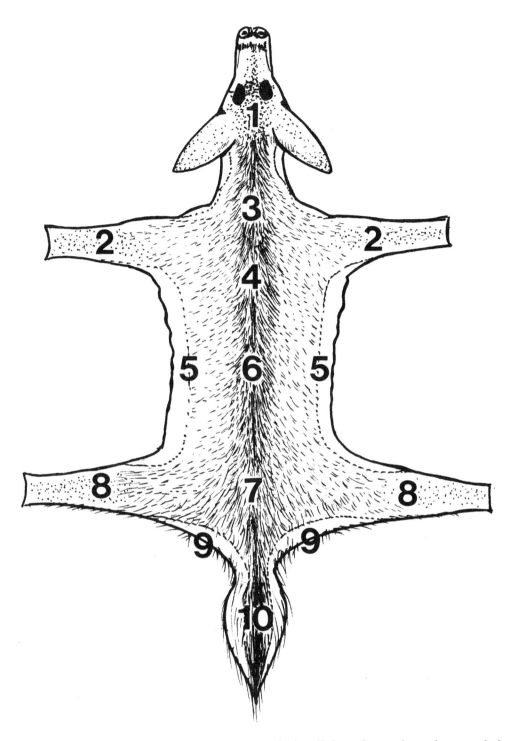

4. Shoulder and Chest: Dark-grizzled along spine, tinting lighter deeper into chest, and shortening somewhat from spine down. Hair is coarse, thick and compact. Excellent for most deer-hair body and head patterns such as muddlers, sculpins, XE series mayflies, bass bugs and mice.

5. Belly: Light-gray to pure-white, thick, short, coarse hair. Ideal white or dyed for bass bugs, spinner wings, Trude and coachman wings and saltwater flies. The gray to light-gray hair is ideal for bleaching to a true white for dyeing bright colors. Natural pure-white deer hair is always limited on skin and always in short supply.

6. Back Hair: Long wire-tough tips and a heavy-texture base hair. Very dark-marked, going lighter and shorter down the sides toward the flanks. Excellent for muddlers, bass bugs, mice, Drake's sliders, large hairwings, underwings and extended bodies, etc.

7. Rump Hair: Very long, thick, coarse hair but less strong than hair on back. Somewhat lighter in color and marking. Excellent for Drake's sliders, large muddler and sculpin heads, bass bugs, extended bodies and saltwater bug heads.

8. Rear Legs: Similar to front legs except more white hair and generally longer, coarser hair. Same uses as front legs.

9. Crotch Hair: Long, silky thin-to-thick pure-white hair. Excellent white or dyed bright colors for streamers, bucktails, saltwater flies, jigs, etc.

10. Bucktail (*Doe Also*): Tail has long, brown and white, thin to coarse hair (bucktail), traditionally used for bucktail streamers, saltwater flies, jig wings, Wulff wings (brown tips straightened) and bass flies.

Other Deer Family Hairs

Southern Whitetail: Identical to the northern whitetail except that the hair is more wiry and shorter. It does not flare as well but is superior for hackle, wings and tail on Western patterns, grasshoppers and caddis.

Summer Whitetail: A whitetail that is killed before fall. Hair has a more reddish cast and is much shorter and finer grained. Especially ideal for hairwings and tails of dry flies such as caddis and Wulffs. Legs and mask hair very similar to many African deer and antelope.

Sitka Whitetail: Very similar to northern whitetail, but more vividly marked hair. Excellent for muddlers, hoppers, caddis and hairbugs.

Mule Deer: A Western plains and mountain deer that is usually more coarse and colored more grayish than the whitetail. Excellent for tails, clipped bodies and hairwings.

Pacific Black-tailed Deer: Very similar to Midwestern whitetail in length and size. Hair is more black and gray. Excellent for muddler collars, caddis wings, Wulffs, etc.

Antelope: This rather coarse hair is either white with a gray base or rich cinnamon-brown with a gray base. This hair dyes easily and flares better than any other I've seen. It is very tender but has superior floating ability.

Elk: Elk is a very dense dun-gray/cream/light-brown hair that flares very well. It is somewhat more durable than most deer hair. It is tough to beat for hair bass bugs, extended bodies and wings. It takes dyes very well, but it (and antelope hair) lacks the interesting grizzled markings of mule and white-tailed deer. Elk varies greatly in length and texture. Rump hair is outstanding for extended bodies.

Caribou: A fairly short, dense, dun-gray to light-cream hair that is extremely soft and light but somewhat tender. It is very easy to flare with light pressure, and its texture is perfect for smaller deer-hair-bodied trout flies. It does not dye well because of its tender texture. The rump hair is similar to the elk's.

Dall Sheep: A dense, pure-white hair that is soft and fairly tender. It flares well but is not particularly suited for general all-purpose use. It makes nice dense trout fly bodies and will dye light shades easily.

Moose: A coarse, tough, very dark slate/dun-brown/black hair that varies greatly in length. It is ideal for wings, tails and bodies. It does not flare easily but does make great bass bugs if you use a strong thread to tie. Moose is ideal for ants and patterns that use special knotted legs. The mane hair is different from the body hair and is used for imitation quill bodies and insect legs.

SYNTHETICS

When I wrote about synthetics in the first *Almanac,* I was apprehensive about their general acceptance by most fly-tyers. Well, it's a different story now. The great majority of tyers have embraced synthetics with such enthusiasm that new ones are being developed specifically for fly-tying. In many cases the synthetics surpass the natural materials. However, the sheer number of synthetics, plus the brand names used, has caused some confusion. Here is a list of synthetics and their uses to do away with the confusion.

Synthetic Dubbing

Orlon Knitting Wool: An ideal medium-soft shiny fiber for blending with natural coarse furs such as seal or other soft furs or synthetics. Cut into lengths of ¼ to ½ inch and put into blender for dubbing on fly sizes 8 to 16.

Kodel Polyester Rug Yarn: Coarse fiber, a good substitute for seal fur or polar bear underfur for medium- to large-bodied flies, sizes 1/0 to 8. Cut into ¼- to ⅝-inch pieces and blend.

Seal-ex: Very similar to Kodel polyester but blended with two sizes of fiber. Excellent substitute for seal or polar bear underfur as is, or blended with other synthetics or natural furs. For flies 1/0 down to 16.

Andra Spectrum: A fine new synthetic dubbing that comes in fifty colors especially for fly-tying. It is an ideal small dry-fly and nymph-body material because of its very fine fibers and wide color range. It is the best substitute I've found for beaver belly. For fly sizes 18 to 26.

Fly-Rite Standard: A polypropylene dubbing that is medium-fine fibered. It is very easy to dub flies down to 16s, and it comes in forty great varieties of natural and bright colors.

Poly II: A fine sheet dubbing that comes in a very useful range of sixteen colors. It is excellent for small dry- and wet-fly bodies. The flat sheets are easy to carry in streamside tying kits.

Mohlon: An orlon acrylic fiber that is useful dubbing for fly sizes 1/0 to 16. It comes in a yarn but can be separated and dubbed or blended.

Frostlon: Another acrylic-fiber blended dubbing that makes very shiny bodies. Its sparkle makes it a good choice for emerging caddis pupa bodies. Best used on fly sizes 8 to 16.

Orvis Poly Body: A medium-textured polypropylene dubbing available in thirty colors. It is a little coarser than standard Fly-Rite and finer than Seal-ex. All colors are solid, not spectrum-blended. Makes very nice medium-size fly bodies.

Orvis Poly Caddis: Extra-fine poly dubbing in twenty-four blended or heathered colors. An excellent working kit to simulate closely most natural nymph and adult aquatic insects. Excellent for tying bodies sizes 8 to 18.

Fireside's Poly X: One of the original and best poly dubbings for sizes 2 to 16. With blend cards, it mixes and blends beautifully with other synthetics or natural furs. Comes singly or in a kit of twenty-four natural colors.

Fireside's Poly XXX Fine and XXX Blend: A very fine poly dubbing or blended dubbing for size 18 or smaller. A most effective and easy-to-work-with synthetic. The manufacturer recommends use of blend cards for mixing colors or other furs.

Fly-Rite Extra Fine Poly: Similar to Fly-Rite Standard except much finer, for tying size 16 or smaller. Works and blends easily to create beautiful tight or loose bodies. Some of the forty colors are blended, and others are solid.

Synthetic Wing Materials

Swiss Straw: A folded rayon-fiber ribbon that looks like straw or raffia. It comes in a very large variety of bright and natural colors. Folded, it is an excellent nymph wing-case material. Unfolded, it makes nice spinner or dun wings, but it absorbs water rapidly and softens if not waterproofed. It is a super scud or shrimp back material, and the stillborn shucks when not waterproofed.

Polypropylene Sheeting: Cut from various thicknesses of poly sheet (e.g., Ziploc bags, sandwich bags), it makes nice cut wings or wing cases. Can be colored with dyes or marking pencils. It is almost indispensable to me.

Fly-Rite Poly Wiggle: Long, fine, slightly crinkled poly fibers for making streamer wings for fresh- and saltwater flies. Cut short, it also makes glassy poly wing spinners and emerger wing cases. It is a beautiful synthetic.

Fireside and Orvis Poly Wing Material: This is a 100 percent medium-size poly nonabsorbent yarn material that has a lustrous sparkle. It comes in the nine most practical and useful colors to match most natural aquatic insect wings. For Gary Borger's Poly Caddis (Chapter 9) it has no equal. Also makes terrific spinner and hairwings. For emerging nymph or stillborn patterns, it is fantastic.

Fly-Rite Extra Fine Poly and Standard Poly: These two Fly-Rite dubbings also make excellent floating nymph caddis and stillborn wings in suitable colors.

FisHair: This modacrylic fiber very similar to synthetic human hair wigs has fantastic potential for substitutes for all types of fly-tying hair. It can be made in any length, denier, taper, color or color barring. Margie Duescher, FisHair manager, said they are eager to expand their types of FisHair to best accommodate fly-tyers and jig-makers. I've seen perfect FisHair substitutes for kip tail, polar bear, bucktail and squirrel tail. At present, FisHair is available in twenty-four colors and lengths from 2½ up to 10 inches. It is very reasonable, plentiful and ties up easily. It is also "rooted" in a base, so that, like animal skin, all the hair is in place until you are ready to cut a portion off. Our tests with it show FisHair to be every bit as effective as natural hair, on both salt- and freshwater fly designs.

Microweb Wing Material: Distributed by Barry Beck's Cahill House and Orvis, it was developed by Bill Luzardo and Hank Leonhard (see chapters 7 and 8, L&L Mayfly and L&L Caddis). This new synthetic mat wing material has excellent potential. It comes in two thicknesses and is easily colored by most waterproof markers or by dyeing. For almost any terrestrial or aquatic insect adult cut wings, it has no equal for durability and realism. It is so easy to shape, color and tie that I get the feeling I'm cheating.

Metallic Materials

The variety of flashy materials for ribbing, bodies and wings continues to grow. Metallic coating of mylar and other plastics has all but made tinsels obsolete, as plastics are stronger, tougher, less expensive and will not discolor or corrode. Creative Sports Enterprises has come up with some very interesting metallics. One is Colored Mylar Thread, which can be used as a tying thread or as a tinsel. It is very strong and ties flat and smooth. It comes on standard-sized spools in silver, gold, copper, red, green and blue.

CSE also sells colored fine-diameter wire. This strong, small wire is exactly what I want for ribbing perfect Matuka wings. It is also superb for ribbing nymphs, dries and streamer bodies. It is on a standard bobbin spool and comes in the same finishes as the mylar thread.

The Fly Fisherman's Bookcase has Poly Flash, a soft, oval mylar braid that gives streamers a high sparkle. It wraps and ties bulky or flat, depending on how tightly you wrap it down.

Sunrise of India has recently marketed two assortments of mylar tinsel and floss. There are a dozen spools in each practical dispenser box. I consider them almost a must for any fly-tyer.

Fly-tying Threads

Nylon continues to be the most popular tying thread, despite all the bad-mouthing it gets from diehard silk purists. Danville's Herb Howard's prewaxed 6/0 to 7/0 is still the most popular medium-to-small fly-tying thread. With Nymo almost all gone now, several other threads have begun to replace it. Monocord and prewaxed Monocord seem heir to the heavy fly-thread throne. However, I've never felt it could be totally trusted for really heavy tying, as Nymo could be.

In my opinion, the best replacement for Nymo is single-strand nylon floss, introduced by Creative Sports Enterprises. The name sounds all wrong for tying thread, but it is as strong as stainless-steel cable, works easily and covers and holds like a dream. For streamers, hairbugs, most western hairwings, salmon and steelhead flies, it is greatly superior to Nymo or Monocord. Since I started using it a year ago, it has replaced all my other tying threads except for those used on flies under size 12. It should be used with a flared tube-type bobbin for best results.

Dave Engerbretson's Ultra Midge Thread goes on the other side of Herb Howard's prewaxed thread for tying the tiniest flies. It is quite strong enough for any fly size 16 or smaller, especially if a very high-quality lightweight bobbin such as Matarelli's Midge Bobbin is used.

FLY-TYING TOOLS AND ACCESSORIES

I can hardly believe the amount of new or improved tying tools that has come on the market since the first *Almanac* appeared. There is almost an excess.

Vises

The most dramatic increase has come with vises. At least a dozen new vises have hit the market in the past few years. Happily, there seems to be room for every one, as vises costing from $10 to $150 are really moving. The most significant advances are multi-jaw units, better pedestals and clamps, rotary operation and adjustable angle jaws.

Sunrise of India has made the widest entry into the market with no less than ten models, which often resemble successful American and European vises. Workmanship, durability, finish and function are good to excellent. Best of all, they are usually available, dealers say, but spare parts often are not.

D. H. Thompson Company, thanks to Jim Chestney, has made a strong effort to improve their once-famous vises. From what Jim has said and shown me, I'm very impressed by and pleased with the improvements. A special Ultra Vise has completely vertical jaw adjustment and an accessory midge jaw. There is also a new "black body" pro vise that is the standard Thompson A dressed in black matte finish. The standard jaw shape and the midge jaws have been slimmed to make it easier to work around all hook sizes.

Al Price of La Pine, Oregon, and his son, Eric, have introduced a new quality vise that resembles the Salmo in outline. It has a fine all-black matte finish and all-angle adjustable jaws. It operates off a rotating handle to tighten the jaws. The single universal set of jaws holds all sizes of hooks almost equally well. Al told me to put all hooks in the same position for long life and best performance. Al's vise has probably the most unique and versatile table C-clamp yet devised. It tightens instantly to flat surfaces up to 4 inches thick. The clamp alone is almost worth the "Price" of the vise, which by the way is in the $60 range. Al says his vise is made for a lifetime of hard tying use.

To me, Bill Hunter's new HMH vises are the ultimate today in traditional cam-operated fly-tying tools. During development of the HMH standard and premium models, nothing was spared in time, engineering and field testing to make a product that leaves nothing to be desired. I personally feel they are the finest vises I've ever used. Both standard and premium models have three functional sets of no-tool fast-change jaws, magnum, medium and midge. All three are specifically shaped to best accommodate flies tied in these size ranges.

HMH vises are available in either pedestal or C-clamp mounts. They can be operated as stationary vises at any jaw angle or put into rotary mode for that type of tying just as easily. Cams have grooves in them to accommodate spring-material clips. The HMH vises are in the $80 to $100 price range. You may someday buy another vise, but if you own an HMH, you will never need another one.

New HMH Vises. Includes standard with C clamp and premium with pedestal mount. Extra jaws and Darrel Martin custom HMH carrying case.

Orvis has improved the operation of the original vise that I wrote about in the first *Almanac*. My sample remains durable and functional. But the real news in Manchester is the Orvis-Renzetti Presentation Vise. It comes with two sets of fine positive holding jaws covering hook sizes from 28 to 5/0. A custom-fitted spring-material clip and bobbin cradle holder and suede case are included in the package, which costs $150. Orvis gives a lifetime guarantee. I have not had time to give this vise a full test, but my initial one found it to be well engineered and interesting. It has a radical look and feel, and it needs getting used to if you've worked with more conventional models.

Special Vise Mountings

There are times and places where an ordinary C-clamp or pedestal-mounted vise will not work. Here are three new alternatives.

On page 191 of Art Flick's *Master Flytying Guide* (1972) I suggested that some company adapt a suction mount to a vise stand rod. With the Mini Vac Vise Base by Fly Tyers Carry All, it would seem such a useful mount is on the market.

Sunrise makes a special wood screw attachment for their Majestic Vise that can also be easily adapted to other vises. It allows you to mount a vise on a fence post, picnic table or log with ease.

Dr. Fred Oswalt of Battle Creek, Michigan, adapted a mini camera tripod to take a screw-in shortened Thompson Model A standard head. It works well. It can be set up on almost any flat or moderately irregular surface. You need to bore out the stand-rod end to accommodate the standard screw on the tripod's head base. If you are tying on smooth surfaces, little suction caps on each leg prevent slipping.

Bobbins

The Matarelli-type bobbin has become extremely popular for a multitude of tying jobs. Floss, tinsel, mylar thread, nylon monofilament, lead wire, ribbing wire and all threads can be used more efficiently with this style of bobbin.

Frank Matarelli has made two important additions to his famous line of quality bobbins. Frank has a new mini-midge bobbin that uses the Singer sewing machine plastic or metal bobbin spools. This petite barrel bobbin is just great for tying the tiniest fly and using the very smallest threads. Its great weight reduction also prevents binding, breaking or damage to the hook and finest threads. Matarelli also has just introduced the true hardened stainless-steel flared-tube bobbin.

Frank Matarelli's Custom Tying Tools. From left to right: Dubbing twister, Matarelli whip finisher, midge bobbin threader and cleaner tool, midge bobbin, standard bobbin, long barrel bobbin, standard bobbin threader and cleaner tool and new inner flared barrel bobbin.

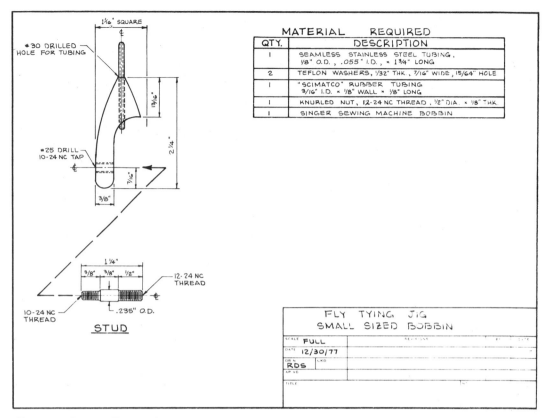

Creative Sports Enterprises' flared-tube bobbin is perhaps the best all-around tool for using single-strand nylon floss, lead wire and tinsel. Though not as durable as Matarelli's, the bobbin accommodates all sizes and helps eliminate fraying, kinking, clogging and breakage. CSE is also working on an adjustable-length barrel.

Thompson has a new Matarelli-style bobbin with an offset thread tube, but I cannot say how well it works, as I've yet to test it.

Sunrise also has several look-alike models of CSE-Matarelli–type bobbins. These other copies of spring bobbins are available under various names.

Wayne Moore of Mountain Home, Arkansas, whom I met just last year, is a remarkable maker of tools. He has spent fifty years devising tying tools and tying flies, but his contributions to toolmaking are not known to the public at all. He has quietly shared his ideas and inventions with tyers and toolmakers throughout the world and never charged a cent. He has designed more tools and accessories than anyone else I've ever known or heard of, but he is the most modest person you could meet. Here is a list of his inventions: a loop-dubbing chenille-maker, flywing-sizer, several bobbin holders and cradles, metal hackle guards, auxiliary bobbin-holder stand for pedestal vises, knot-tightener, hair-evener (stacker or aligner), technique for mixing types and colors of hair in the eveners, three types of dubbing twisters, two half-hitch tools, mini double-surgeon loop-knot tool, special hand nylon bobbin threader and straightener, and a unique dubbed-body conditioner that allows easy fast-fuzzing of bodies such as are made from burlap, synthetics and furs.

Wayne has also invented a bobbin that is beautiful to see, hold and use. I have one made from hand-rubbed rosewood that must rank as a collector's gem. Wayne designed it, Bill Charles made it, and it contains a Matarelli midge barrel. It is always the subject of conversation when I tie in public.

Wayne Moore's bobbin is not sold commercially, but it is quite easy to make one yourself, and I want to thank Wayne for his generosity in giving us the directions and blueprint for the *Almanac*.

Wayne uses any tight-grained wood, such as walnut, rosewood or cedar, for the handle. Draw pattern for handle on block of wood $1^1/_{16}$ inches square and 2¼ inches long. Drill holes for barrel and bobbin axial first. With a band saw, cut out pattern and either whittle, rasp or disk-sand to shape. Finish with hand rub. Stain or varnish as desired.

Fit in barrel and cement with epoxy. Allow to set for more than twenty-four hours. Wayne polishes the barrel tube with a linen thread and 500-grit valve-grinding compound to prevent thread fraying and promote smoothest operation. Tap threads and insert stud and add other axial accessories and sewing bobbin spool. Wayne says that a flathead bolt will substitute for the stud.

Bobbin spools can be filled directly from a thread spool, using a sewing machine or electric or hand drill. Extra spools of either plastic or metal allow complete quick-change choice of colors, sizes, etc. Wayne prefers the plastic type, as many metal ones are not made well and tend to rust.

Hackle Pliers

There are dozens of hackle pliers on the market, but try the simple and inexpensive E-Z Hook. It works so well it is almost perfect on all quills, feathers, hackles and so on. I am amazed at its proficiency, as it was not originally designed for fly-tying, but for use in wiring and soldering.

New Tying Tools. From top, clockwise: Gausdal hair aligners; Matarelli flared barrel and midge bobbins with threader and cleaner tool; CSE Fuz Comb and double flared tube bobbin; HMH spring material clips; Orvis-Renzetti wing formers; larva forceps; Bookcase's mini needlenose pliers; Sunrise angle and curved blade tying scissors.

New Hooks

There has been an encouraging emphasis on developing new, better and more specialized fly-tying hooks. This is the result of several factors. First, the number of fly-tyers is growing rapidly. Then, fly-tyers are often willing to pay more than a cent or two for a desired hook. A number of fly-tying materials firms are contracting with manufacturers for special "lot" runs on hard-to-get standards, new models and more sizes. Mustad, Wright & McGill (Eagle Claw) and Partridge of Redditch are the three most active fly-tying hook manufacturers today. I consider the products of all three certainly worth the price charged.

Last year I visited the Wright & McGill Company at Denver, and John Sweeney showed me through the hook-manufacturing facilities. It was a most interesting experience. Making hooks of any size and design is an incredibly complex process, and making each smaller-size hook below 14 literally doubles in difficulty.

Here is what's new in hooks:

Mustad 94859: Special straight ringed-eye "midge" hook in sizes 20 to 26. Equal or better hooking than the 94842 on tiny patterns.

Mustad 3532-C: Highest-quality double salmon hook. Sizes 10 through 1/0. Looped-up eye on heavy wire hook. An excellent all-purpose double hook.

Mustad 7986-B: Single salmon hook with extra-long shank, turned-up eye, 2X strong wire, Dublin point and Limerick forged bend. Black finish. Sizes 3/0 to 10. This is an outstanding hook for sculpins, Matukas, Rabbit Muddlers and other salmon and bass streamers.

Mustad 36620: Straight ringed-eye 4X long Limerick bend. Sizes 12 to 1/0. A special hook for tying streamers, long-bodied nymphs, woolyworms, bucktails and Matukas.

Mustad 90240: Dry-fly low-water salmon hook. Turned-up looped eye, extra-long shank and 2X fine black wire. Sizes 4 through 10. An exceptionally nice hook for salmon, Western dry flies, low-water nymphs and fry patterns.

Mustad 37160: Wide-gape hollow-point bronzed turned-up ball eye. Sizes 10 to 26. Size 16 equals standard 10 hook. A hook that takes caddis larva, pupa, shrimp and Tarcher nymphs especially well.

Special Bass Bug Stinger: This special extra-wide-gape straight ringed-eye bronzed hook is available in sizes 10, 6 and 2. It is the finest bass bug hook ever made, in my opinion. It is a custom-made model from Mustad and can be purchased retail only from Porky Loucks, 2846 East 38th Street, Tulsa, Oklahoma 74105. Phone: 918-742-1088. I use this to tie 90 percent of my hairbugs and hardhead bugs.

Orvis Supreme Hook by Partridge: Turned-down eye, round-bend 1X long-shank, 4X fine wire. A very fine high-quality dry-fly hook for standards and no-hackle-type flies.

Orvis Premium: Regular length, forged round bend, 4X fine turned-down eye. Sizes 8 to 22. A very high-quality, lightweight, all-purpose dry-fly hook.

Orvis Partridge Hook: 3XL, sproat bend, turned-down eye, regular wire. An excellent all-purpose nymph hook.

Eagle Claw No. 281: 4XL medium-wire, turned-down eye, bronzed. Sizes 6 to 10. An especially good hook for woolyworms, large nymphs and streamers.

Flymph, Kaufmanns' Streamborn Fly Shop: Turned-up eye, 2XL shank, offset bend. Very sharp point! Sizes 8 to 16. For tying flymph patterns or emergers.

The more I experiment with various hook-eye designs, the more it becomes apparent that shape and size have a great deal to do with the types of knots you should use and the way the tied fly fishes. I suggest each of you stop and consider these facts before you just grab any hook and tie a particular pattern and tippet knot to it.

Straight-Ring Eye: Does not affect fly's attitude if shank is or is not unweighted. Straight pull from improved clinch knot or Duncan loop. Turle knot not recommended.

Turned-Up Looped Eye: Traditional salmon fly and steelhead hook. Unweighted shank fly has more tendency to swim true with point under shank. With clinch knot to eye, fly has tendency to travel canted up or on side. Pull is not direct. Turle knot causes truer swimming and more direct pull in line with point. Turned-up looped eye makes it easier to stack materials on top and below in head area. Muddler heads are difficult to spin, however.

Turned-Down Tapered Eye: Unweighted or weighted shank fly tends to turn over and ride sideways or with hook point up. Clinch knot further encourages that keeling effect for good or bad. This knot moves direct line of pull away from point. The Turle knot is much better for true ride and direct point in line pull.

Scissors and Other Cutting Instruments

There really is nothing radically new in scissor designs, but many more to choose from in the various dealers' catalogs. I'm particularly impressed with the wide line of Sunrise scissors, as they are reasonable, well designed for tying and stay sharp and free quite well. The 4-inch curved blade Sunrise scissors are my favorite sculpin and hairbug trimming tools.

The Kaufmanns have two pairs of Italian custom-made tying scissors that come in both curved and straight blades that any fly-tyer will find extremely useful. The prices are very reasonable.

The tyer who really hacks away at heavy feathers and hair should try the sewing shears made by Wiss called Quick-Clip Speed Scissors. They are reasonable, easy to use and very durable, and extra sets of quick-exchange blades are available.

For cutting latex and sheet mylars, use a small paper cutter and board. Tape each sheet to a thin piece of cardboard; then cut both into strips. There are several multi-strip cutters available that rug hookers use that do a fantastic job cutting even strips of latex. Inquire about them at hobby and sewing-material shops.

Fly-Tying Lights

One of the most important accessories any tyer must have both for day and night tying is a good lighting system. By using either natural indirect sunlight, filament or daylight fluorescent bulbs and good contrasting backgrounds, fly-tying is easier, better done and much more fun. Other than indirect sunlight, I most prefer daylight fluorescent lighting, particularly the dual-purpose Luxo Magnifying lamp.

Al Price is coming out with a Price Vise light made and adapted especially for his new vise. It should be available by the time this book is published.

Portable Fly-Tying Cases

While it is always best to have what flies you need tied and ready, many times traveling to fish even a few miles away from home bench can cause a dilemma if you don't have the right flies or enough of them. Carrying a portable case is also a lifesaver on dull motel-bound evenings. I average one to two weeks each month on the road and used to carry my materials in plastic bags, shoeboxes and old camera cases until I started using Plano Tackle Boxes, particularly the 777 and 777S models. I first purchased a 777 unit and over a two-and-a-half-year period put sixty-eight commercial airline baggage flights on it, plus dozens of car and private plane trips. Except for losing one brass eye on the lid lock and a small piece of plastic guard, it came through without anything but scratches. I'm now using the 777S model. It has one less drawer than the 777, but the four other shelf drawers are much deeper.

On a smaller scale, the Laggie Vest Pocket Leather Pouch kit, the Streamside Tyer, is a high-quality unit. It has a nice set of tools and a very well designed system of material storage.

Although I've not tried it, the Flytyer's Carry All Kit would seem to be a good carry-on choice between the Plano units and the Laggie kit.

Portable Fly-tying Equipment. Includes Tensor two-bulb Lamp; Plano 777S (open), Plano 777 and Plano 737 tackle boxes; Laggie's Streamside Tyer Kit and extra tray for Plano boxes.

Cements and Coatings

There are several new cements and coatings that are worth notice.

Laggie's Gloss Cote: A thin, crystal-clear head and body cement that is deep-penetrating and quick-drying. It usually requires three coats to build up a smooth, hard, glossy head. Gloss Cote does not discolor materials, and I like to use it to undercoat eye spots on Matuka Marabou Shad–type patterns. It works nicely as a base cement on hairbugs.

Al Price's Anglers Corner Professional-Quality Head Cement: A rather heavy, viscous, clear cement with applicator brush bottle. The cement has no ketones in it, so it has far less tendency to run, drip or shrink up while drying. It gives a hard, shiny head with one or two coats of cement. Not recommended for flies under size 18. An excellent overcoating to protect painted eyes or bass bug paint finish.

Orvis Super Cement: A special new two-in-one head and vinyl cement. It is clear, no-staining and fast-drying. Works on heads, underbodies and overcoats for feather surfaces.

Rocket Cylinder Crystal Cement: A jeweler's cement for watch crystals. Extremely easy to handle and apply as a head cement, thanks to its small tube container and delicate applicator tip. Allows for very neat cementing of tiny flyheads. My thanks to Lory Watkins of Seattle for telling me about it.

Five-Minute Epoxies: Several brands including Leech, Devcon and Ross in two-tube sets. All make very fine, fast, clear, hard-gloss durable heads for all types of flies. Especially good for saltwater fly bodies, wing bases and head overcoating, as well as bass-bug gluing. The trick is to mix only a drop or two at a time. Devcon comes in a neat, efficient double-barrel syringe unit for fast, easy, economical use. Not recommended for epoxy line splices.

Dow Corning Silicone Rubber Sealer: Comes in tubes of several sizes and in clear, white and black. An outstanding cement to glue two soft, flexible materials together without stiffening or distorting them. Especially good for gluing plastic, glass eyes or feathers to hair or hard-bodied bass bugs. Applications to fly-tying are many.

Scotch-Weld Structural Adhesive No. 3520: The best flexible two-part slow-setting epoxy made, in my opinion. Excellent for gluing bug bodies to hook, overcoating balsa or soft plastic bugs, all epoxy line splices and rod-guide under- and overcoating.

Grumbacher Tuffilm Plastic Spray: A graphic arts overcoating spray that comes in 8- and 16-ounce cans. The finest overcoating for all feathers. Will not discolor, misshape, stiffen or add excessive weight if used properly.

3M Scotchgard: A special silicone-type compound that enhances the durability and water repellency of any material. Will not discolor or change the texture of materials unless used excessively or on damp materials. Either spray on, or spray into a container and dip materials in it. Shake excess out and allow to dry a few minutes. Dipping gives best deep penetration. Does not create an oily look, as some greasy water repellents do on feathers or hair.

Tanning, Dyes and Bleaching

The fly-tyer who takes a little extra effort to learn how to wash, preserve, tan, bleach and dye materials will greatly expand his or her range of useful and unique tying materials.

Most raw or fresh animal and bird skins can be easily and safely preserved with salt or borax, applied after skinning. However, tanned hides with hair are more desirable for fly-tying purposes. Until now, most skins tanned by taxidermists cost a good sum and usually took a long time to prepare. Now a simple home tanning kit is available from George Lawrence Company, 306 Southwest First Avenue, Portland, Oregon 97204. It is a very inexpensive kit, since you do most of the labor. Instructions and enough tanning salts and chemicals are included to tan two or three deer hides or the skins of dozens of smaller animals, such as muskrat, rabbit or squirrel.

Bleaching skins and feathers should be done with great care in order to avoid damage to natural shape, luster and texture. You can obtain human hair-bleaching agents at most beauty supply stores, drugstores, or beauty shops. I use Clairol Pure White Creme Developer, a better hydrogen peroxide substitute, and Roux Creme Delight Extra Light hair lightener. Instructions are included in the package.

With these agents you can bleach hair and feathers to any tint down to pure white without undue fiber damage in just minutes to an hour or so. A brown neck goes to honey ginger to cream to white, for example. Dark muskrat fur goes to a rich fox tan to ginger to cream to white. At any stage, washing with water stops the action.

Home fabric dyes, such as Rit, Tintex and HiDye, are ideal for overdyeing most natural materials, such as hair and feathers. Follow instructions, use very concentrated solutions and *do not allow water temperature to exceed 180 degrees F*. Stir frequently and be patient. Some colors and materials take an hour to two hours to dye a rich true color.

For rich, dark, natural shades of brown, auburn, brown-black and blue-black, use human hair dye for best results. Hot-solution fabric dyes fall short of color intensity before they begin to break down the feather or hair fibers. Cold human hair dye formulas will not cause this problem if used properly. These dyes can be purchased in kits from drugstores and beauty shop supply stores, and they all include full instructions.

Kaufmann, Herter and Veniard have excellent feather and hair dyes in a very useful range of bright and natural colors. Kaufmann's and Buz's Fly and Tackle Shop will custom-dye large lots of material for you on advance orders.

Photo dyeing is not cheap, but the best results are easily obtained in a few tries. Silver nitrate, developer and fixer are expensive, but if shared by several tyers they are affordable. Check Eric Leiser's *Fly Tying Materials* for easy-to-follow instructions on photo dyeing.

Latex and rubber hackle must be dyed with a special organic-base solution dye. Water-base dyes will not work on them. Keystone Aniline and Chemical Company, Inc., of Chicago manufactures dyes for latex or rubber-based materials. Dealers may contact Frank Stover, 321 North Loomis Street, Chicago, Illinois 60607, phone (312) 666-2015. Also the Morton Chemical Company (110 North Wacker Drive, Chicago, Illinois 60606) puts out an excellent single-phase liquid dye called Automate. You may contact T. E. Nowakowski, product sales manager of dyestuffs, for information on these dyes.

Thanks to a tip from Rick Warner and Bill Bernstein of the art department at *Sports Illustrated*, Bob Boyle was put on to Dr. Ph. Martin's dyes. These radiant concentrated watercolors cost $1.10 each for a half-ounce bottle with an eyedropper. There are forty-two radiant colors available, ranging from lemon yellow to slate blue and antelope brown. Bob uses Dr. Martin's dyes on church-window feathers from a pheasant. He applies the dye—say, lemon yellow—to the feather so that the white portion becomes yellow. It dries in a few minutes, and Bob then dips the dyed feather in Pliobond or fly-tying vinyl cement. This encases the color so that it will not wash out. Trimmed to shape, the dyed feather now makes a striking wing case for a stonefly nymph. Bob gets his dyes from one of the best art-supply stores he has ever seen, A. I. Friedman, 25 West 45th Street, New York, New York 10019. Friedman issues a catalog, and in it you may find numerous other items of interest, ranging from industrial razor blades to what seems like an endless variety of marking pens.

Other Goodies

Here are some unusual items:

Renzetti-Orvis Wingmaker: A novel but excellent way of forming full-stem cut wings. Simply place one or two feathers in the tip of one of the three sizes of the forcepslike tool and burn away the excess with a match, candle or butane lighter. The result is a pair of neatly shaped cut wings in just seconds. There are three sizes for sizes 8 to 12, 12 to 18 and 18 to 22 wings. Look for tools similar to this for making wing cases, legs and so on to become the new rage in tying.

Lance Kaufmann's Deer-Hair Spinning Tool: This spins deer hair into a perfect flared deer-hair chenille that can be wrapped to the hook shank. Makes anyone an expert at making deer-hair bodies in about thirty minutes of practice.

Sierra Tackle Icky-Poo: A really super new dubbing wax liquid. Just rub a drop on a needle loop or tying thread, and dubbing sticks to it like contact cement.

Fly Fisherman's Bookcase Mini Needle-Nose Pliers: Perfect for bending down hook barbs and a thousand other tying tasks. I don't see how I ever did without them. The handle has a hole in it for attachment to vest or tying table to prevent loss.

Prism-Lite Mylar Tape: This new material comes in all metallic colors, including red, blue and green. Great for use on fly bodies, wings and bug bodies. Buz Ramsey, manager of Luhr Jensen, Hood River, Oregon, supplied me with a wide assortment. It is sold in many fishing-tackle stores. This is the prismatic tape I use for the threadfin Prismatic Marabou Shad in this volume. Many applications.

Creative Sports Enterprises Fuz-Comb: For removing underfur or fuzz from guard hairs. Also useful for George Grant's hair weaving or for cleaning deer hairs before putting them into a hair straightener or stacker.

Custom Cases by Darrel Martin: For HMH vise or almost any other quality tool kits, Darrel Martin makes a fine leather and velcro carrying or storage case. Designed and sewn by Darrel. For information, write Darrel Martin, 7410 48th Avenue East, Tacoma, Washington 98443.

Hassle Out of Hair: Ron and Dottie Vivit of Kalispell, Montana, suggested we use women's hair-setting tape to hold hair and feathers down or keep them out of our way when tying or trimming such various bushy flies as hoppers, muddlers, sculpins and hairbugs. The tape and small clamps made from safety pins make tying and trimming much easier.

Movable Doll Eyes: These neat, light, durable, inexpensive eyes add life and charm to any bug or streamer calling for painted or feather eyes. They are available in fine sizes in most hobby and craft stores and some fly-tying materials shops. Use silicone rubber aquarium cement to attach to feathers, or Duco-type cements for plastic, cork or balsa wood.

IX. A Special Section on Stoneflies

23. The Plecoptera, or Stoneflies
by STEPHEN W. HITCHCOCK

(Editor's note: *In* The Fly-Tyer's Almanac *published in 1975, we presented scientific papers on the Odonata (dragonflies and damselflies) and the Trichoptera (caddis flies), two orders of aquatic insects that had largely been ignored. Now* The Second Fly-Tyer's Almanac *presents a special section on stoneflies, a most important order for fly fishermen and one long ignored, and once again we have turned to the Geological and Natural History Survey of the State of Connecticut. The article by Dr. Stephen W. Hitchcock originally appeared as part of* The Plecoptera or Stoneflies of Connecticut, Bulletin *107 (1974), State Geological and Natural History Survey of Connecticut. This edited version, brought up to date, appears here through the kind permission of the survey. R.H.B.)*

INTRODUCTION

The Plecoptera are a small order of aquatic insects, with more than 465 described species in America north of Mexico. Almost all species pass their larval life in streams in temperate climes. Some of the same species are also found in lakes in colder areas. Adults are terrestrial. Exceptions are found in the Southern Hemisphere, where a few stoneflies are terrestrial in the larval stage (Wisely, 1953; Illies, 1960a; 1964b; McLellan, 1967). In California one species of *Capnia* is aquatic as an adult (Jewett, 1963, 1965).

There is a great need for biological and behavioral studies of various species of stoneflies. Unfortunately, the immature stages of most stoneflies are not known. Rearing the larvae and developing means of identifying them, together with biological studies, should prove a productive field for the amateur and professional entomologist alike. Fly-tyers could contribute greatly in this regard.

For the fly-tyer who wishes to identify the stoneflies that he might capture, there are a variety of publications available. Two pioneering works by Needham and Claassen (1925) and Claassen (1931) are now badly dated but do contain useful pictures. Specific works for particular sections of the country are Hitchcock (1974) for the northeastern United States and eastern Canada; Surdick and Kim (1976) for Pennsylvania; Frison (1935, 1942) for Illinois; Hilsenhoff (1975) for Wisconsin; Harden and Mickel (1952) for Minnesota; Gaufin, Nebeker and Sessions (1966) for Utah; Gaufin, Ricker, Miner, Milam and Hays (1972) for Montana; Baumann, Gaufin and Surdick (1977) for the Rocky Mountains; Jewett (1959b) for the Pacific Northwest; Ricker (1943) for British Columbia; Jewett (1960a) for California; Syczytko and Stewart (1977) for Texas; and Stewart, Stark and Huggins (1976) for Louisiana. There have also been detailed revisions of specific genera or families. Recent state checklists that do not contain keys or figures but would be useful in determining the species present in a state are Cather, Stark and Gaufin (1975) for Nevada and Ricker and Scudder (1975) for British Columbia.*

Most of the known biological information about the stoneflies is scattered in bits and pieces over many journals and years. I have attempted to summarize it in the body of the text.

PHYLOGENY

The Plecoptera belong to the general orthopteroid group of insects, although this group has been variously subdivided. Of present orders, they are most closely related to the Embioptera (Crampton, 1932; Ford, 1923; Hudson, 1948; Nutting, 1951; Walker, 1922, and others).

The present-day order probably originated in Late Carboniferous time from insects close to the family Narkemidae in the extinct order Paraplecoptera. Paraplecoptera adults all had five tarsal segments, whereas even the most primitive Plecoptera today have only three. Abdominal gills are found on the larvae of both Paraplecoptera and the more primitive Plecoptera. The first true Plecoptera appear in the fossil record of the Lower Permian.

SUBORDERS AND FAMILIES

In North America, stoneflies are divided into two groups, the Euholognatha and the Systellognatha. The Euholognatha, which are generally herbivorous, have glossae and paraglossae of about the same length, while in the Systellognatha, many of which are carnivorous, the glossae may be much reduced, in some genera appearing only as small projections on the inner side of the paraglossae, as shown in the illustration. Within the two groups, there is a total of nine families.†

The families in the Euholognatha are:

The Capniidae, small, dark stoneflies, mostly less than 10 millimeters long, with the adults having tails (cerci) that are well segmented and usually as long or longer than the body. Many species in this family emerge during midwinter.

Editor's note: Complete titles for these references, plus others of special importance to fly-tyers and fly fishermen, are to be found in this section under Selected References. Because of space limitations, we have had to omit the numerous other references cited by Dr. Hitchcock in this paper. Those interested in pursuing a particular reference cited by him but omitted here are advised to consult his original 262-page study which is obtainable from the State Geological and Natural History Survey, Department of Environmental Protection, Hartford, Connecticut 06115.

†*Editor's note:* Portraits of members of these nine families will be found at the back of this section.

The Leuctridae, very small and dark-colored stoneflies, with the wings *rolled* around the body when at rest. Members of the genus *Leuctra,* commonly called the willow fly, are brownish and from 6 to 11 millimeters in length. Many species of *Leuctra* are spring emergers and as such are favored by trout, but members of the genus are among the few adult stoneflies to be found from spring until autumn.

The Nemouridae, small and inconspicuously colored (dull brown or blackish) stoneflies. Gills are either absent or in the cervical region. The adult cerci have only one segment.

The Taeniopterygidae, a family of medium-sized stoneflies, mostly under 15 millimeters long. Usually dark brown or blackish, with very short cerci with six or fewer segments.

The families in the Systellognatha are:

The Peltoperlidae. The nymphs are readily recognized because they are cockroachlike, with a broad and flattened body. The gills are fleshy and fingerlike, and the adult cerci are many segmented.

The Perlidae, a family characterized by thoracic gills that are finely branched tufts appearing on all three thoracic segments. The members of the genus *Acroneuria* are large stoneflies, strikingly patterned in brown and yellow, ranging from 25 to 42 millimeters in length. The nymphs are predacious. In the East, two important species are *A. lycorias* and *A. carolinensis.* In the West, *A. pacifica* ranges from British Columbia to California and Montana to Colorado. In Utah, it is probably the most widespread and common species of stonefly in the state, abundant in creeks and rivers. The adults emerge from April to September. Another important species is *A. californica,* commonly called the California salmon fly.

The Chloroperlidae, a family of small to medium-sized stoneflies, 9 to 22 millimeters in length. The adult cerci are long. In genus *Alloperla,* the body is most often yellow (but sometimes greenish), and the fly is known in this country as the yellow Sally. Emergence is usually from late spring to midsummer; in the West, trout can be extraordinarily energetic when *Alloperla* adults become active in late evening.

The Perlodidae, a family of varied size and structure. Members of the genus *Isoperla* are generally yellow and brown and not much more than 10 millimeters long. They are found throughout the United States and are of importance as a food for trout and other fish.

The Pteronarcidae, a family of large (up to 60 millimeters in length) and primitive stoneflies that are found only in North America and eastern Asia. The celebrated salmon fly hatch on many Western rivers is occasioned by the emergence of *Pteronarcys californica.*

LARVAL FEEDING

Several investigations have been made of the food of larval stoneflies. In the Nearctic families we find:

Capniidae, Leuctridae, Nemouridae

Wu (1923), Frison (1929), Hynes (1941), Brinck (1949) and Jones (1950) all agree that the larvae feed on dead leaves of higher plants. Early instars of nemourids apparently feed on detritus (Hynes, 1941).

Taeniopterygidae

Frison (1929) noted that the larvae of this family feed on decaying leaves and on seven species of diatoms. Hynes (1941), Brinck (1949) and Richardson and Gaufin (1971) found the gut contents to be principally detritus, with appreciable amounts of the tissue of higher plants, together with diatoms, algae and mineral matter—the latter undoubtedly picked up inadvertently. *Brachyptera* can graze on the surface of stones.

Peltoperlidae

Chapman and Demory (1963) stated that *Peltoperla brevis* feeds chiefly on algae. In stream cages, I found that *P. maria* skeletonized dead leaves of maple and beech but fed only sparingly on oak. The guts of captured specimens contained detrital material, probably the remains of the dead leaves and associated flora. Wallace, Woodhall and Sherberger (1970) found that *P. maria* (?) feeds on leaves of fifteen species of trees, with elm, alder and sourwood preferred.

Perlidae

Samal (1923) stated that first instar *Perla burmeisteriana* probably do not feed and that second instar eat algae. Chisholm (1962) found that first instar *Dinocras cephalotes* feed on diatoms. Later instars of Perlidae are carnivorous and apparently feed on any stream animals that they can catch and swallow. Although plant material is occasionally found in the gut, it probably comes from the gut content of the prey or is only a minor food source (Smith, 1913; Grau, 1926; Muttkowski and Smith, 1929; Hynes, 1941; Brinck, 1949; Jones, 1949; Mackereth, 1957; Chisholm, 1962; Sheldon, 1969; Richardson and Gaufin, 1971; Tarter and Krumholz, 1971).

Chloroperlidae

This family appears to be less restricted to a carnivorous diet than either of the last two. Frison (1935) said that *Hastaperla* is herbivorous, but Hynes (1941) and Jones (1950) found *Chloroperla* to take either plant or animal material. Nicola (1968) found *Alloperla* scavenging on dead trout embryos. Chapman and Demory (1963) claimed that *Kathroperla perdita* feeds in equal parts on algae and detritus.

Perlodidae

Food habits are similar to those of the Perlidae. Whereas an occasional perlid specimen has only vegetable matter in the gut (Hynes, 1941), at least two of the small *Isoperla* species appear to be completely herbivorous (Frison, 1935). Jones (1950) found that the diet of *I. grammatica* shifted toward animal food as the larvae became larger. Grown larvae in this family are principally predacious but do take plant materials on occasion (Dunn, 1954; Richardson and Gaufin, 1971).

Pteronarcidae

The first instar of *Pteronarcys proteus* takes no food but digests the remains of yolk in the midgut. The second instar feeds on algae (Miller, 1939). Older *P. dorsata* larvae have been reared on dead elm leaves, which they skeletonize (Harden and Mickel, 1952), and *P. scotti* prefers alder leaves. When an energy budget was tabulated for the latter, the assimilation and growth efficiencies were found to be quite low (McDiffett, 1970). Muttkowski and Smith (1929) found the guts of 26 specimens of *P. californica* to contain 42 percent detritus, 4 percent animal matter and 54 percent plant material. The latter was principally wood fibers and moss. Richardson and Gaufin (1971) found that 275 specimens of the same species contained 80 percent detritus, 9 percent plant material and 11 percent animal matter. More than half the specimens contained animal matter. These investigators found *Pteronarcella badia* to be omnivorous but to eat less detritus and more plant and animal matter than does *Pteronarcys*. They observed *Pteronarcys californica* preying occasionally on other insects.

The food of larval Plecoptera is dependent on the size of the larva. Very young larvae feed on particles of detritus and other material small enough for them to handle. As the carnivorous forms become larger, they eat progressively larger and more active prey. They are apparently somewhat selective, either through choice or chance. Mackereth (1957) found that the gut content of *Perla bipunctata* was 5 percent *Rithrogena* in December, when the latter formed 25 percent of the stream fauna. However, in early spring *Baetis* made up 23 percent of the gut content but only 11 percent of the fauna. *Acroneuria californica* feeds mostly on Diptera when small, Ephemeroptera when of intermediate size and Trichoptera when large. The choice of prey also depends on the season: Diptera are taken most often in summer, Trichoptera in winter, and Ephemeroptera at all seasons (Sheldon, 1969).

My own observations bear out those of Brinck (1949), who found that the larger predatory stoneflies recognize prey only on antennal contact. Unlike him, however, I have observed *Acroneuria* and *Paragnetina* actively searching for prey during the day. That such means is adequate is borne out by the work of Davis and Warren (1965), who found that *Acroneuria pacifica* individuals were able to crop the common food source more efficiently than do sculpins. The presence of these stoneflies reduced the food consumption and production of the fish.

ADULT FEEDING

For many years it was believed that adult stoneflies did not feed, an idea apparently based on the flabby condition of the mouthparts of the large perlids and pteronarcids.

Newcomer (1918) found, however, that adult *Brachyptera* feed on the buds and young fruit of various fruit trees, as well as on the leaves of several trees and on the catkins of willow. Subsequently Wu (1923) determined that *Nemoura vallicularia* feeds on the leaves of the touch-me-not. Frison (1929) discovered that all Illinois specimens of *Taeniopteryx* and *Allocapnia* feed on the blue-green alga *Protococcus vulgaris* and that *Brachyptera fasciata* feeds on the blossoms of elm trees. He (1935) further stated that *Leuctra* and *Nemoura* adults are also herbivores. Hynes (1942), studying *Nemoura cinerea* in England, found that adults given lichen and Protococcales lived thirty-two to thirty-seven days, whereas unfed adults lived only four to five days. He also surmised that food is necessary to allow egg maturation. I have observed *Nemoura depressa* in the laboratory feeding on algal growth from twigs collected by the stream where they emerged. Dissection showed their guts filled with this material. Hynes (1941) starved representatives of twenty-five species of stoneflies for a few days and then provided them with water, lichens and algae. All Taeniopterygidae, Capniidae, Leuctridae and Nemouridae fed on this material and all species of both sexes drank water. Brinck (1949) observed in nature that certain nemourids, capniids, taeniopterygids, and leuctrids feed on lichens and green algae, and a lesser number also feed on decaying leaves near the stream bank.

All the above genera belong to the superfamily Taeniopterygoidae. The evidence for adult feeding in other groups is less secure. Miller (1939) obtained viable eggs from unfed *Pteronarcys proteus* that had been reared from late instar nymphs. They required water but apparently do not take, and obviously do not require, any food. I have provided adult *Peltoperla maria* with a variety of substances from their normal habitat but did not observe any feeding. However, they avidly drank a mixture of honey and water. Hynes (1941), in the tests mentioned above, found that adult Perlodidae and Perlidae drank water but would not eat lichens or algae. Brinck (1949) agreed that most Setipalpia do not feed, but he did find food in the gut of an adult *Chloroperla burmeisteri*. Smith (1913) found that adult *Paragnetina immarginata* do not require food, but their lives were shortened by several days if denied water. Her unfed specimens apparently produced viable eggs. Arnold (1966) observed *Acroneuria arenosa* adults drinking water. Claassen (1931) reported that adult *Alloperla pallidula* had been observed feeding on honeydew secreted by aphids on alder. Frison (1935) saw adults of *Isoperla nana* feeding on the pollen of dock (*Rumex*) and wild grape. He found their mandibles to be well sclerotized. He states that the mandibles of *I. decepta* also appear functional but those of other *Isoperla* do not.

Generally it appears that the smaller larval herbivores feed as adults but that the carnivores and large herbivores do not.

NATURAL ENEMIES

Although trout and birds feast avidly during the salmon fly hatch on large Western rivers—angling literature often gives a vivid picture of this awesome phenomenon of nature—adult stoneflies appear to be surprisingly free from predators. Spiders catch some, and often as a first check on what is emerging from a stream the collector can examine nearby spiderwebs. Occasionally in the early spring, I have observed hunting spiders attacking winter stoneflies. I have also captured an immature *Pityohyphantes phrygianus* (determination by J. Anderson) feeding on a male *Taeniopteryx burksi* on February 29.

There seem to be few records of other insects preying on adult stoneflies. Odonata capture mostly small Diptera (Pritchard, 1964) and apparently do not hesitate to attack any prey. However, of numerous publications of dragonfly prey records that I have examined, none mentions the capture of adult stoneflies. Nor have I seen any record of empids, asilids or other predacious insects attacking adult Plecoptera. There seems to be no reason why these predators should not include stoneflies in their diet, and Plecoptera possibly are a very small component of their menu. Rohwer (1913) recorded a sawfly, *Tenthredo rurigena*, feeding on adult *Alloperla signata*, but this would not be a significant cause of mortality.

Aside from hatches on large Western rivers, birds do not seem to eat stoneflies as much as might be expected. Although stoneflies were numerous near their nests, only one bank swallow out of sixty took any stoneflies (two *Alloperla mediana*) and this was only about 1 percent of the food in the bird's stomach (Stoner, 1935). As stoneflies have but feeble powers of flight, swallows are not likely to take them on the wing.

Other reports of individual birds feeding on identified stoneflies are: a robin on *Perlesta placida* (Frison, 1935), a chickadee on *Allocapnia pygmaea* (Willey, 1936), a bluejay on "*Capnia vernalis*" (Hamilton, 1932)—probably *Paracapnia opis* or *P. angulata*—and a golden crowned kinglet and a chickadee probably feeding on *Allocapnia recta* (Hamilton, 1933).

Although adult stoneflies apparently are not the principal food of any bird, they are palatable to a wide variety of bird species. McAtee (1932) identified Plecoptera in the stomachs of 41 species of Nearctic birds, but these insects represented only 0.0419 percent of all insects taken. Knappen (1934) found Plecoptera in 122 stomachs of 50 species of Nearctic birds. These were generally adult insects, although a few larvae were also found. Nighthawks were the most persistent feeders, with stoneflies found in 21 stomachs. The stomach and gullet of one had 41 and 42 adult stoneflies, respectively. Other birds that appear to feed extensively on stoneflies are the American golden-eye, Swainson's hawk, and the western grebe. As might be expected, the greatest number were ingested in late spring and early summer.

Frost (1924) found adult Plecoptera in the stomachs of frogs, and Minckley (1963) reported an adult *Paragnetina* in the stomach of a bat.

Larval forms suffer more from predators than do adults. Fish take a considerable number of stoneflies, as recorded in the voluminous fisheries literature. In New Zealand, according to Tillyard (1921b), introduced trout eliminated certain native stoneflies. However, most earlier workers indicated that fish eat insects in general relationship to availability of the prey. This is not necessarily related to the total numbers of the insects. Elliott (1967c) found that the species of stonefly larvae taken by fish show a seasonal as well as a diurnal change. Gerald (1966) noted that the long-nose dace (*Rhinichthys cataractae*) feed proportionally more on small Plecoptera than on large. In some cases, more than the size of the insect is involved. Hartman (1958) found that active and long-legged stoneflies were taken less often (or rejected more often), as compared with Trichoptera, than would be expected merely from their size in relation to the mouth size of trout. Many fish have been recorded feeding on larval Plecoptera, and I have seen nothing to indicate that any fish does not. Maitland (1966) found five species of fish feeding on *Amphinemura sulcicollis*, and others (for example, Lochman [1955]) have recorded various fish species preying on these insects.

Other vertebrates have been noted feeding on stoneflies. Two out of twenty-five water shrews (*Sorex palustris*) had fed on Plecoptera, which made up 2.8 percent by volume of the ingested material (Connor, 1966). Three out of twenty-seven spotted turtles (*Clemmys guttata*) contained stoneflies (Surface, 1908). Bakus (1959) reported a dipper, *Cinclus mexicanus*, putting its head into the water and picking Plecoptera off rocks in the stream. Salamanders have been found eating *Acroneuria californica* (Anderson, Martin and Pratt, 1966).

Larval stoneflies are also preyed upon by crayfish (Prins, 1968).

Larvae are also subject to predation by the larvae of other insects; in fact, they probably take a major share of the stonefly population.

The predacious caddisworms feed on stoneflies but, except on *Leuctra* (Jones, 1950), less so than on Ephemeroptera and Diptera (Muttkowski and Smith, 1929; Jones, 1949). Slack (1936) lists no Plecoptera in the diet of caddisworms, but there were apprently few in the stream he studied. Thut (1969) found *Rhyacophila vaccua* feeding on *Nemoura spp.*, but four other species of *Rhyacophila* feed very little or not at all on stoneflies. Generally the caddisworms do not seem to take a heavy toll, perhaps because the larval stoneflies are either too quick or too well concealed. The predacious stoneflies take many of their stonefly brethren and are one of the chief causes of mortality. Coleoptera apparently feed only lightly on Plecoptera (Muttkowski and Smith, 1929; Hynes, 1941; Brinck, 1949; Jones, 1950). However, Wu (1923) reported that hydrophilid beetle larvae are common predators of *Nemoura vallicularia*. I have seen only one record of aquatic Neuroptera preying on stoneflies (Helson, 1934), but we can assume that they do because they eat almost any insect.

Few parasites have been recorded; undoubtedly this reflects only the rarity of close examinations for parasites in stoneflies. Winkler (1956), Schoenemund (1924) and Kühtreiber (1934) have all found mermithid worms in stoneflies. Imamura (1950) discussed a parasitic mite found on six species of stoneflies in Japan. Léger and Gauthier (1932) described the endomycete *Orphella coronata* from the larva of a *Protonemura,* and Helson (1934) discovered a gregarine parasite in *Stenoperla prasina.* Muttkowski and Smith (1929) found that 12 percent of larval *Acroneuria pacifica* contained gregarines. Desportes (1963) included a figure of a gregarine found in *Perla* and *Isoperla.* She also gave additional references to gregarine infections. Weiser found two species of microsporidia on *Chloroperla* (Thomson, 1960). Cercariae of trematodes infect stoneflies but apparently do little harm (Hall, Weaver and Gomez-Miranda, 1969). Cercariae appear to be most common in the Perlidae, Perlodidae and Pteronarcidae (Hall, 1960; Hall and Groves, 1963; Anderson, Martin and Pratt, 1966).

Frison (1935) described what he called "anal gills" on *Leuctra claasseni* and later (1942) stated that *L. tenuis* and *L. ferruginea* had similar gills. I have observed such structures on a *Nemoura* larva and, because it does not seem likely that such delicate gills would grow sporadically in diverse genera, conclude that they are probably fungal growths on the living larva.

MATING AND OVIPOSITION

It was noted in the mid-1800s that some stoneflies beat the ends of their abdomens on the surfaces where they were resting. This drumming, observed many times subsequently, was assumed to be a mating signal. Rupprecht (1965, 1968, 1969) has recently studied it in some detail. Drumming has been found in *Acroneuria, Pteronarcys, Taeniopteryx, Capnia, Dinocras, Diura, Isoperla* and *Perla.* The signal is specific to each species in frequency and duration. Drumming is not necessary before mating to release the sexual response; it serves only to bring the two sexes into close proximity. The males drum and unmated females respond. Depending on genus (and perhaps species?), the two sexes either actively search for each other or the females remain in place while the males seek them out. The signal is not given by the sound of the drumming but by the vibrations of the substrate and is perceived by the subgenual organs of the tibiae. Once a female is mated, she no longer responds to the drumming signal of a male.

The manner in which exact immediate recognition of the sexes is made is not known but it is probably tactile. Males often try to mate with unreceptive females, and I have even observed a male *Allocapnia* apparently trying to mate with a female *Taeniopteryx,* which would imply a lack of fine discrimination. *Perlesta placida* apparently depends on visual recognition or chance encounters (Stewart, Atmar and Solon, 1969). Other senses may be involved, however. Hynes (1941) observed a male *Capnia nigra* attempting to mate with a female *Leuctra nigra* that had been in contact with a female *C. nigra.* He therefore suggested the presence of a pheromone. Coleman and Hynes (1970) state that *Allocapnia pygmaea* males can recognize females at distances of 15 centimeters.

Mating is usually necessary to produce viable eggs. However, Degrange (1958) discovered that a small percentage of eggs from virgin females of at least two species would hatch. Because females would not oviposit, the eggs had to be obtained by dissection, but it is possible that in nature there may be occasional young produced without fertilization.

In mating, the male mounts the back of the female, puts his abdomen to the side of the female and recurves the tip to bring his genitalia into position against hers on the ventral side of her abdomen. The male has a variety of projections, varying by species, with which to accomplish mating. Various genital hooks or protrusions are present on any of the distal abdominal segments, including, in some species, the epiproct and paraprocts. Either of two principal means of sperm transference occurs in Nearctic stoneflies. The first, in the Setipalpia and some Filipalpia, is a simple extrusion of the eversible copulatory organ, apparently made turgid by body fluid. The second, found in some Filipalpia, is the use of the epiproct as a sperm conveyor. *Notonemoura* males use the ventral process of the subgenital plate as a sperm conveyor (McLellan, 1968). Some Plecoptera have accessory glands, and in at least one species, *Arcynopteryx compacta,* there is a spermatophore (Brinck, 1962). Brinck (1955) examined the reproductive system and mating of a number of stoneflies from different families in some detail and gave a valuable comparative study of the order. Berthélmy (1969) made additional comments on mating in *Leuctra.* The limited information available on individual North American species is given in the accounts that follow.

In at least some species, several matings can occur and several batches of eggs can be laid. This is probably a common occurrence, so that counts of single egg masses probably do not represent the full complement of eggs. Percival and Whitehead (1928) state that five *Perlodes microcephala* (=*mortoni*) laid 11 egg masses in 11 days, thus averaging 2.2 egg masses per female. Brinck (1949) found that *Dinocras cephalotes* extruded 3 successive masses of 600, 470 and 250 eggs. *Paragnetina immarginata* mates more than once, perhaps before each oviposition, and in *P. media* the egg mass is formed with one hour of copulation (Heiman and Knight, 1970). The number of egg masses varies between 2 and 4, the number of eggs decreasing with each successive mass (Smith, 1913). *Pteronarcys proteus* will mate between successive ovipositions, but this is not necessary in order to deposit the full number of eggs. Again, successive egg masses decrease in size with time; for example, 386, 134, 88, 25, 45 eggs per mass (Miller, 1939). All of the above species are Setipalpia, but Khoo found that *Brachyptera risi* also laid up to 1,500 eggs in 4 batches with eight to eleven days between successive batches. However, *Capnia bifrons* deposits only a single group of eggs, generally 300 to 400 but with a range of 110 to 713 (Khoo, 1964), and *Allocapnia pygmaea* also lays but a single batch (Coleman and Hynes, 1970).

To deposit the eggs, females either crawl to the edge of the water (and sometimes into the water) or run across the water, dipping the tip of the abdomen. The exact method apparently depends on species and circumstances.

When the egg mass is deposited in the water, the gelatinous coating surrounding each egg swells and the eggs separate and fall free. Upon reaching the substrate, each egg becomes glued to the surface. Setipalpian eggs are variable in shape and reticulation but generally possess a collar at one end (apparent exceptions are found in several *Alloperla,* according to Knight and his co-workers, 1965a, b). This collar bears a circular white structure, the basal plate, which upon contact with the substrate sticks the egg in place. The sticky material of the basal plate is elastic, allowing the eggs to return to position when displaced.

In some Setipalpia, there are additional adhesive knobs on the gelatinous covering of the egg, or the eggs bear hooked filaments (*Perlesta placida*). Filipalpian eggs are round or oval, without a collar or anchor plate. These eggs are attached to the substrate by the gelatinous coating that swells and becomes sticky when wetted. In those few species whose embryos develop while the egg is still in the female, there is no sticky material on the eggs, but these larvae hatch as soon as the eggs are deposited in the water (Percival and Whitehead, 1928; Miller, 1939; Brinck, 1949; Berthélemy, 1964; Knight, Nebeker and Gaufin, 1965a, b; Stewart, Atmar and Solon, 1969).

INCUBATION OF EGGS AND LARVAL DEVELOPMENT

The period from oviposition to the hatching of the egg varies greatly, from a few minutes for the European *Capnia bifrons* to ten months in *Pteronarcys proteus* and *Diura bicaudata.*

Dinocras cephalotes spends up to a year in the egg stage (Ulfstrand, 1968). In the laboratory under cold temperatures, eggs of *Brachyptera risi* can have an incubation period of as long as fourteen months (Khoo, 1968c). In nature, the range of most species is apparently from three weeks to a month, with some species needing up to three months (Frison, 1929; Percival and Whitehead, 1928; Helson, 1934; Hynes, 1941; Brinck, 1949; Komatsû, 1971).

Our knowledge of diapause (a period of arrested development) in the egg or larval stage comes in part from Miller (1939) but more particularly from the interesting work of Khoo (1964, 1968a, b, c). Not all stoneflies have diapause; studies show that at least two *Leuctra* species, one species of *Taenopteryx,* and one *Nemoura* species do not.

Diapause in the *Pteronarcys proteus* egg is initiated by freezing temperatures in the fall and is broken by warmer temperatures in the spring. No photoperiodic phenomenon is involved, for if the eggs are kept warm, they develop normally and hatching occurs in December. In nature, egg diapause occurs from November to April. *Capnia bifrons* diapauses in the larval stage. It hatches from the egg immediately following oviposition in the spring, develops to the fourth or fifth instar and then, following higher temperatures and lengthening days, enters diapause. Diapause ends in the fall, and larval growth resumes. Diapause is shortened by low temperatures. *Brachyptera risi* also diapauses over the summer but in the early stage just after formation of the germ disc. In contrast to *C. bifrons,* diapause was lengthened by low temperatures. Different environmental conditions affecting the egg did not initiate or break diapause, so probably diapause is initiated in the mother, as it is in some other insects. Diapause in *Diura bicaudata* is genetically determined in part. In two different populations, one laid diapause eggs and one did not. Diapause occurred in the egg stage just before the revolution of the embryo and lasted four to four and a half months over the summer, until broken by chilling in the fall. Nondiapause eggs had a three-month incubation period and the insect a one-year life cycle, whereas diapause eggs had a nine- to eleven-month incubation period and the insect a two-year life cycle.

Of the four stoneflies known to diapause that have been carefully studied, three diapause in the egg state (although at different periods of embryonic life), one as a larva; three diapause in the summer, one over the winter; two have diapause initiated in the egg stage, one in the larval, and one apparently in the adult mother; two have diapause broken by cooler temperatures, one by warmer, and for one the temperature effect is unknown.

In Plecoptera, larval diapause is possibly of wider occurrence than realized. Various North American species emerge from the egg in the spring but exhibit little or no growth until fall. Others, such as *Perlesta placida,* do not appear to have a synchronized emergence period and perhaps do not diapause. Harper and Hynes (1970) found diapausing larvae of several winter stoneflies in the genera *Taeniopteryx, Brachyptera, Allocapnia* and *Capnia,* but not in *Paracapnia*.

In the latter part of embryonic life, the hypodermis secretes an embryonic cuticle about the body. On the head, this cuticle is formed into a conical hollow egg-tooth. At hatching, the egg-tooth presses against a preexisting rupture line, causing the shell to split. In the Setipalpia this rupture line separates a cap from the rest of the egg, whereas in the Filipalpia it is a longitudinal division. The embryonic cuticle and egg-tooth are usually left in the empty eggshell when the first instar larva emerges (Miller, 1939, 1940; Degrange, 1957).

The number of larval instars has been investigated in only a few species. *Capnia bifrons* has 14 to 15 in the male, 15 to 16 in the female (Khoo, 1968a); *Nemoura vallicularia* has 22 (Wu, 1923); *Amphinemura decemceta* has 24 (Komatsû, 1971); *Perla burmeisteriana* has 23 (Šámal, 1923); *Pteronarcys proteus* has 12 in the male and 13 in the female (Holdsworth, 1941b).

Larval development occurs at a variable rate, depending on species. Brinck (1949) has divided the stoneflies into various growth classes—(a) rapid growth in late summer or early fall and again in late spring but little or no growth through the winter, (b) greatest growth in fall and early winter, with adult emergence in late winter, (c) steady growth throughout the year, somewhat retarded in the coldest part of the winter, (d) even growth throughout the year and (e) most growth occurring in the warm weather of late spring and early summer.

There is a relationship between temperature and light that regulates larval growth. The influence of each depends somewhat on the species. Hirvenoja (1960) found that the uniform temperature of a spring in Finland apparently disrupts the normal growth pattern of *Nemoura picteti*, so that adults and larvae of all ages could be taken simultaneously. This is in contrast to *Nemoura cinerea* (Hirvenoja, 1960) and *Brachyptera risi, Leuctra hippopus* and *Nemoura picteti* in Denmark (Thorup, 1963), whose growth rates were not correlated with temperature; they grew at seasonally regulated rates throughout the year, even though found in the uniform water temperature of a spring. Thorup suggested that this variable growth rate may reflect the degree of plant growth or the presence of detritus from decomposing leaves in the fall. It is also possible that there may be a direct effect of photoperiod on the insect itself. I have collected adults of *Nemoura depressa* in all months of the year at a single location in California.

In northern Sweden there is a cessation of larval growth in the winter, but in a less rigorous climate, winter temperatures play a less decisive part in the growth pattern, and speed of growth may vary from one year to another (Svensson, 1966).

ECOLOGY, BEHAVIOR AND LOCAL DISTRIBUTION

The presence or absence of a stonefly in a stream can be the result of a multitude of interacting factors. For example, cold water may slow metabolism, but it also holds more oxygen. The movement of the water and the character of the stream substrate affect aeration, insect drift, collection of detritus and plant composition. These, in turn, feed back to the patterns of water movement and available oxygen. For general reviews of these factors on stream organisms, one may consult Macan (1961, 1963) or Hynes (1970). Although much of the information on other aquatic insect orders is applicable to stoneflies, in the discussions below I will include only those studies that were concerned specifically with the Plecoptera.

In more temperate areas, winter does not seem to be a time of exceptional danger to stoneflies. Some damage to Plecopteran populations comes from anchor ice, both physical damage to the insect itself and damage from lifting the benthic Plecoptera into the stream where fish can feed on them. Brown, Clothier and Alvord (1953) found Plecoptera even in areas where anchor ice formed several times a season, and Benson (1955) found a few Plecoptera in floating anchor ice. As long as any free water remained on the bottom, the insects could survive. Farther north, winter temperatures are more crucial. Clifford (1969) determined that larval *Nemoura cinctipes* suffered very heavy mortality when a dry autumn allowed the reduced amount of water to be frozen down into the substrate. A severe winter considerably reduced the numbers of *Perlodes* and *Nemoura* in England but left other species little affected (Elliott, 1967b). Pattée (1959) discovered that the larvae of *Perla abdominalis* became acclimated to the lowering temperatures and that small specimens consumed even more oxygen in February than in September and October. Kamler (1965), working in Poland, found Plecoptera more abundant in the cooler streams, and that even in the warmer streams they were more likely to be found in the cooler parts.

Needham and Usinger (1956), in sampling the organisms, water velocity and depth across a stream, found that *Alloperla* and *Isoperla* were collected in inverse ratio to the depth and speed of the water. The velocity ranged up to about 5 feet per second, but these stoneflies were most common at velocities of 1 to 2½ feet per second. The presence of *Isogenus* bore no relationship to water speed or depth.

However, the speed of the water measured at the surface does not necessarily reflect the velocity at the spot occupied by an insect, and close to the substrate there may be relatively little current. The insect responds to the stream velocity of its microhabitat. The European *Brachyptera risi* is found on the upper parts of stones in the current but in slack water will swim or hang from the water surface. Individuals do not necessarily face directly upstream but, rather, orient to the flow of the water over the substrate. As the current increases, they maintain position but press their bodies more closely to the surface (Madsen, 1969). Moreover, the velocity and pattern of the current also regulate the deposition of sediment and detritus. Egglishaw (1964, 1969) studied the relationship between detritus and several stonefly species and found that, for species of *Nemoura, Leuctra, Isoperla, Chloroperla* and *Perla,* an increase in detritus means an increase in the number of stoneflies. Presumably the insects were aggregating for food rather than as a direct response to the current. Too much deposition of matter is, of course, detrimental and Plecoptera disappear, to be replaced by chironomids when inorganic sedimentation becomes too heavy (Cordone and Kelley, 1961).

Many stoneflies feed on allochthonous detritus, derived from plant material falling into the stream, rather than on living plant growth within the stream (Minshall, 1967). Consequently, the stream cover probably regulates the species of stonefly to be found in a stream, but this effect has never been closely examined. *Pteronarcys dorsata* was not found in a stream below a productive lake rich in nutrients but was common in the stream above the lake (Cushing, 1963), even though there was more food available in the former location. Likewise, *Aeroneuria theodora* was found only in riffles above geyser basins in Yellowstone, not below, although other stoneflies were not affected by the ion concentration and higher temperature (Vincent, 1967). Whether these differences are due to the availability of certain food or whether the insects are directly affected by the quality of the water is not known. Larval *Pteronarcys californica* can regulate its internal salt balance from the surrounding water, even without access to food (Colby, 1970). However, stonefly populations can be related to general ecological conditions within streams (Marlier, 1954; Gaufin, 1959). Pollution studies have shown that some stoneflies are quite resistant to certain chemical changes in their environment, whereas such changes cause other Plecoptera to disappear quickly. *Chloroperla tripunctata* was common in a river with a heavy zinc concentration (Jones, 1958), and nemourids and capniids common in acidic waters (Maitland, 1966; Ochiai, 1962). Bell and Nebeker (1969) give the median lethal pH level for several species of stonefly in the laboratory, with the most hardy reaching a pH of about 3. Gaufin and Hern (1971) and Nebeker (1971c) give information on the tolerance of various stoneflies to heated water, with the most sensitive dying at 16°C. However, even at temperatures that permitted larval survival, there was an adverse effect on adult emergence.

The amount of available oxygen is related both to water temperature and current speed. *Brachyptera risi* is found on top of stones, where there is a high oxygen content in the water, whereas *Nemoura flexuosa* is found beneath the stones, where the oxygen content is low. Although oxygen is available within leaf packets. *B. risi* remains on the surface of the packet. This probably reflects the greater current speed at the surface. The water current brings fresh oxygenated water to the insect after the animal has exhausted the oxygen immediately adjacent to its body. *B. risi* dies sooner than *N. flexuosa* under conditions of declining oxygen unless the water is agitated (Madsen, 1968). There are day-night differences in oxygen consumption in some species, with oxygen uptake greater in the dark (Zoladek and Kapoor, 1971).

The variation in oxygen consumption between individual larval specimens is very great—various workers have reported results that vary by many hundredfold.

Olson and Rueger (1968) determined that, unlike other aquatic insects, larger specimens of the stoneflies *Pteronarcys pictetii* and *Paragnetina media* have higher oxygen-consumption rates than do smaller individuals of these species. That is, large specimens consume more oxygen per milligram of body weight than do small ones. By contrast, *Pteronarcys californica* and *Acroneuria pacifica* fit the usual pattern of greater oxygen consumption by smaller individuals (Knight and Gaufin, 1966b). This is an unsolved discrepancy. However, the relationship of size to oxygen consumption is possibly correlated with body surface rather than with weight (Istenic, 1963).

Pattée (1955), working with *Perla abdominalis,* found that the oxygen consumption of larvae shifted sharply with a change in temperature; greater consumption with a rise in temperature, less consumption with a decrease.

As the larvae became accustomed to the new temperature, the difference in oxygen consumption lessened; that is, a sudden rise in temperature caused a great increase in oxygen consumption that later was somewhat moderated.

In response to respiratory distress, stoneflies often make rapid up-and-down body movements by flexing the legs, so that they appear to be doing "pushups." Presumably this is to increase the amount of oxygen-bearing water in contact with the gills. As the water immediately adjacent to the larva becomes deficient in oxygen, this movement creates currents and also moves the position of the gills in the water.

Using the number of movements per minute as an indication of respiratory demand, one can compare the relationship between the concentration of dissolved oxygen, the velocity and the temperature of the water. *Acroneuria pacifica* was observed to begin these "pushups" sooner and at a faster rate, the higher the temperature and the lower the water velocity. These undulatory movements increased as the oxygen concentration dropped, until the insect could no longer increase the rate of movement to compensate for the oxygen lack in the water. There was then a sharply decreasing amount of movement until death occurred. Stonefly larvae with gills can apparently stand lower oxygen concentrations than can those without gills (Knight and Gaufin, 1963, 1966a). Kamler (1970) likewise found respiratory movements in *Perlodes intricata* greater with higher temperatures and lower oxygen.

Both *Acroneuria pacifica* and *Pteronarcys californica* can survive lower dissolved-oxygen concentrations better at lower temperatures, probably because of reduced metabolism, but *A. pacifica* is killed at water temperatures above 60°F, even when oxygen is abundant (Gaufin and Gaufin, 1961; Knight and Gaufin, 1964).

Possibly there are more subtle effects than oxygen starvation alone. At low levels of oxygen, *P. californica* is unable to regulate body-fluid volume and becomes distended. Even if removed to oxygen-rich water, it is apparently unable to rid itself of this excess fluid and dies, although if the fluid is removed with a hypodermic syringe, normal life resumes (Knight and Gaufin, 1964).

For stoneflies, therefore, there is an intimate relationship between water velocity, oxygen content and temperature. The papers of Knight and the Gaufins cited above should be consulted for the exact figures on these parameters for the survival of the two stonefly species which they studied.

Several studies have correlated species or species groups of immature stoneflies with various types of streams. It appears from these studies that there are additional factors that help to regulate the kind and number of stoneflies in a stream. Ulfstrand (1967) studied the distribution of larval plecopterans within a stream, correlating the effects of stream depth, current and substrate. *Diura nanseni* was found in areas of strong current and bare rock, whereas other stoneflies were found in areas of less current and more sediment and detritus. Ulfstrand concluded that distribution within the stream is related more closely to food than to any other factor; a conclusion with which Egglishaw (1964, 1969) concurred.

Water temperature determines the emergence of adult stoneflies, and altitudinal differences in adult-emergence time probably reflect only temperature differences (Sprules, 1947; Gledhill, 1960; A. W. Knapp *in* Scott, 1961; Nebeker, 1971b; Radford and Hartland-Rowe, 1971b). The emergence time of any one species becomes progressively later as the altitude increases, and there is also a shift in species toward the more predacious forms (Knight and Gaufin, 1966c). It has not been determined whether the water must reach a certain critical temperature for adults to emerge or if emergence time is determined by a summation of accumulated heat (Radford and Hartland-Rowe, 1971a). There is possibly an interaction of photoperiod and temperature that determines maturation and size. Khoo (1964) found that photoperiod initiates adult development whereas cold temperatures restrict growth, causing the formation of adult characters within the larval skin. However, Nebeker and Gaufin (1967) stated that wing brachyptery is genetically determined, rather than a response to lengthening days and cool temperatures.

Emergence usually occurs at the time of day when humidity is highest (Brinck, 1949) or perhaps when water temperature is lowest and oxygen tension highest (Radford and Hartland-Rowe, 1971a), although I have observed *Paracapnia* emerging at midday. Closely related species are usually temporally isolated when emerging from the same stream. Although closely related species may emerge at the same time from two separate streams, if they are together in the same stream, one species will usually emerge several days ahead of the other. Males emerge first (Sheldon and Jewett, 1967), although there may be exceptions in some stoneflies with extended emergence periods (Harper and Pilon, 1970).

The effects of light on stoneflies have been little examined. Light traps in Connecticut have caught some adult perlids, particularly *Perlesta placida*. Other stoneflies (principally *Leuctra*) were caught in a light trap only occasionally and singly. In Africa, where *Neoperla spio* adults emerge year round, a mercury-vapor light trap made peak catches of this stonefly from thirty to ninety minutes after sunset (Tjonneland, 1961). The larval European *Dinocras cephalotes* is photonegative (Scherer, 1962).

Larval stoneflies are commonly collected in insect drift in streams. The considerable information on this subject has been summarized by Elliott (1967a, b). Plecoptera are more active at night and are, therefore, most commonly found in the drift at night. This stonefly activity is correlated with changes in light rather than with other factors (Elliott, 1967a; Chaston, 1969). Although stoneflies in drift have been described as reattaching themselves to the substrate within a short time, there is one bit of evidence indicating that this is not always so. The trematode *Cephalouterina dicamptodoni* has as its first intermediate host a snail that is not found below 2,000-foot altitude. The second intermediate host is the stonefly *Acroneuria californica*. Cysts of *C. dicamptodoni* have been found in *A. californica* as far down the watershed as 200 feet above sea level (Anderson, Martin and Pratt, 1966). As the stonefly could have obtained these cysts only at the higher elevations, at least some larval stoneflies are carried longer distances downstream than previously thought.

In addition to downstream drift, both adults and larvae can move upstream. Both sexes fly with the wind (Elliott, 1967a) and so, if the wind is right, presumably can go considerable distances and populate denuded areas upstream. Thomas (1966) reported that adult *Capnia atra* emerging from a stream moved preferentially toward a nearby forest. Once inside the bordering woods, they walked upstream. If no woods were visible as the stoneflies emerged, the insects tended to move upstream immediately. Adult *Allocapnia pygmaea* moved directly away at a right angle from the stream but were not seen to turn upstream (Coleman and Hynes, 1970).

Although the larvae of many arthropods have been recorded moving upstream, there is little information on Plecoptera. Hultin and his co-workers (1969) found larval *Nemoura flexuosa*, and Bishop and Hynes (1969) found larval *Allocapnia pygmaea* moving upstream in midwinter.

ECONOMIC IMPORTANCE

Apart from their great value as a food for fish, stoneflies are of little direct economic importance to man. In the Pacific Northwest, *Brachyptera pacifica* has been reported as a minor pest in orchards (Newcomer, 1918, 1950) and on ornamental plants (Schuh and Mote, 1948). The adults feed on the foliage, buds and fruit, and are most injurious to apricots, peaches and plums. Kawai (1967) stated that Japanese workers have found the closely related *Rhabdiopteryx nohirae* as an occasional pest on soft fruits in Japan. Tsukiji and Suzuki (1957) found larval nemourids causing damage by feeding on the underwater parts of the edible *Wasabia* plant.

Winter *Allocapnia* stoneflies, upon adult emergence, commonly crawl up any vertical surface. If large numbers emerge, they sometimes cause annoyance to nearby residents. In the spring of 1967, a school in Connecticut sought to control adult allocapnids that were crawling up the building and into the classrooms. In Pennsylvania, *Allocapnia recta* was reported crawling into a milkhouse and contaminating milk cans and other equipment (Anon., 1960).

Acroneuria pacifica is the alternate host to at least one internal fluke of birds (Macy and Bell, 1968). Hall and Groves (1963) found that seven out of nine species of cercariae in a species of river snail entered Plecoptera.

A. pacifica has also been observed attacking and killing eggs and small alevins of the steelhead or rainbow trout, *Salmo gairdneri* (Claire and Phillips, 1968). Nicola (1968), however, found that larvae of *Alloperla sp.* are beneficial in one way: they scavenge dead salmon eggs, thereby preventing the spread of fungus to living eggs.

Indirectly, stoneflies are probably of greatest economic importance as a natural fish food and as biological indicators of unpolluted waters. Generally, fish feed on stoneflies in the proportion in which they are available, relative to other foods. A decrease in stonefly availability merely causes the fish to shift to other prey. Stoneflies are usually indicative of clean water and, in conjunction with other aquatic organisms, have been used as a measure of water purity. Hynes (1960) summarizes much of the work on this subject. Gaufin (1958) lists those stoneflies found in the zone of clean water and those in the zone of degradation. None was found in grossly polluted waters.

In addition to the above references, an interesting and more extended discussion on the practical importance of stoneflies is given by Winkler (1964).

EFFECTS OF INSECTICIDES AND POLLUTION

Like many other aquatic insects, stoneflies are quite sensitive to insecticides. These chemicals are usually applied to control forest defoliaters and reach streams only incidentally. The effects on stoneflies of such spraying were summarized by Hitchcock (1965). More recent studies are by Ide (1967) and Sprague (1968). Laboratory studies defining more exact levels of stonefly mortality were made by Hitchcock (1965) and by Jensen and Gaufin (1964, 1966).

Resistance to insecticides varies by species, and, unfortunately, most North American stoneflies cannot be identified in the immature stages. However, some stoneflies are quite resistant to certain chemicals (Jones, 1958), and possibly there are also considerable differences in resistance to insecticides. Certain species, such as larval *Peltoperla maria*, recover from insecticidal treatment but show a reduced adult emergence (Hitchcock, 1965). No resistance has yet been acquired by field populations following 7 successive years of spraying (Sprague, 1968).

Most of the larger streams in Connecticut have suffered from varying degrees of pollution. Some, such as the Naugatuck River, are devoid of stoneflies. Although pollution and land use undoubtedly affect the distribution and movement of stoneflies, this has never been examined in detail.

DISTRIBUTION IN CONNECTICUT

Because most Plecoptera are poor fliers and restricted to watercourses, they are good subjects for zoogeographical studies. Several faunal movements of stoneflies in eastern North America have been postulated (Ricker, 1964; Ross, 1965; Ricker, Malouin, Harper and Ross, 1968; Ross and Ricker, 1971). Most of these apply only indirectly to New England.

The present distribution of stoneflies in Connecticut is of recent origin, dating back to the last glaciation of 15,000 to 20,000 years ago. Consequently, our population is somewhat depauperate compared to those of the Appalachians and Cumberlands to the south, which remained ice free. Preglacial stoneflies were forced southward by the advancing ice, and only the more active species were able to return after its retreat.

To reenter this area, stoneflies needed to find a suitable habitat and a means of access. Unfortunately, little is known of the absolute requirements of stoneflies, particularly for food. Probably the plant cover that contributes dead leaves to a stream determines in part what Plecoptera are found there. This aspect of stonefly distribution has yet to be examined.

According to Davis (1965, 1969), there probably was tundra vegetation in Connecticut 12,000 to 14,000 years ago. At 12,000 B.P. (years before the present) there was a gradual increase of woodland, with a sharp rise at 9,000 B.P. These woodlands consisted of white pine and other trees now typical of the forests of the northern Great Lakes region. At 8,000 B.P., with a warmer, drier climate, deciduous trees became more common. Subsequently, beech (6,500 B.P.), hickory (5,500 B.P.) and chestnut (2,000 B.P.) appeared.

A large number of stonefly species that are not found in Connecticut or other parts of New England have penetrated from unglaciated regions into the Great Lakes area, New York State and the Saint Lawrence River plain to the Maritimes (Hitchcock, 1968; Ricker, Malouin, Harper and Ross, 1968; Ross and Ricker, 1971). A barrier running along the Hudson River–Lake Champlain line apparently denied them access to New England. The lower Hudson Valley was an estuary of the sea 12,000 B.P. and, as recently as 4,000 B.P. and perhaps even later, was saline enough to support oysters (Newman and his co-workers, 1969). This condition would be fatal to any stoneflies that tried to establish themselves there or that were carried downstream into this brackish water. To the north there were several postglacial lakes that interrupted eastward movement. The present-day Hudson River drains only a narrow strip of land on its eastern boundary, providing only limited access to aquatic insects moving eastward. Its small eastern drainage basin and its general southward flow contrast sharply with those of its principal tributary, the Mohawk River to the west. That river aids east–west movement of stoneflies and its numerous tributaries help north–south movement. North of the Hudson River, Lake Champlain and the relatively high Adirondacks prevent eastward stonefly movement.

Within Connecticut there are nine principal drainage basins, of which only three (Housatonic, Connecticut, Thames) extend over any considerable area (Flint, 1930). Because all these streams debouch into saline Long Island Sound, it would be difficult for a species to move from the mouth of one stream to the mouth of another along the coast, as may have occurred along the tributaries of the Mississippi River (Ross and Ricker, 1971). However, since the tributary headwaters of the various streams are in close proximity, there seems no reason why east–west movement should not take place there.

The topography of Connecticut is divided generally into eastern and western uplands and a central lowland. Few stoneflies appear to be restricted to any one of these areas.

Allocapnia zola and *Capnia manitoba* are restricted to the western upland in small brooks in Hartland and Goshen, respectively. The former species occurs on the Cumberland Plateau with outlying populations in previously glaciated areas in Connecticut and New Brunswick. This distribution is difficult to explain unless there are other undiscovered populations in limited areas of New England. *C. manitoba* is found in Canada from Manitoba eastward, with collections also from various parts of New England (Hanson and Hitchcock, 1961). As all its closest relatives are western and its distribution unique, it seems clear that it must be a recent immigrant from western Canada, with Connecticut representing its southernmost extension.

Brachyptera glacialis has been collected only in the eastern uplands. Enough collections have been made to show that it is not a collecting artifact. There is no apparent reason why this species should not also be present in western Connecticut.

Species that are found in both the eastern and western uplands but not in the central lowlands or along the coast are: *Allocapnia minima, Brachyptera pacifica, Alloperla imbecilla* and *Neoperla clymene*. With the exception of the last named, these are either northern or mountainous species.

Presumably the first stonefly colonizers in Connecticut were those species that can survive near-tundra conditions and/or are now found only to the north of us. These would probably not include such northern species as *Claassenia sabulosa* or *Capnia vernalis,* which have western affinities, no immediate relatives to the south, and have probably only recently extended their range eastward. More likely candidates are *Arcynopteryx compacta* and *Diura nanseni*. These presumed Pilgrim Fathers of the Connecticut stoneflies are northern Holarctic species and were pushed southward ahead of the advancing glaciation, then retreated with the melting ice sheet, to be trapped eventually as isolated populations near or above timberline in the White Mountains of New Hampshire, probably at about the time of the Valderan glacial substage some 10,500 years ago. Because of long distributional gaps, it is extremely unlikely that they could have attained the peaks of the White Mountains from a northern population after the disappearance of the ice sheet from northern Canada. *Allocapnia minima* occurs over most of the previously glaciated area of North America. It perhaps survived the Wisconsin ice sheet in an unglaciated part of Newfoundland (Ross and Ricker, 1971; Ross, Rotramel, Martin and McAlpine, 1967), then moved down the East Coast.

From 12,000 years ago, the gradual increase of woodland and the amelioration of climate allowed stoneflies that had survived glaciation south of the ice to move north again. The Great Lakes watershed alternately drained to the west and south or to the east, depending on the advance or retreat of lesser glacial ice sheets in the colder Middletown (13,000 B.P.), the warm Two Creek (11,500 B.P.), the colder Valders (10,500 B.P.) stages, and the warm thermal maximum of the Mankata (5,000 B.P.). Depending on the glaciation to the north, western New York was drained either eastward through the Hudson or northward to the Saint Lawrence (Flint, 1953, 1956, 1957). These changes in streamflow and drainage basins provided ample opportunity for stoneflies to move from the area of the present Ohio River drainage into the Great Lakes drainage. Although the Saint Lawrence plain was covered by intrusions of the sea, when land emerged, the stoneflies could easily follow the Saint Lawrence downstream to the Maritimes, although this movement must be of relatively recent date.

Movement directly eastward past the Hudson River and its succession of glacial lakes was more difficult, and only some species extended their range into southern New England. Presumably some of the less active species should also be found in the lower (northern) Lake Champlain Valley, an area that has never been searched thoroughly for stoneflies. There are some indications that as these species reached the Maritimes, their range extended southward along the coast. Perhaps, over a long period of time, they will reach southern New England if their way is not blocked by grossly polluted streams.

From 8,000 to 2,000 years ago, the woodlands of Connecticut assumed approximately their present composition, with a decline of conifers and an increase in deciduous trees. There was probably a continuing trickle of new species from the Appalachian hardwood forests.

There thus appear to be four main elements of the stonefly population in Connecticut: (1) Species that could survive near-tundra conditions and were probably the first colonizers following glacial retreat. Those that were sufficiently adaptable remained as the climate warmed. Example: *Allocapnia minima*. (2) Midwestern species that are typical of the Great Lakes region and the Saint Lawrence River plain. Several species have penetrated the Hudson River barrier. Example: *Leuctra ferruginea*. (3) Appalachian species that moved northward as deciduous trees increased in this area. Example: *Peltoperla maria*. (4) Species from western North America that moved southward into New England. These are the most recent invaders of only a few thousand years ago. Example: *Capnia manitoba*.

COLLECTING

Immature stoneflies in the eastern United States usually live in running water and can be captured by stirring rocks with the feet or hands and letting the insects drift onto a screen held a few feet downstream. Moss and bunches of dead leaves should also be removed from the water and carefully examined for stoneflies in a water-filled white pan or taken back to the laboratory for examination. Seepage areas, small trickles and intermittent streams should not be neglected when collecting. Cast skins may be found on bridges or rocks over streams.

Adults are usually collected by sweeping the vegetation near streams or by examining bridges, posts and tree trunks near running water. Some adults may be found hiding under rocks on shore, although turning over rocks is a tedious and often unproductive way to collect. The winter forms (*Allocapnia, Taeniopteryx, Brachyptera*) can be collected in numbers where they have come out of the water and crawled up on bridges and highway posts. Some species come readily to light traps (*Perlesta, Acroneuria*). Occasionally, good collecting may be had by netting adults as they fly over the stream. A Malaise trap, a large, funnel-type trap made from fine mesh, will capture some specimens flying upstream.

Whenever possible, late instar larvae should be reared in order to associate them with known adults. All instars may be preserved in 80 percent alcohol. With large specimens, it is usual to change the liquid in a week or two, as the body contents of the insect will dilute the alcohol.

24. Glossary of Descriptive Terms

This glossary is not exhaustive, and the definitions are applicable only to stoneflies. Some of them may make purists cringe. Nevertheless, it is hoped that they will make biological discussions intelligible to those who have not previously studied entomology.

A: anal vein.
aedeagus: the penis or intromittent organ.
anal cell: an area between two longitudinal anal veins that is delineated by crossveins.
anal vein: (A): longitudinal vein in the posterior area of the wing (fig. 6).
anterior: toward the forward part.
anterolateral: the front corner.
apical segment: the segment farthest from the base to which the series of segments is attached; the last segment.
apically: at the extremity.
apophyseal pit: the external pit (or pits) on the thorax that marks a cuticular ingrowth.
apterous: without wings.

basal lobe: a rounded lobe found on the seventh, eighth, or ninth sternite of some species.
basal processes: accessory sclerotic structures at the base of the epiproct.
basisternum (bs): the largest thoracic sternite.
brachypterous: with short, abbreviated wings.
bs: basisternum.

C: costa.
carina: a ridge or low keel.
ce: cercus.
cell: wing area bounded on all sides by veins.
cephalad: toward the head.

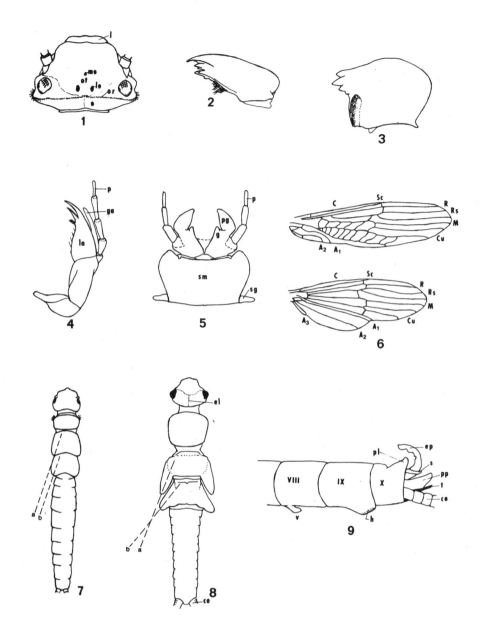

A=anal vein	la=lacinia	pp=paraproct
C=costa	lo=lateral ocellus	R=radius
ce=cercus	M=media	Rs=radial sector
Cu=cubitus	mo=median ocellus	s=stylet or basal process
el=ecdysial line	o=occipital region	Sc=subcosta
ep=epiproct	or=occipital ridge	sg=submental gill
g=glossa	ot=ocellar triangle	sm=submentum
ga=galea	p=palpus	t=titillator
h=hammer	pg=paraglossa	v=vesicle or basal lobe
l=labrum	pl=posterior lobe	

1. Head of larval *Paragnetina media*.
2. Mandible of larval *Isogenus subvarians*.
3. Mandible of larval *Nemoura* sp.
4. Maxilla of larval *Isogenus subvarians*.
5. Labium of larval *Isogenus subvarians*.
6. Forewing and hindwing of *Paraleuctra sara*.
7. Unknown larva from Gale River, New Hampshire. The eyes are at a distance from the posterior margin of the head greater than their own length. The fore-wing pad (a) is parallel to the hindwing pad (b).
8. Larval *Nemoura* sp. The eyes are "normal"; that is, they are at a distance from the posterior margin of the head less than their own length. The fore-wing pad (a) is divergent from the hind-wing pad (b).
9. Adult male genitalia.

cercus (pl cerci) (ce): terminal paired appendages at the posterior extremity of the abdomen (fig. 9).
cervix (adj. cervical): the neck, the area between head and thorax.
clypeus: the most anterior part of the head, to which the labrum is attached.
cord: a transverse line in the wings, made of crossveins and bases of main veins, generally running from the apex of the subcosta to the cubitus.
costa (C): the anterior vein of the wing (fig. 6).
coxa: the basal segment that connects the leg to the body.
crossvein: a short vein connecting two longitudinal veins.
Cu: cubitus.
cu-a: a crossvein connecting the cubitus with the first anal vein.
cubitus (Cu): the longitudinal wing veins lying between the media and the anal veins (fig. 6).
cusp: a pointed process resembling a sharp tooth.
cuticle: the outermost layer of the integument.

detritus: very small pieces of organic matter derived from larger pieces by mechanical or bacterial action.
diapause: a state of arrested development, usually initiated by temperature or light.
distal: farthest from the center of the body.

ecdysical line: the Y-shaped line on the head, marking where the cuticle splits at time of molting.
egg-tooth: a projecting point on the head used by the embryonic insect to break the eggshell at hatching.
ep: epiproct.
epiproct (ep): a raised (generally), unpaired, sclerotic structure attached to the tenth tergite of the male and used in mating.
eversible: able to be turned inside out.

femur (pl. = femora): the large basal segment of the leg, connected to the thorax by the coxa.
fs: furcasternum.
furcal pit: apophyseal pit.
furcasternum (fs): a sclerotized thoracic plate posterior to the basisternum.

g: glossa.
ga: galea.
galea (ga): a process on the maxilla (fig. 4).
ganglia: disclike structures along the ventral nerve cord.
genital hook: a sclerotized process on the male terminalia used in mating; it can originate from the tenth tergite or from a paraproct.
gill: a fleshy protuberance, either single or branched, serving as a respiratory organ.
glossa (g): the paired inner lobes of the labium (fig. 5).
glabrous: without hairs.

h: hammer.
hammer (h): a raised tubercle on the posterior margin of the ninth sternite of *Acroneuria* (fig. 9).
hemitergal lobe: either segment of the cleft tenth tergite of the male.

Holarctic: pertaining to the northern hemisphere.
hypodermis: the cellular layer of the integument that secretes the cuticle.
hypopharynx: the "tongue."

imago: the adult insect.
incised: cut or narrowly notched.
instar: the form of the insect between each moult.
intercubital: crossveins running between the cubital veins.
intersegmental membrane: thin, flexible tissue connecting the sclerites of the body segments.

l: labium.
la: lacinia.
labium: the lower "lip" (fig. 5).
labrum (l): the upper "lip" (fig. 1).
lacinia (la): the inner projecting process of the maxilla (fig. 4).
larva: an immature insect.
lateral: pertaining to the side.

M: media.
MA vein: anterior media.
macropterous: with normal-size wings.
mandibles: the first pair of jaws (figs. 2, 3).
maxilla: the second pair of jaws (fig. 4).
media (M): longitudinal wing vein situated between the radial sector and cubitus (fig. 6).
median: middle.
mentum: a sclerite on the labium that bears the distal processes.
mesal: on the median plane of the body.
mesally: along the median plane of the body.
meso: a prefix pertaining to the second thoracic segment; for example, the mesonotum is the dorsal surface of the second thoracic segment.
meta: a prefix pertaining to the third thoracic segment; for example, the metabasisternum is the basisternum of the third thoracic segment.
MP vein: posterior media.

Nearctic: pertaining to North America and adjacent islands.
notum: dorsal surface.

occipital region: the posterior area of the head.
occipital ridge (or): a ridge or line of bristles running laterally across the head behind the eyes.
ocellar triangle: the area included within an imaginary line connecting all three ocelli (fig. 1).
ocellus: a simple eye located on the head between the compound eyes; stoneflies have either two or three.
or: occipital ridge.
ovoviviparous: living young produced by the hatching of the egg within the mother's body.

p: palpus.
palpus (p): an antennalike process on the maxilla and labium (fig. 4, 5).
paragenital plate: a paired sclerotized plate at the base of the epiproct.

paraglossa (pg): the paired outer lobes of the labium (fig. 5).
paraproct (pp): a pair of sclerotized lobes or plates located behind the tenth sternum (fig. 9); in some species they are curved forward as genital hooks or otherwise modified.
pfs: postfurcasternum.
pg: paraglossa.
pheromone: a chemical released by one insect that modifies the behavior of another.
phytophagous: feeds on plant material.
posterior: toward the rear.
posterior lobe: a produced hemitergal lobe.
postfucasternum (pfs): a sclerotized thoracic plate posterior to the furcasternum.
pp: paraproct.
pro: a prefix pertaining to the first thoracic segment; for instance, a proleg is a leg on the first thoracic segment.
process: a projection or outgrowth.
proximal: closest to the center of the body.
prothoracic stripe: a longitudinal colored mark on the pronotum.
pterostigma: a thickened and/or darkened spot on costal margin of the wing.

R: radius.
r-m: a crossvein between the radius and media.
radial sector (Rs): a longitudinal wing vein branching from the radius (fig. 6).
radius (R): a longitudinal anterior wing vein (fig. 6).
reticulation: a network of fine lines.
Rs: radial sector.
rugose: wrinkled, roughened.

s: stylets.
Sc: subcosta.
sclerite: an area of the integument that is hardened and darkened.
sclerotized: hardened and darkened.
scutellum: the posterior dorsal sclerite of the meso- and metanotum.
seta: stiff "hair."
setose: covered with setae.
sinuate: wavy.
specilla: terminal processes in *Leuctra*. If fig. 9 were a *Leuctra*, *pp* would be the specillum and *t* the paraproct or titilla.
spermatophore: a capsule containing sperm.
spinasternum (ss): an intersegmental sclerite of the thoracic sternum.
ss: spinasternum.
sternite: a sclerite on the sternum.
sternum: ventral surface.
stylets (s): accessory lateral processes at the base of the epiproct.
subanal lobes: paraprocts.
subcosta (Sc): longitudinal vein just behind the leading edge of the wing (fig. 6).
subgenital plate: produced part of the female seventh or eighth sternite, covering the genital opening.
subgenual organ: a receptor in the tibia for perceiving vibrations of the leg.
submentum (sm): the basal sclerite of the labium (fig. 5).

supra-anal apparatus: the epiproct and associated structures.

t: titillator.
tarsus (adj. tarsal; pl. tarsi): the distal part of the leg, consisting of three segments and bearing the claws.
teneral: a newly emerged adult, soft and light colored.
tergum: dorsal surface.
thorax (adj. thoracic): the middle section of the body, between the head and abdomen.
tibia: a segment of the leg connected proximally with the femur, distally with the tarsi.
titillator (t): a lateral pair of apical processes in *Leuctra* (fig. 9).
tubercle: a small rounded projection.

v: vesicle.
vannal area: the wing region of the anal veins.
ventral lobe: a rounded projection or fleshy lobe on the posterior margin of a male abdominal sternite.
vesicle (v): a lobe on the anterior part of an abdominal sternite (fig. 9).

wing pad: in larvae, the projections on the meso- and metathorax that contain the developing wings.

25. Selected References

Baumann, R. W., A. R. Gaufin and R. F. Surdick. 1977. The stoneflies (Plecoptera) of the Rocky Mountains. Mem. Am. Ent. Soc. 31: 1–208.

Brinck, P. 1949. Studies on Swedish stoneflies. Opusc. Entomol. Suppl. 11, 250 pp.

Cather, M., B. P. Stark and A. R. Gaufin. 1975. Records of stoneflies (Plecoptera) from Nevada. Great Basin Nat. 35: 49–50.

Claassen, P. 1931. Plecoptera nymphs of America. Thos. Say Found., 199 pp.

Frison, T. 1929. Fall and winter stoneflies, or Plecoptera, of Illinois. Ill. Nat. Hist. Surv. Bull. 18: 343–409.

———. 1935. The stoneflies, or Plecoptera, of Illinois. Ill. Nat. Hist. Surv. Bull. 20: 277–471.

———. 1942. Studies of North American Plecoptera. Ill. Nat. Hist. Surv. Bull. 22: 233–255.

Gaufin, A. R., A. Nebeker and J. Sessions. 1966. The stoneflies (Plecoptera) of Utah. Univ. Utah Biol. Ser. 14: 1–89.

———, W. E. Ricker, M. Miner, P. Milam, and R. A. Hays. 1972. The stoneflies (Plecoptera) of Montana. Trans. Am. Entomol. Soc. 98: 1–161.

Harden, P., and C. Mickel. 1952. The stoneflies of Minnesota (Plecoptera). Univ. Minn. Agric. Exp. Sta. Tech. Bull. 201, 84 pp.

Hilsenhoff, W. 1975. Aquatic insects of Wisconsin. Tech. Bull. 89 Dept. Nat. Resources. Madison, Wis.: 1–52.

Hitchcock, S. W. 1974. The Plecoptera or stoneflies of Connecticut. Conn. State Geol. and Nat. Hist. Surv. Bull. 107: 1–262.

Hynes, H. B. N. 1960. The biology of polluted waters. Liverpool Univ. Press, 202 pp.

Jewett, S. G. 1959b. The stoneflies of the Pacific Northwest. Oreg. State Monogr. Stud. Entomol. 3: 1–95.

———. 1960a. The stoneflies (Plecoptera) of California. Bull. Calif. Insect Surv. 6: 122–177.

Needham, J., and P. Claassen. 1925. A monograph of the Plecoptera or stoneflies of America north of Mexico. Thos. Say Found., 397 pp.

Ricker, W. E. 1943. Stoneflies of southwestern British Columbia. Ind. Univ. Publ. Sci. Ser. 12: 1–145.

———. 1952. Systematic studies in Plecoptera. Ind. Univ. Publ. Sci. Ser. 18: 1–200.

———. 1959b. Plecoptera in freshwater biology, ed. W. Edmondson. John Wiley & Sons, N.Y. pp. 941–957.

Ricker, W. E., R. Malouin, P. Harper and H. H. Ross. 1968. Distribution of Quebec stoneflies. Nat. Can. 95: 1085–1123.

——— and G. Scudder. 1975. An annotated checklist of the Plecoptera (Insecta) of British Columbia. Syesis 8: 333–348.

Ross, H. H., and W. E. Ricker. 1971. The classification, evolution, and dispersal of the winter stonefly genus *Allocapnia*. Ill. Biol. Monogr. 45: 1–66.

Stewart, K. W., B. P. Stark and T. G. Huggins. 1976. The stoneflies (Plecoptera) of Louisiana. Great Basin Nat. 36(3): 366–384.

Surdick, R. F., and K. C. Kim. 1976. Stoneflies (Plecoptera) of Pennsylvania. Bull. 808, Penn. State Univ. Agric. Exp. Sta. 73 pp.

Szczytko, S. W., and K. W. Stewart. 1977. The stoneflies (Plecoptera) of Texas. Trans. Am. Ent. Soc. 103: 327–378.

Tarter, D. C., and L. A. Krumholz. 1971. Life history and ecology of *Paragnetina media* (Walker) in Doe Run, Meade County, Kentucky. Am. Midl. Nat. 86: 169–180.

Wu, C. 1923. Morphology, anatomy, and ethology of *Nemoura*. Bull. Lloyd Lib. Entomol. Ser. 3: 1081.

26. Portraits of Members of the Nine Families of Plecoptera

The editors wish to thank the following:

The American Entomological Society for permission to reproduce drawings from Arden R. Gaufin, William E. Ricker, Michael Miner, Paul Milam and Richard A. Hays, "The Stoneflies (Plecoptera) of Montana," *Transactions of the American Entomological Society,* Volume 98, 1972.

Entomological Society of America and The Thomas Say Foundation for permission to reproduce drawings from J. G. Needham and P. W. Claassen, *A Monograph of the Plecoptera or Stoneflies of America North of Mexico* (The Thomas Say Foundation, Lafayette, Indiana, 1925; reprinted without change, 1970) and Peter W. Claassen, *Plecoptera Nymphs of America* (*North of Mexico*) (The Thomas Say Foundation, Charles C Thomas, Springfield, Ill., and Baltimore, 1931).

Cooperative Extension Service, The Pennsylvania State University, for permission to reproduce drawings from Rebecca F. Surdick and Ke Chung Kim, "Stoneflies (Plecoptera) of Pennsylvania," Pennsylvania Experiment Station *Bulletin 808,* May, 1976.

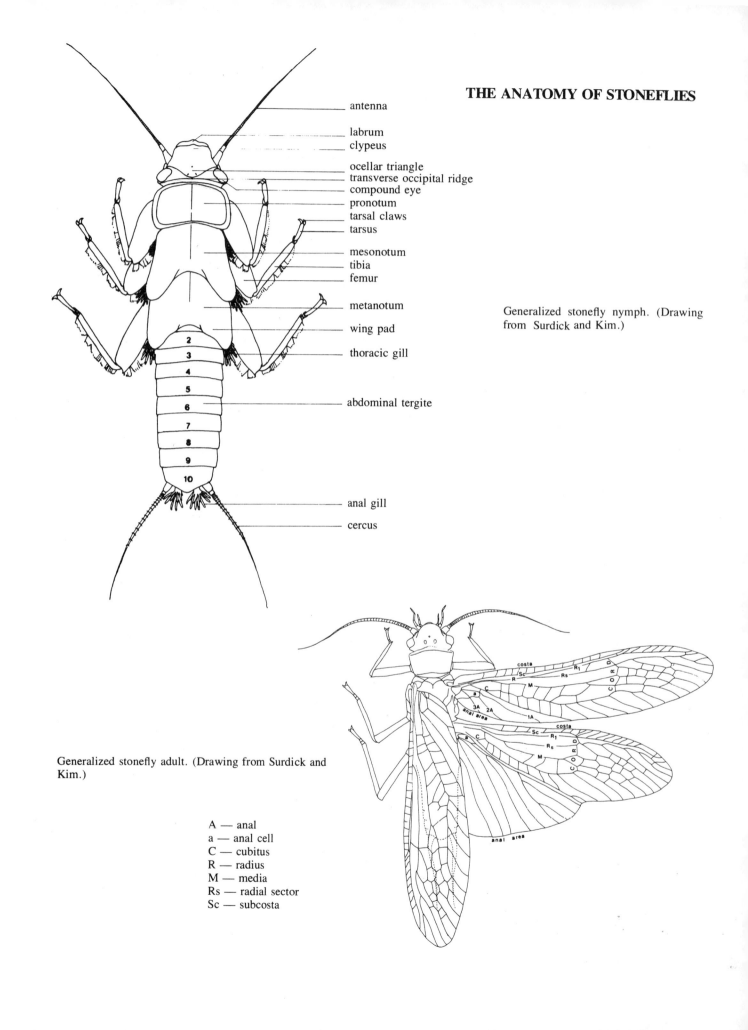

FAMILY CAPNIIDAE

Capnia nana adult, one of the so-called winter stoneflies. Members of this genus are small (mostly less than 10 mm. long) black stoneflies. According to "The Stoneflies (Plecoptera) of Montana," by Gaufin, Ricker and colleagues, *nana* ranges from British Columbia south to Oregon and Utah and "occurs commonly in creeks and small rivers with the adults emerging from November through May." (Drawing of adult from Gaufin, Ricker and colleagues.)

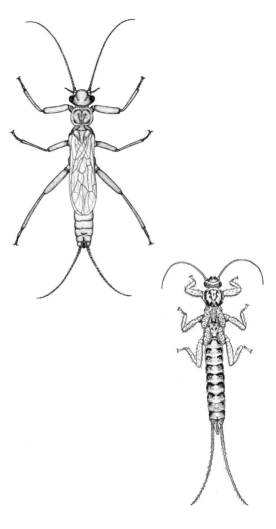

Allocapnia pygmaea nymph, 5 to 8 mm long and generally brown in color. Ranges from Quebec south to Virginia and almost to Alabama in the mountains, west to Minnesota and Missouri but not found in the tier of states from Ohio to Iowa. Members of this genus have been the subject of a monumental study by Ross and Ricker and other members of the "Winter Stonefly Club," who have keyed, figured and mapped every species. The genus appears to be undergoing unusually great evolutionary change. (Drawing from Claassen.)

FAMILY LEUCTRIDAE

Leuctra hamula adult. Length to tip of wings in male, 7.5 mm; in females, 9 mm. General color brown to dark brown with slightly smoky wings which characteristically are partially rolled over the body. Recorded from Maine and New York. Of the genus *Leuctra*, Hitchcock writes, "These are small, brownish, inconspicuous stoneflies that may, at times, be exceedingly numerous. Generally they seem to favor the smaller, slower streams and are among the few adult stoneflies that are to be found from spring until autumn." (Drawing from Needham and Claassen.)

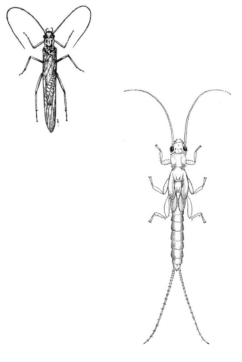

L. decepta nymph, general color brown with length of body up to 8 mm. Recorded from New York. (Drawing from Claassen.)

FAMILY NEMOURIDAE

Nemoura flexura nymph. This small and inconspicuously colored stonefly is common in creeks in eastern Oregon and Washington but rare in Montana. (Drawing from Gaufin, Ricker and colleagues.)

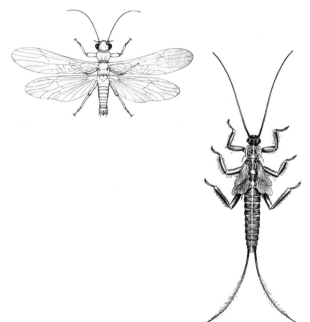

N. flexura adult. General color brown; length to tip of wings in males, 6.5 to 7 mm; in females, 8 to 9 mm. In the Pacific Northwest, adults emerge from April to June, but as late as September in Montana. (Drawing from Gaufin, Ricker and colleagues.)

FAMILY TAENIOPTERYGIDAE

Taeniopteryx nivalis nymph, length of body up to 14 (maybe 17) mm, antennae up to 9 mm, and cerci up to 8 mm. General color dark brown to blackish with lighter markings and a very distinct median yellow line on the dorsum extending from the head to the tip of the abdomen. Range is from the Maritimes south to Pennsylvania and west to Minnesota and Illinois. It is also reported to occur in northern California, Oregon and Idaho. (Drawing from Claassen.)

T. nivalis adult. General color dark brown to blackish with wings glassy to smoky gray-brown. Adults emerge in late winter and may be separated from other winter stoneflies by having the tarsal segments subequal in length. (Drawing from Needham and Claassen.)

FAMILY PELTOPERLIDAE

Peltoperla arcuata. Dorsal and ventral views of nymph found from southern Quebec to Virginia and westward into New York and Pennsylvania. Roachlike in appearance, brown in color, the nymph looks extraordinarily wide and short because of the deflexed condition of the head. The actual length is 14 to 18 mm. The males of this species differ from all other *Peltoperla* by having the cerci sharply curved toward each other a short distance from the base. This difference distinguishes *arcuata* from *maria,* the only other northeastern *Peltoperla. Maria* is common in small streams where dead leaves accumulate. It prefers to eat the leaves of elm, alder, sourwood and dogwood, and this probably holds true for most, if not all eastern *Peltoperla.* (Drawing from Claassen.)

P. cora adult found in California and Nevada. Head yellowish to almost black; prothorax brown to blackish; legs brown; abdomen brownish, lighter underneath; and wings smoky gray-brown to blackish. Length to tip of wings in males, 18 to 21 mm; in females, 23 to 26 mm. (Drawing from Needham and Claassen.)

FAMILY PERLIDAE

Paragnetina immarginata, one of the largest (24–39 mm) and most beautiful nymphs found in eastern North America. The species ranges from James Bay and the Maritimes south to Georgia. It is sometimes confused with *P. capitata,* but *immarginata* has no anal gills. The nymphs, which feed on mayflies, dipterans and other stoneflies, have been found in three sizes, suggesting a three-year life cycle. They are common in large, fast streams with stony bottoms. Adult emergence takes place over an extended period. (Drawing from Surdick and Kim.)

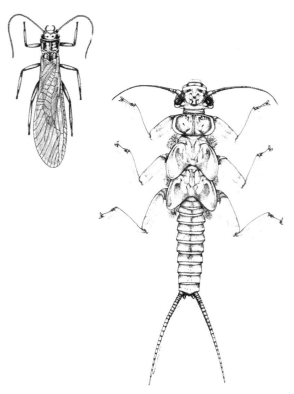

The general color of the adult *immarginata* is dark brown varied with yellow. The head is dark brown to blackish, prothorax the same, ditto the legs, abdomen yellowish, and the wings slightly smoky. (Drawing from Needham and Claassen.)

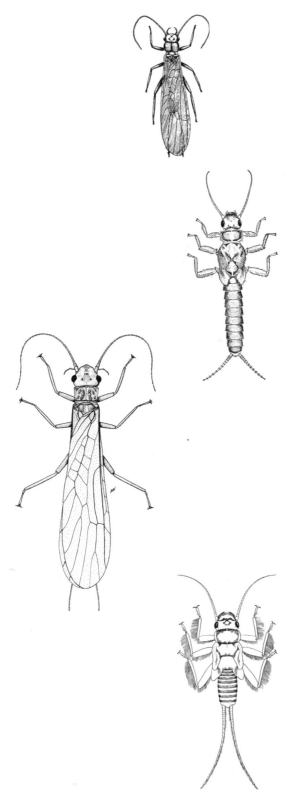

FAMILY CHLOROPERLIDAE

Alloperla marginata adult. Length to tip of wings in male, 8 mm; in female, 9–10 mm. General color yellowish, usually blackish on lateral margins of prothorax. Hitchcock notes, "This species is easily distinguished by the inward-pointing process at the base of each cercus, a characteristic shared by the Western *A. pallidula* but by no other Eastern species." Harper and Pilon studied adult emergence. Mainly an Eastern species ranging from Labrador south to New York and west to Wisconsin. (Drawing from Needham and Claassen.)

A. borealis nymph. Length up to 13 mm, antennae up to 4 mm, cerci up to 3 mm. General color is light brown. Abdomen is hairy. Claassen notes, "The large size and relative shortness of the cerci differentiate *borealis* from related forms." Ranges from Colorado and California to Alaska. In Montana, the species is common in small rivers and creeks. Adult emergence is from April through October. (Drawing from Claassen.)

FAMILY PERLODIDAE

Isoperla mormona adult. Length to tip of wings in male, 10 mm; in female, 11 mm. General color yellow-brown with greenish hyaline wings. Ranges from British Columbia to California and Wyoming and Arizona. Adults emerge from May to August. (Drawing from Gaufin, Ricker and colleagues.)

I. stgnata nymph. Lenth of body up to 10 mm, antennal up to 5.5 mm, cerci up to 5.5 mm. Yellow with brown markings. Two dark transverse bands across the head. Ranges from the Maritimes to southern New England, west to Minnesota. (Drawing from Claassen.)

FAMILY PTERONARCIDAE

Pteronarcella badia resembles members of the genus *Pteronarcys* but is only about half as large. In the adult there are fewer cross-veins in the wing than in *Pteronarcys*. In *Pteronarcella*, cross-veins are absent from the radial areas in the middle of the wing. *Badia* is found in the Rocky Mountain states from Montana to Arizona, and Gaufin, Ricker and colleagues write, "The nymphs of this species are very common in creeks and rivers at altitudes below 7,700 feet. Their distribution closely parallels that of *Pteronarcys californica*. A two-year life cycle is probable, with the adults emerging from early May through July." (Drawing of nymph from Claassen.)

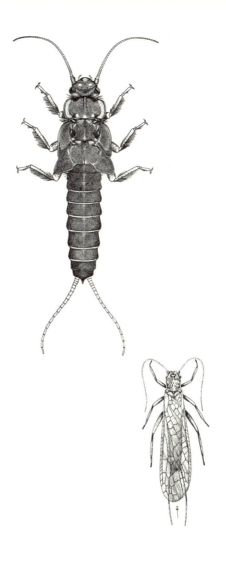

P. badia adult. (Drawing of adult from Needham and Claassen.)

FAMILY PTERONARCIDAE

Pteronarcys californica adult male with wings outspread. Hatches of this "Salmon Fly" on western rivers are legendary. Gaufin, Ricker and colleagues note in "The Stoneflies of Montana," "Nymphs of this species generally occur in beds of higher aquatic plants or under large rocks, where there is an accumulation of debris. The food consists primarily of vegetable material, although specimens held in an aquarium became carnivorous. The species has a three-year life cycle with the adults emerging from mid-April through early August, depending primarily on the temperature and altitude." The species ranges from Montana to New Mexico and from California to British Columbia. (Drawing from Gaufin, Ricker and colleagues.)

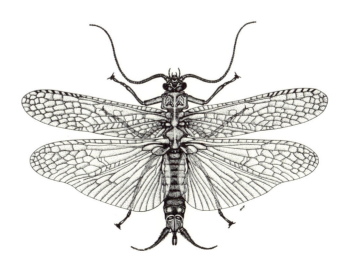

Appendixes

Dealers in Fly-Tying Materials, Tools, New Books and Accessories

When ordering fly-tying materials that you have earmarked for specific patterns (saltwater hackle streamers, bass-bug tails, tails and legs for nymphs, No-Hackle spinner-wing hen hackle, and so forth), it is always best to include this special information on the order blank or in any accompanying letter. Most materials dealers will understand more clearly what you need with this directive. The order-and-hope technique will create problems for both you and the dealer, whereas customized ordering will help your supplier both to choose material you really want and to order future stocks accordingly.

If you cannot find a particular material, color or size listed in these catalogs, don't hesitate to write or call the firm and make known your need. Often, dealers will actually have the material or be able to get it, or will refer you to another source. Some available items are simply not practical to catalog.

Many of these dealers also sell books in print.

We advise each tyer to collect a complete library of material catalogs, for they are both useful and informative and are the best means for the average tyer to keep abreast of fly-tying. No one shop will have everything you might need, but you will surely find certain dealers particularly geared to your kind of tying.

The designation (OS) is an Orvis Shop dealing in fly-tying materials.

American Anglers
P.O. Box 521
Bethlehem, Pennsylvania 18015

Angler's Roost
141 East 44th Street
New York, New York 10017

    Jim Deren holding forth as usual amid extraordinary clutter. A must stop for anyone passing through New York City.

Dan Bailey's Fly Shop
209 West Park Street
Livingston, Montana 59047

    Free catalog. Retail and wholesale. A very reliable source for flies, fly-tying tools, hooks, limited selection of materials. Complete stock of fly-fishing tackle and accessories. Western specialists. Excellent in-shop customer service and prompt, efficient mail-order services.

The Barbless Hook
23 Northwest 23rd Place
Portland, Oregon 97210

    Quality retail materials and West Coast flies.

The Battenkill Anglers Nook
Route 313
Shushan, New York 12873
(518) 854-7525

Black's Custom Flies
Idleyld Route, Box 95
North Umpqua Highway
Roseburg, Oregon 97470

Raleigh Boaze, Jr.
P.O. Box 115
Brunswick, Maryland 21716

    Latex sheets.

Bodmer's Fly Shop
2404 East Boulder
Colorado Springs, Colorado 80909

    Free catalog. Shop and retail mail-order service. Good personalized service by George Bodmer. Regular newsletter to customers. Good assortment of flies, fly-tying materials, tools, hooks and fly-fishing tackle and accessories for the Rocky Mountain area.

T. D. Brooke, Ltd. (OS)
726 East 65th
Indianapolis, Indiana 46220

The Brown Trout (OS)
Chagrin River Road
Gates Mills, Ohio 44040

Sue Burgess
"Glyn Celyni"
Felin Fach, Brecon
Powys, Wales

> The latest in European materials and a very special hook selection.

Buz's Fly and Tackle Shop
805 West Tulare Avenue
Visalia, California 93277

> Free catalog upon request. Retail and wholesale. An up-to-date, complete stock of highest-quality hand-selected materials and tools, flies, popular fly-fishing tackle and angling books. Extremely high-quality, fast, personal service (by Mickey Powell and Virginia Buszeck) in the shop and mail order. Direct importers. All-country specialists.

The Caddis Fly
688 Olive Street
Eugene, Oregon 97401

Cahill House
R.D.2
Benton, Pennsylvania 17814

> Barry Beck's establishment.

The Compleat Angler
61 Madison Street
Oswego, Illinois 60543
(312) 554-8707

Creative Anglers
2964 Peak Avenue
Boulder, Colorado 80302
(303) 443-5720

Creative Sports Enterprises
2333 Boulevard Circle
Walnut Creek, California 94595

> Free catalog. Wholesale and retail. An up-to-date, complete stock of high-quality standard and unusual fly-tying materials, flies and quality tackle. Fly-tying school. Good custom service in shop and mail order, managed by Andre Puyans. Many items available that are not listed in catalog. Direct importers. Western and West Coast specialists, and arrangers of foreign fly-fishing trips.

E. B. and H. A. Darbee
Livingston Manor, New York 12758

An excellent source of flies and materials.

Fireside Angler, Inc.
P.O. Box 823
Melville, New York 11746
(516) 427-6881

Free catalog. Retail and wholesale. Under new management since 1974. A complete line of up-to-date fly-tying materials, tools, hooks, fly-fishing books, flies, tackle and accessories. Good custom shop (managed by Glen Mikkleson) and mail-order services. Direct importer.

The Fisherman's Fly
941 Chicago Avenue
Evanston, Illinois 60202

The Fish Hawk
283 Buckhead Avenue, Northeast
Atlanta, Georgia 30305
(404) 237-3473

Fish 'N Hole (OS)
127 North Tejon Street
Colorado Springs, Colorado 80907

The Fly Fisher (OS)
315 Columbine Street
Denver, Colorado 80206

Fly Fisherman's Bookcase
3890 Stewart Road
Eugene, Oregon 97402

The pioneer discounter has moved west, with Sam Melner at the head of the wagon train. Seasonal catalogs.

Fly Fisherman's Headquarters
169 Route 46
Mine Hill, New Jersey 07801

Flyfisher's Paradise
P.O. Box 448
Lemont, Pennsylvania 16851
(814) 234-4189

The Fly Line, Inc.
3935 Washington Boulevard
Ogden, Utah 84401
(801) 394-1812

The Fly Tyer's Supply Shop
P.O. Box 153
Downington, Pennsylvania 19335

Forest County Sports Center (OS)
Elm Street
Tionesta, Pennsylvania 16353

Greenwich Sportsman's Center, Inc.
398 Greenwich Avenue
Greenwich, Connecticut 06830
(203) 661-2796

The Hackle House
P.O. Box 505
Oakville, Ontario, Canada

> Catalog 50 cents, refunded on first order. Discount prices and wholesale. Importer and exporter. A Canadian fly-tying mail-order service that is specializing in custom-service orders and a wide choice of standard and unusual tying materials, tools, imported quality English hooks and many unusual accessory items.

Hackle & Tackle
Department FF11-4
Central Square, New York 13036

> Free catalog. Broad supply of fly-tying tools, materials and equipment at discount prices.

The Hatch
P.O. Box 5624
Tucson, Arizona 85705

> Free catalog.

The Hatch
DeBruce Road
Livingston Manor, New York 12758
(914) 439-4944

Henrys Fork Anglers, Inc.
P.O. Box 487
St. Anthony, Idaho 83445
(208) 624-3595, winter; 558-7525, summer

Herter's, Inc.
R.F.D. 2, Interstate 90
Mitchell, South Dakota 57301

   One of the biggies.

High Country Flies
Box 1022 S
Jackson, Wyoming 83001
(307) 733-4944

   Free catalog.

E. Hille
P.O. Box 996, Department FF
Williamsport, Pennsylvania 17701

   Retail and wholesale. Wide selection. Free catalog.

Hoffman's Fly Shop
Route 2, Box 41A
Dauphin, Pennsylvania 17018
(717) 921-2020

   Conducted by Ben and Sandy Hoffman. Winter tying classes.

Houston Orvis Shop, Inc. (OS)
3115 South Post Oak Road
Houston, Texas 77056

Hunter Bradlee Co. (OS)
291 The Quadrangle
2800 Routh Street
Dallas, Texas 75201

Hunter's Fly Shop
P.O. Box 55A
New Boston, New Hampshire 03070

   Bill Hunter of the HMH Vises.

Robert Jacklin
P.O. Box 406
West Yellowstone, Montana 59758

   Free catalog.

Jack's Tackle
301 Bridge Street
Phoenixville, Pennsylvania 19460

   Jack Mickievicz is a top specialist in fur blending and dyeing.

Joe's Tackle Shop
P.O. Box 156
Danforth, Maine 04424

Send $1 for list.

Jorgensens, Inc. (OS)
6226 Covington Road
Fort Wayne, Indiana 46804

Kaufmann's Streamborn Fly Shop
P.O. Box 23032
Portland, Oregon 97223
(503) 639-6400

Discount shop and mail-order service. Quality selection of materials, special goodies and books. Free catalog. Run by Randall and Lance Kaufmann.

Lake George Angler's Shop
Route 9
Lake George, New York 12845
(518) 668-2233

Mark Francato is, in his own words, "hyper" about fly-tying. Mark has taught tyers who turn out 10,000 dozen quality flies a year for him. "I'll teach anybody to tie flies who will tie for me," he says. But watch out. If Mark doesn't like your fly, he'll clip it apart with a pair of footlong scissors. As he says, he's hyper.

H. L. Leonard
25 Cottage Street
Midland Park, New Jersey 07432

Free catalog. Retail and wholesale. Quality service to fly-tyers and fly fishermen by this old, renowned company. Fly-tying materials, tools, hooks, Leonard rods, fly-fishing tackle and accessories, books and flies. Eastern specialist.

Bud Lilly's Trout Shop
West Yellowstone, Montana 59758

Free catalog. High-quality service. Good selection of tools and materials, excellent selection of fly-fishing tackle. Western specialist. First-rate information on flies and fishing for West Yellowstone area.

Line and Shot, Inc. (OS)
2646 Erie Avenue
Cincinnati, Ohio 45208

McLaughlins Orvis Shop (OS)
1150 Old Freeport Road
Pittsburgh, Pennsylvania 15238

The Millpond, Inc.
59 North Santa Cruz Avenue
Los Gatos, California 95030
(408) 354-5291

>Free catalog on materials, tools, books, plus regular fly-tying schools and expert seminars. Special master fly-tyers listing of original flies. Managed by Billy Butts.

Ojai Fisherman
218 North Encinal Avenue
Ojai, California 93023

Oliver's Orvis Shop (OS)
44 Main Street
Clinton, New Jersey 08809

The Orvis Company, Inc.
Manchester, Vermont 05254

>Free catalog. Retail and wholesale business. An up-to-date, complete stock of high-quality fly-tying materials, tools, hooks, fly-rod kits, tying accessories, fly-fishing books, wide selection of flies and Orvis fly-fishing tackle. Fly-tying schools. Very high quality in-shop and mail-order service. Fly-fishing information and travel specialist for this and other countries. Interesting and elaborate seasonal catalogs and regular news bulletins that allow customers to keep well informed on schools, trends, sales and new products.

Orvis Shop of Arkansas (OS)
7710 Cantrell Road
Little Rock, Arkansas 72207

Orvis Shop of Boston, Inc. (OS)
213 West Plain Street
Wayland, Massachusetts 01778

Orvis of Tulsa, Inc. (OS)
506 South Boston
Tulsa, Oklahoma 74103

The Orvis Shop (OS)
5655 Main Street
Williamsville, New York 14221

Orvis Pole and Paddle Shop (OS)
12525 West Lisbon Road
Brookfield, Wisconsin 53005

Patrick's
2237 Eastlake Drive
Seattle, Washington 98188

The Plumlea Angler (OS)
1 Swan Street
Biltmore Village, North Carolina 28802

Price's Feathers
P.O. Box 53
Three Rivers, California 93271

   Discounts. Free catalog.

Rangeley Region Sport Shop
Box 850
Rangeley, Maine 04970

   Free catalog. Good selection of tools, materials, books and tackle. Eastern specialist.

Reed Tackle
Box 1348
Fairfield, New Jersey 07006

   Catalog. Retail and wholesale. Very independent shop service and excellent mail-order service. High-quality, complete, up-to-date stock of materials, tools, hooks, lure-making parts, accessories, rod blanks and books. Eastern specialist.

Reesers Sporting Goods, Inc. (OS)
123 West Lancaster Avenue
Shillington, Pennsylvania 19607

The Rivergate
Route 9, Box 275
Cold Spring, New York 10516
(914) 265-2318

   Author Eric Leiser offers books, materials, tools and accessories. Shop and fast mail-order service. Fly-tying school in winter. Eric has an eye for new materials such as Swannundaze. Free catalog. Retail and wholesale.

Hank Roberts
1035 Walnut Street
Boulder, Colorado 80302

Rod and Gun of Central Florida, Inc. (OS)
501 Park Avenue North
Winter Park, Florida 32789

The Rod & Reel
P.O. Box 132
Leola, Pennsylvania 17540
(717) 397-8551

Raymond C. Rumpf & Son
P.O. Box 176
Ferndale, Pennsylvania 18921

Shorelines South (OS)
617 East Las Olas Boulevard
Fort Lauderdale, Florida 33301

Hank Shotwell
Box 3761
New Haven, Connecticut 06525

Sierra Tackle
Box 373
Montrose, California 91020

Free catalog. Wholesale and retail. An up-to-date stock of quality fly-tying materials, tools, hooks, books and fly-fishing tackle. Pacific Coast fresh- and saltwater fly-fishing specialist. An excellent shop and mail-order service. Direct importer.

Sporting Adventure (OS)
9191 Baltimore National Pike
Ellicott City, Maryland 21043

The Sporting Gentleman (OS)
306 East Baltimore Avenue
Media, Pennsylvania 19063

Steckler-Tibor
P.O. Box 21
Stoneboro, Pennsylvania 16153

Materials, tools and books. Catalog.

Robert J. Stone
20 Brookside Circle
Springfield, Massachusetts 01129

Straightline Fly and Tackle
Box AJ
Steamboat Springs, Colorado 80477
(303) 879-4080; (800) 525-2501

Clinics and workshops on entomology, fly-tying, reading water and casting.

Streamside Anglers
P.O. Box 2158
Missoula, Montana 59806
(406) 728-1085

Free catalog. Limited supply of Henry Hoffman super necks.

Dick Surette Fly Fishing Shop
Route 16, Box 686
North Conway, New Hampshire 03860

Catalog. Surette is editor and publisher of a new quarterly, *Fly Tyer*. See periodicals section.

W. W. Swalef & Son
P.O. Box 5574
Fresno, California 93755

Wholesale only.

Thornapple Orvis Shop (OS)
Thornapple Village
Ada, Michigan 49301

Trout and Grouse (OS)
1147 Wilmette Avenue
Wilmette, Illinois 60091

The Trout Shop
Box 2158
Missoula, Montana 59801

Twin Rivers Tackle
1206 North River Avenue
Sunbury, Pennsylvania 17801

Jim Hepner is a go-getter.

Universal Imports
P.O. 1581
Ann Arbor, Michigan 48106

Van Dorens Orvis Shoppe (OS)
5703A Grove Avenue
Richmond, Virginia 23226

E. Veniard, Ltd.
138 Northwood Road
Thornton Heath, Surrey, England CR48YG

A complete stock of common and rare fly-tying materials, most foreign books, hooks, tools, dyes and accessory items. Excellent mail-order service. Specialist in world fly-tying material market.

Yellow Breeches Shoppe (OS)
Allenberry Road
Boiling Springs, Pennsylvania 17007

Dealers in
Out-of-Print Books

The editors are acquainted with the following specialists in out-of-print books and periodicals.

American Sporting Collector
Arden Drive
Amawalk, New York 10501

    Allan J. Liu deals in rare books, rods, reels, flies, decoys and other sporting collectibles of field and stream. Prices often high, but quality is there.

Anglebooks Limited
12 Boxwell Road
Herts., England

    Highly recommended by Tony Shuffrey. A large and varied stock of out-of-print angling books.

Angler's and Shooter's Bookshelf
Goshen, Connecticut 06756
(203) 491-2500

    Out-of-print and rare hunting and fishing books; also sporting art. Prices often high, but a bargain now and then from the colonel. Without question, the best stock in the country of out-of-print angling works. Send $2 for catalog, rebated against the first order of $10 or more—worth it because the catalogs themselves are becoming collector's items.

E. W. Classey, Ltd.
Park Road, Faringdon
Oxon, SN7, 7 DR.
England

Publications on natural history, rare and antiquarian, new titles, and a small number of Classey's own publications. There are occasionally books for the angler, but the Classey catalog is must reading for entomologists and other serious students of natural history.

The Crossroads of Sport, Inc.
5 East 47th Street
New York, N.Y. 10017
(212) 755-6100

Fly-tying, fly fishing, and sporting books, including Derrydales. Sporting art galore. Catalogs.

E. B. and H. A. Darbee
Livingston Manor, New York 12758

Out-of-print angling.

Entomological Reprint Specialists
P.O. Box 77224
Dockweiler Station
Los Angeles, California 90007
(213) 227-1285

In addition to publishing and reprinting books, Entomological Reprint Specialists offers for sale any insect book in print. Write for the list on aquatic entomology. Truly outstanding stock with fast mail order provided by Julian Donahue, an entomologist. Highly recommended for entomological books.

E. Chalmers Hallam
Earlswood
Egmont Drive
Avon Castle, Hampshire
England

Out-of-print books on angling and fishes, mainly British. An excellent stock.

Morris Heller
R.D. 1
Swan Lake, New York 12783

Out-of-print books on natural history, hunting and fishing. His spring 1978 catalog offered a first edition of Jack Atherton's *The Fly and the Fish,* in dust jacket, at $50; A. J. McClane's *The Practical Fly Fisherman,* first edition, at $85; and Vincent Marinaro's *A Modern Dry Fly Code,* first edition, near-fine condition, $70.

John Johnson
R.F.D. 2
North Bennington, Vermont 05257

Out-of-print natural history, including entomology and fishes. Very reasonable prices. The catalogs bear reading for hard-to-find books.

Kraus Periodicals Co.
Route 100
Millwood, New York 10546

An enormous, modern warehouse in the countryside, absolutely stuffed with runs and odd volumes of periodicals dealing with entomology, fishes and just about any subject you can name.

Julian J. Nadolny
121 Hickory Hill Road
Kensington, Connecticut 06037

Natural history books; occasionally some really good ones on entomology and fishes. Very reasonable prices.

Periodicals of Interest to Fly-Tyers

The Flyfisher
4500 Beach Drive, Southwest
Seattle, Washington 98116

    The official magazine of the Federation of Fly Fishermen, published quarterly. Membership in FFF includes subscription to magazine.

Fly Fisherman
Circulation Department
P.O. Box 2F05
Boulder, Colorado 80322

    Editorial correspondence should be sent to
Fly Fisherman
Dorset, Vermont 05251
(802) 867-5951

Fly Tyer
Box 1231
North Conway, New Hampshire 03860

    A new quarterly. $2 a copy or $7 for one year.

International Flyfisher
39 Mayfield Road
Belvedere, Kent, England

    A new magazine edited by Brian Harris. The subscription rate is not given in the June/July 1978 issue we saw, but individual copies sell for 75 pence in Britain. Interesting articles on flies.

The Roundtable
United Fly Tyers, Inc.
P.O. Box 723
Boston, Massachusetts 02102

> Membership in UFT, a nonprofit international organization founded to preserve, promote and develop the art of fly-tying, includes a subscription to the bimonthly magazine.

Salmon Trout Steelheader
P.O. Box 02112
Portland, Oregon 97202

> Often describes how to tie best Western patterns.

Trout
Editorial Office
737 South Sparks Street
State College, Pennsylvania 16801

> The official magazine of Trout Unlimited, published quarterly. Annual TU membership includes a subscription to *Trout*.

Notes on the Contributors

DEL BEDINOTTI is an intuitive tyer whose area of expertise is tiny dry flies. His size 24 cut-wing duns are something to see. Del prefers to maintain a low profile; he says the reason is that he wouldn't want to contribute to the death of a trout, and he expressed to us his hope that anyone benefiting from this book would release his trout. He is a past president of Trout Unlimited's Clearwater Chapter and works at the New York State Department of Environmental Conservation, where he avidly promotes energy-saving recycling programs. He lives in Castleton, New York, with his wife, two children and a beautiful Brittany spaniel.

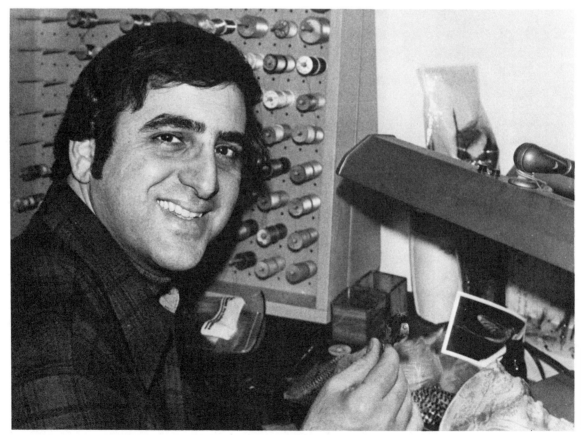

PHOTO BY DICK TALLEUR

ROBERT H. BOYLE is a senior writer of *Sports Illustrated*. He began tying flies in the early 1960s when doing a story on Harry and Elsie Darbee. His interest in fishing led him to write *The Hudson River: A Natural and Unnatural History,* published in 1969, and into collaboration with members of the Environmental Defense Fund on a book on cancer and its environmental causes which will be published next year. The first journalist to win the annual Outdoor Life Conservation Award, Bob, his wife, Kathryn, and three children live in Cold Spring, New York.

RAY DOLLING, a scientist, lives in Burling, Ontario, and works as a consultant in data processing. He makes regular forays with sampling net and camera to the top trout waters of the East as well as his native Canada, and he attributes his angling success to keen observation of the insect-trout relationship.

Don Hathaway, an energetic and most productive professional fly-tyer, learned to fly-fish in Southern California. Now thirty-one, he and his wife, Mary, operate a custom fly and gunsmith shop in McCall, Idaho, where they live with their two sons. Don's specialties are quality saltwater flies, salmon and steelhead flies and streamers. His Matuka streamers are superb.

STEPHEN W. HITCHCOCK was born in Vermont and became interested in insects while wandering the hills and woods of New England as a boy. Following undergraduate work at Grinnell College in Iowa, he earned his M.S. and Ph.D. in Entomology at the University of California (Berkeley). He is Director of Pesticide Compliance for the Connecticut Department of Environmental Protection. In addition to writing numerous scientific papers, he has also done articles for *National Geographic, Natural History, Audubon* and other magazines.

KEN IWAMASA is a professor of art at the University of Colorado in Boulder. He first began fly-tying and fly-fishing in Los Angeles at the age of nine to catch frogs, not fish, sneaking his brother's South Bend bamboo rod and a box of flies out of the house to angle for the frogs in the stream of a nearby meadow. Since then, however, Ken has used flies for fish in both fresh and salt water. His beautifully wrought flies reflect his considerable talent as an artist and keen student of entomology. He has lectured at a number of institutions including the University of Texas and the Denver Museum of Art, and he has served as visiting artist at Cal Tech and other schools. His work has been shown at a number of national, invitational and international exhibitions. Ken says, "I've learned so much from nature that it is impossible for me to say that I go out just to catch and release trout anymore."

LAYTON (SKIP) JAMES lives in St. Mary's Point, Minnesota, on the St. Croix River with his wife and two sons. He is a harpsichordist and pianist with the St. Paul Chamber Orchestra and makes his living giving concerts. In his spare time, he builds furniture and harpsichords, ties flies, fishes for trout and smallmouth bass and is as active as possible in the Kian-Tu Wish Chapter of Trout Unlimited.

LEW JEWETT of Lake Elmo, Minnesota, has fly-fished in more parts of the world than most of us can name. He manages Scientific Anglers/3M, the largest fly line company in the world. Lew loves trout fishing and bass bugging, but he is happiest fishing saltwater flats.

FRANK JOHNSON drives an eighteen-wheeler for a freight trucking company out of Baltimore. He lives in Lyndhurst, New Jersey, with his wife, Kathy, and their two daughters, Suzanne and Dawn. "I started fishing and fly-tying at the age of fourteen," Frank says, "and I killed every trout I caught until a few years ago. I then started fishing New York's Catskills and threw away my Jersey license. I have had to kill only one trout in the past three years. I firmly believe in barbless hooks and no-kill fishing."

DMITRI KOTYIK is of Russian and Siamese background. He and his twin brother, Alyosha, have been interested in fish as long as they can remember. Together they run their own exterminating business in Philipstown, New York.

HANK LEONHARD (right) and BILL LUZARDO, the co-creators of the L&L mayfly and caddis patterns, are also the inventors of Microweb, the realistic winging material, and Spin-a-fly, a handy reference for anglers and tyers. A commercial artist, Bill, wife Mary, and their two children, Lizabeth and Richard, make their home in Westbury, New York. Hank works in the casualty and environmental restoration field and lives in Bethpage, New York, with his wife, Estelle, and children Michael and Michele.

Mike Praznovsky, Jr., his wife and three children live in Hialeah, Florida. A sporting goods salesman and a past vice-president of the Miami Sportfishing Club, Mike started fly-tying ten years ago. His sixteen-foot boat, *Polish Popper*, is set up for backcountry fishing.

RICK RUOFF has made his home in Islamorada in the Florida Keys since graduating from the University of Miami. He has been a light-tackle angling guide for the past seven years. Fly-fishing is his first love, and tarpon and bonefish are his specialties, but he enjoys pursuing the lesser-known gamefish, too. He is currently president of the Islamorada Fishing Guides Association and is concentrating his attention on water quality and further fisheries development in South Florida. Ruoff is fortunate enough to be able to spend most of the summer and fall fishing the Rockies and the Northwest. If offered a choice between salt water and fresh, he would have to ask for a lengthy time out. During the summer and fall he lives in Jackson, Wyoming.

A. L. (Tony) Shuffrey lives near London, England. A physicist by profession, Tony recently took early retirement from the photographic manufacturing industry and is devoting his time to fly-tying, fly-fishing and collecting old angling books. He has twice taken first prize of the Fly Dressers Guild.

JOHN TIBBS began tying flies at the age of twelve when he received a small tying kit for his birthday. Within a few weeks, he found that tying flies was easier than mowing lawns and soon began supplementing his pocket money by selling his own flies. By the time he entered law school, he was tying 12,000 to 15,000 a year. He literally paid his way through law school by fly-tying, with most of his flies going to Orvis and Eddie Bauer. Now twenty-seven, John is a staff attorney for the St. Paul Insurance Company in Seattle, but he continues to maintain a small wholesale quality fly-tying supplies business. He is also a lecturer and field consultant for Berkley and Company, Inc.

Howard West has been fly fishing for nineteen years and raising his own hackle for nine. The marketing supervisor for Scientific Anglers/3M in St. Paul, Howard is active with Trout Unlimited and the Federation of Fly Fishermen. His favorite fishing is "for trout—and as much salt water as I can get."

Dave Whitlock, born in Muskogee, Oklahoma, holds B.S. degrees in chemistry, physics and biology. Prior to devoting himself professionally to the art of fly-fishing, he was associated for more than a dozen years with the U.S. Bureau of Mines and Standard Oil of New Jersey. The recipient of the Buz Buzek Memorial Fly Tying Award and the Anders Wild Trout Conservation Award, Dave, his wife, Joan, and their two sons live in Cotter, Arkansas.

Index

Al Price's Anglers Corner Professional-Quality Head Cement, 147
Alewives, 113
Andra spectrum, 137
Antelope hair, 136
Atherton, Jack, 59
Atkin, Darwin, 108
Automate, 148

Bailey, Dan, 107
Bally Hoo Tail Streamer, 82–85
Barracuda, 83
Bass, smallmouth, Humpy for, 67
Bass Bug Stinger, 144
Bear hair, 134
Beck, Barry, 50
Berry, Randy, 65
Birds. *See also* Roosters and hens
  stoneflies eaten by, 156–57
Black cats, 108
Black-tailed deer hair, 136
Blades, Bill, 126
Bleaching, 148
Blueback herring, 113
Blue Crab, Lew Jewett's, 79–81
Boar bristles, 134
Boaze, Raleigh, Jr., 91
Bobbins, 141–43
Bobcat fur, 134
Borger, Gary, Poly Caddis by, 53
Boyle, Robert (Bob), 17, 112, 148
Bristles, boar and pig, 134
British Columbia, stoneflies in, 152
Brook trout
  fry flies, 104–5
  Kat's Meow streamer used for, 113

Brown trout fry flies, 104
Brunn, Paul, 65
Buchner, Jay, 65–67
  Buchner Caddis by, 54
  Jay Dave's Hopper by, 71–78
Buchner, Kathy, 65–67
  Humpy by, 67–70

Caddis fly, 151, 155
  Buchner, by Jay Buchner, 54
  Hunter, by Bill Hunter, 55
  L&L, 49–52
  Lawson, by Mike Lawson, 55
  Poly, by Gary Borger, 53
  pupae, 95
  spent, 29–30
Caddisworms, 157
California, stoneflies in, 152
California salmon fly, 153
Canada, stoneflies in, 152
Capniidae, 152, 154–56
Caratex, 91
Caribou hair, 136
Cases
  custom, by Darrel Martin, 149
  portable, 146
Catskill Flytier (Darbee), 130
Cements, 147
Char egg fly, single, 96–97
Charles, Bill, 91, 142
Chestney, Jim, 139–40
Chickens. *See* Roosters and hens
Chinook salmon fry, 106
Chloroperlidae, 153, 154
Claassen, Peter W., 177, 179–83
Coating, 147

Coho fry flies, 105
Combs, Trey, 101
Connecticut, stonefly distribution in, 166–68
Connequoit River, 113
Copydex, 91
Coyote fur, 134
Crab, Blue, Lew Jewett's, 79–81
Creative Sports Enterprises, 139
    bobbins, 142
    Fuz-Comb, 149
Crockett, Dan, 115
Cutthroat fry, 105
Cutting tools, 145

Dall sheep hair, 136
Darbee, Harry, 129–30
Dealers in materials, tools, new books and accessories, 185–96
Dealers in out-of-print books, 197–99
Deer hair, 134–36
    for mayfly legs, 43
    for XT system mayflies, 34, 35
Deer-Hair Spinning Tool, Lance Kaufmann's, 149
DeFeo, Charlie, 59
Dennis, Jack, 65
Dette, Walt, 59
Diptera, 155
Dr. Ph. Martin's dyes, 148
Doll eyes, movable, 149
Dolly Varden trout fry flies, 104–5
Donnell, John, 82
Dorato, Bill, 28–29
Dow Corning Silicone Rubber Sealer, 147
Dragonflies, 156
Draper, Keith, 107–8
Duescher, Margie, 138
Duncum, Alan, 107
Dyeing, photo, 148
Dyes, 148

Egg fly, single, 96–97
Egg sperm, 96
Eggs, fish, 96
Elk hair, 136
Embioptera, 152
Engerbretson, Dave, 139
Ephemeroptera, 155
Euholognatha, 152–53
Eyes, doll, 149
E-Z hook, 143

Feathers, 133–34. *See also* Hackle
  bleaches and dyes for, 148
    saddle, 124
    spade, 124, 126
Filipalpia, 159
Fireside's Poly X, 137
Fireside's Poly XXX Fine and XXX Blend, 138
Fish as stonefly predators, 157
FisHair, 138
Fishing Creek, 50
Five-Minute epoxies, 147

Flick, Art, 124, 127
Floss, 139
Fly Fisherman's Bookcase, 139
Fly Fisherman's Bookcase Mini Needle-Nose Pliers, 149
Fly Tying Materials (Leiser), 148
Flymph, 145
Fly-Rite Extra Fine Poly, 138
Fly-Rite Poly Wiggle, 138
Fly-Rite Standard, 137
Flytyer's Carry All Kit, 146
Fox fur, 134
Frostlon, 137
Fry, 96
Fry flies, 101–6
Fulsher, Keith, 114
Fuz-Comb, Creative Sports Enterprises', 149

Gapen, Don, 107
Gaufin, Arden R., 177, 179, 180, 182, 183
Goat hair, 134
Golden shiners, 113
Goose quill, Canada, 60
Grasshoppers, 71. *See also* Hopper
Green River, 108
Greenwald, Bob, 13
Grumbacher Tuffilm Plastic Spray, 147

Hackle, 119–32
  dyed and bleached, 133–34
  dyes and bleaches for, 148
  fluorescent, 133
  hen, 133–34
  imported, 120, 121
  judging, 123–24
  latex and rubber, 148
  pliers for, 143
  price of, 121, 124
  raisers of birds for, 126–27
    Harry Darbee, 129–30
    Ted Hebert, 130
    Henry Hoffman, 130–33
    Bucky Metz, 132
    Andy Miner, 128–29
    Bill Tobin, 128
  saddle, 124
  spade, 124, 126
  throat, 124, 126
Haig-Brown, Roderick, 101
Hair, 134–37
  bleaching, 148
  deer, 134–36. *See also* Deer hair
  dyes for, 148
Hair-setting tape, 149
Harrop, Bonnie, 66
Harrop, René, 66
Harvey, George, 132
Hathaway, Don, 66, 96–97
Hathaway, Mary, 66
Hays, Richard A., 177
Hebert, Ted, 127, 129, 130
Hellgrammite, Niemeyer's Swannundaze, 59–64

Hens. *See* Roosters and hens
Herring, 113
High Country Flies, 66
Hitchcock, Stephen W., 151, 179, 182
HMH vises, 140
Hoffman, Henry, 121, 127, 130–32
Hook-eye designs, 145
Hooks
   new, 144–45
   on Tarcher patterns, 25–26
   for XT system mayflies, 35
Hopper, Jay Dave's, 71–78
Hudson River, 113
Humpy, Kathy Buchner's, 67–70
Hunter, Bill, 133–34, 140
Hunter Caddis by Bill Hunter, 55

Idaho, sea-run fish in, 101
Illies, 151
Illinois, stoneflies in, 152, 155
Inks, Dave, 133, 134
Insect pins, 35
Inverta Sulphur Dun, Skip's, 39–42

Jack, 83
Jay Dave's Hopper, 71–78
Jennings, Preston, 59
Jewett, Lew, Blue Crab by, 79–81
Jorgensen, Poul, 57, 126

Kat's Meow, 112–14
Kaufmann, Lance, 133
Keystone Aniline and Chemical Co., Inc., 148
Kim, Ke Chung, 177, 181
King, Colonel Joe (USAF ret.), 108
Knots, 145
Kodel Polyester rug yarn, 137
Kokanee fry, 105–6
Kreh, Lefty, 65, 82

Ladyfish, 83
Laggie's Gloss Cote, 147
Laggie Vest Pocket Leather Pouch Kit, 146
L&L Caddis, 49–52
L&L Mayfly, Extended Body, 43–48
Latex hackle, dyes for, 148
Latex Roly-polies, 91–95
Lawson, Mike, 66
Lawson, Sheralee, 66
Lawson Caddis by Mike Lawson, 55
Leisenring, Jim, 58
Leiser, Eric, 57, 112, 121, 148
Leonhard, Hank, 138
Leuctridae, 153–56
Lights, fly-tying, 145
Louisiana, stoneflies in, 152
Luxo Magnifying lamp, 145
Luzardo, Bill, 138

Malencik, Dean, 108
Mallard wing, 58
Hitchcock, Stephen W., 151, 179, 182

Marabou
   stork, 134
   strung white turkey, 134
Marabou Muddler, 107, 108
Marinaro, Vincent, 29, 43
Martin, Darrel, custom cases by, 149
Matarelli, Frank, 141
Matarelli-type bobbins, 141
Materials for fly-tying. *See also* Tools and accessories
   dealers in, 185–96
   feathers, 133–34
   fur, 134
   hair, 134–37
   metallic, 139
   synthetics, 137–38
Matuka Marabou Minnow, 115
Matuka style of dressing, 107
Mayfly (*Ephemera danica*), 94
   L&L, 43–48
   mini-spinners, 28–33
   Skip's Inverta Dun, 39–42
   Tarcher Nymph, 25–27
   wings, 39, 43
   XT System, 34–38
McCabe, Elizabeth, 65
McCabe, Fred, 65
McLellan, 151
Metallic materials, 139
Metz, Robert ("Bucky"), 127, 129, 132
Michigan State University, 130
Microweb Wing Material, 43, 138
Midges, pupae, 94
Milam, Paul, 177
Miner, Andy, 127–30, 132
Miner, Michael, 177
Mini-spinners, 28–33
Mini Vac Base, 141
Minnesota, stoneflies in, 152
Minnows, Matuka Marabou, 115
Modern Dry Fly Code, A (Marinaro), 29, 43
Mohlon, 137
Mono-body knot, 86–88
Monocord, 139
Montana, stoneflies in, 152
Moore, Wayne, 142–43
Moose hair, 137
Morton Chemical Company, 148
Mule deer hair, 136
Mustad hooks, new, 144
Muttkowski, 154, 155
Mylar tape, Prism-Lite, 149

Needham, J. G., 177, 179–83
Nemouridae, 153–56
Nevada, stoneflies in, 152
New Zealand, 107, 108
Niemeyer, Ted, 57–64
   Swannundaze Hellgrammite by, 59–64
Nowakowski, T. E., 148
Nylon thread, 139
Nymo, 139

Nymphs
    glossy versus satin finish for, 58
    Kat's Meow streamers used to imitate, 114
    phantom, 95
    stonefly, *see* Stonefly—nymphs

Odonata (dragonflies and damselflies), 151, 156
Omelet series, 96, 101
Orlon knitting wool, 137
Orvis hooks, 144
Orvis Poly Body, 137
Orvis Poly Caddis, 137
Orvis-Renzetti Presentation Vise, 141
Orvis Super Cement, 147
Oswalt, Fred, 141

Pacific Northwest, stoneflies in, 152
Paraplecoptera, 152
Parasites in stoneflies, 157–58
Patrick, Roy, 58
Peltoperlidae, 153, 154
Pennsylvania, stoneflies in, 152
Periodicals, 200–201
Perlidae, 153, 154, 156
Perlodidae, 153, 154, 156
Phantom nymphs, 95
Photo dyeing, 148
Photo-Plus necks, 133
Pig bristles, 134
Pilchard, 113
Plano Tackle Boxes, 146
Plecoptera. *See* Stoneflies
Pliers, Fly Fisherman's Bookcase Mini Needle-Nose, 149
Plymouth Rock neck, 124
Poly Body, 29
Poly Caddis by Gary Borger, 53
Polyester Rug Yarn, Kodel, 137
Poly Flash, 139
Polypropylene Sheeting, 138
Poly II, 137
Price, Al, 140, 145
Price Vise light, 145
Prismatic Marabou Shad, Whitlock's, 115–18
Prism-Lite, 115
Prism-Lite Mylar Tape, 149
Pryce-Tannatt salmon fly, 59
Pteronarcidae, 153, 155

Quick-Clip Speed Scissors, 145
Quill, Canada goose, 60

Rabbit Fly, 107–8
Rabbit Muddler, 107–11
Raccoon fur, 134
Rainbow trout
    fry flies, 103–4
    Whitlock Prismatic Marabou Shad for, 115–18
Ramsey, Buz, 115
Realistic flies, 57–58
Renzetti-Orvis Wingmaker, 149
Ricker, William E., 177, 179, 180, 182, 183

River Never Sleeps, A (Haig-Brown), 101
Roche, Mike, 59
Rocket Cylinder Crystal Cement, 147
Rocky Mountains, stoneflies in, 152
Roly-polies, Latex, 91–95
Roosters and hens. *See also* Hackle
    diseases of, 126
    fighting among, 127
    grizzly necks, 124
    housing for, 127
    predators of, 126–27
    raising, 126–27
    Super Grizzly strain, 131–33
    using full skins of, 124, 126, 130, 133
Rosenbaum, Seth, 113
Ross, H. H., 179
Rubber hackle, dyes for, 148
Ruhkala, Carl, 101

Sac fry, 96, 103–6
St. Clair, Ernie, 59
Salmon
    fry flies, 101–6
    Single-Egg Fly, 96–97
    Two-Egg-Sperm Fly, 98–100
Salmon fly, 153
    Humpy as, 67
    mono-body knot for, 86
    Pryce-Tannatt, 59
Salmonid fry, 101, 102
Saltwater flies
    Bally Hoo Tail Streamer, 82–85
    Lew Jewett's Blue Crab, 79–81
    mono-body knot for, 86–88
Sawfly, 156
Scissors, 145
Scotchgard, 3M, 147
Scotch-Weld Structural Adhesive No. 3520, 147
Seal-ex, 137
Seal hair, 134
Setipalpia, 156, 158–59
Shrimp, 95
Sierra Tackle Icky-Poo, 149
Sigler, Cam, 108
Sitka whitetail hair, 136
Skip's Inverta Sulphur Dun, 39–42
Snags, 25
Snook, 83
Sockeye fry, 105–6
Soft Stonefly Nymph, Dave's, 17–20
Spawning, 96
Spent Caddis, 29–30
Spiders, stoneflies eaten by, 156
Spinner flies, 58
Spinners, mini-, 28–33
Squirrel hair, 134
Steelhead
    Single-Egg Fly, 97
    Two-Egg-Sperm Fly, 98–100
Steelhead Fly Fishing and Flies (Combs), 101

Stoneflies (Plecoptera), 151–83
  adult
    emergence of, 164
    feeding, 155–56
    predators of, 156–57
  Adult Egg-Laying, Dave's, 21–23
  collecting, 168
  distribution of, 163–64
    in Connecticut, 166–68
  ecological importance of, 165
  ecology of, 161–64
  glossary of terms, 169–74
  identification of, 152
  incubation of eggs, 159–60
  insecticides' effect on, 165
  larval development (or stage), 151
    diapause, 160
    feeding, 154–55
    growth, 160–61
    predators of, 157
  light's effect on, 164
  literature on, 152, 175–76
  mating and oviposition of, 158–59
  nymphs of, 58
    Dave's, Soft, 17–20
    Swannundaze (amber), 13–16
  oxygen consumption of, 162–63
  phylogeny of, 152
  pollution and, 166
  species and genera
    Acroneuria, 153, 158, 168
    A. aremosa, 156
    A. californica, 153, 155, 157, 164
    A. carolinensis, 153
    A. lycorias, 153
    A. pacifica, 155, 158, 163, 165
    A. theodora, 162
    Allocapnia, 155, 158, 160, 165, 168
    A. minima, 167
    A. pygmaea, 156, 158, 159, 164, 165, 179
    A. recta, 156
    A. zola, 167
    Alloperla, 153, 154, 159, 161–62, 165
    A. borealis, 182
    A. imbecilla, 167
    A. marginata, 182
    A. mediana, 156
    A. pallidula, 156, 182
    A. signata, 156
    Amphinemura decemceta, 160
    A. sulcicollis, 157
    Arcynopteryx compacta, 159, 167
    Brachyptera, 154, 155, 160, 168
    B. glacialis, 167
    B. pacifica, 165, 167
    B. risi, 159–62
    Capnia, 158, 160
    C. bifrons, 159, 160
    C. manitoba, 167, 168
    C. nana, 179
    C. nigra, 158
    C. vernalis, 167
    Cephalouterina dicamptodoni, 164
    Chloroperla, 154, 158
    C. burmeisteri, 156
    C. tripunctata, 162
    Claassenia sabulosa, 167
    Dinocras, 158
    D. cephalotes, 154, 159, 160, 164
    Diura, 158
    D. bicaudata, 159, 160
    D. nanseni, 163–64, 167
    Hastaperla, 154
    Isoperla, 154, 158, 161–62
    I. decepta, 156
    I. grammatica, 154
    I. mormona, 182
    I. nana, 156
    I. signata, 182
    Kathroperla perdita, 154
    Leuctra, 153, 155, 157, 159, 160, 162, 164
    L. claasseni, 158
    L. decepta, 179
    L. ferruginea, 158, 168
    L. hamula, 179
    L. hippopus, 161
    L. nigra, 158
    L. tenuis, 158
    Nemoura, 155, 157, 160–62
    N. cinctipes, 161
    N. cinerea, 155, 161
    N. depressa, 155, 161
    N. flexuosa, 162
    N. flexura, 180
    N. picteti, 161
    N. vallicularia, 155, 157, 160
    Neoperla clymene, 167
    N. spio, 164
    Notonemoura, 159
    Paracapnia, 160, 164
    P. angulata, 156
    P. opis, 156
    Paragnetina, 155, 157
    P. immarginata, 156, 159, 181
    P. media, 159, 163
    Peltoperla arcuata, 181
    P. brevis, 154
    P. cora, 181
    P. maria, 154, 168, 181
    Perla, 158
    P. abdominalis, 161
    P. dipunctata, 155
    P. burmeisteriana, 154, 160
    Perlesta, 168
    P. placida, 156, 158, 159, 160, 164
    Perlodes, 161
    P. intricata, 163
    P. microcephala (=*mortoni*), 159
    Protonemura, 158
    Pteronarcella badia, 155, 183
    Pteronarcys, 158
    P. californica, 153, 155, 162, 163, 183

P. dorsata, 154, 162
P. pictetii, 163
P. proteus, 155, 156, 159, 160
Rhabdiopteryx nohirae, 165
Stenoperla prasina, 158
Taeniopteryx, 155, 158, 160, 168
T. burksi, 156
T. nivalis, 180
   suborders and families of, 152–53
   water velocity and depth, 161–62
   winter's effect on, 161
Stork marabou, 134
Stover, Frank, 148
Streamborn Fly Shop, 133
Streamers
   Kat's Meow, 112–14
   Rabbit Muddler, 107–11
   Whitlock Prismatic Marabou Shad, 115
Streamside Tyer, 146
Striped bass, 113
Sunrise of India, 139, 141
Sunrise of India bobbins, 142
Super Grizzlies, 131–33
Surdick, Rebecca F., 177, 181
Swannundaze Hellgrammite, Niemeyer's, 59–64
Swannundaze stonefly nymph (amber), 13–16
Sweeney, John, 144
Swim-up fry, 96, 103–6
Swisher Richards, 26
Swiss Straw, 138
Synthetic materials, 137–38
Systellognatha, 152, 153

Taeniopterygidae, 153–56
Tanning, 147–48
Tape
   hair-setting, 149
   Prism-Lite, 115
Tarcher Nymph, 25–27
Tarcher patterns, 25–26
Tarpon flies, 83
   mono-body knot for, 86
Texas, stoneflies in, 152
Thompson bobbins, 142
Thompson vises, 139–40
Threads, fly-tying, 139
3M Scotchgard, 147
Thundercreek Series, Keith Fulsher's, 114
Tinsel, 129
Tobin, Bill, 128

Tools and accessories, 139–49
   bobbins, 141–43
   cases, 146
   cements and coatings, 147
   dealers in, 185–96
   tanning, bleaching and dyeing, 147–48
   vise mountings, 141
Trout. *See also* Brown trout fry flies; Dolly Varden trout fry flies; Rainbow trout; Steelhead
   nymphing, 25
   Single-Egg Fly, 96–97
   Two-Egg Sperm Fly, 98–100
Trout Brook Hackle Company, 128
Trout Flies in New Zealand (Draper), 107–8
Turkey marabou, 62, 134
Turkey secondaries, speckled, 134
Turle knot, 145

Ultra Midge Thread, 139
Ultra Vise, 140
Umpqua River, 108
Utah, stoneflies in, 152

Vise mountings, 141
Vises, 139–41
Vivit, Dottie, 149
Vivit, Ron, 149

Weakfish, 83
West, Howard, 54
White, Bob, 83
White River, 115
Whitetail deer hair, 136
Whitlock, Dave, 101, 107
Whitlock Prismatic Marabou Shad, 115–18
Wiggle Nymph, Tarcher up-hook concept adapted to, 26
Willow fly, 153
Wingmaker, Renzetti-Orvis, 149
Wings
   mayfly, 39, 43
   synthetic materials for, 138
Wire, 139
Wisconsin, stoneflies in, 152
Wisely, 151
Wright & McGill (Eagle Claw) hooks, 144

XT System Mayflies, 34–38

Yolk-sac fry, 96, 103–6